"*Reasoning Together* is a valuable contribution to the ongoing conversation about faithful, compassionate responses to gay and lesbian persons in our communities of faith. This book retains the format in which these two teachers each presented their own biblical and theological positions in a public debate at Eastern Mennonite University. Grimsrud and Nation model how to differ with one another respectfully while holding a clear position. Especially helpful is their conversation about how hospitality and holiness fit together in the biblical record and in our call to faithfulness today. They end by naming some significant common ground, including the centrality of Jesus' call to love God and neighbor. This book is especially useful for pastors, teachers, students, and for input for study groups within congregations. The extensive annotated reading lists alone would be worth the price of the book."
—*Sue C. Steiner, Mennonite Church Canada*

"As one would expect with a book on homosexuality, there were times the reader wants to murmur, 'Yes, but . . .' However, my overwhelming response to this book is a loud YES. Finally, Mennonites are demonstrating to the world how Christians should fight with each other! We are known, paradoxically, for global peace building but internal schism. Here is a breath of fresh air—Mennonites 'going at it' with each other in a way that befits their biblical faith and peace tradition.

"Ted and Mark are bold in their own declarations and gut-wrenchingly forthright in their critique of each other. But their abiding mutual respect and Christian charity shines through, as well it should. I can personally give witness that both of these friends of mine love the Scripture, love Jesus, and love the church. Christians from all traditions should be grateful they let us in on this conversation. May we learn, not only from their arguments, but from how they argued. This book is a gift to the church."
—*Phil Kniss, Park View Mennonite Church, Harrisonburg, Virginia*

"Dialogue in the Spirit of Christ is an essential discipline in faithful community discernment. The church has been paralyzed by dialogue stoppers in statements like: 'the Bible is absolutely clear about homosexuality,' 'more dialog will not change anyone's mind,' or 'more study of the biblical texts will not relieve this conflict in the church.' But through genuine dialogue, *Reasoning Together* recognizes the complexity of the often quoted Bible texts, demonstrates willingness to listen to each others, to alter one's own views, and seeks faithful application of the biblical message to the human condition. The authors offer a great service to Christians and the church by their honest and vulnerable example of how to discern and align with the will of God and follow Jesus in our conflicted world."

—*Sheldon Burkhalter, Pacific Northwest Mennonite Conference*

"Two brothers in Christ, friends whose life trajectories have intersected and run parallel in many ways, wrestle from deeply held opposite points of view with what the church's call to faithfulness requires regarding same-sex relationships. Ted Grimsrud and Mark Thiessen Nation engage each other with honed skill and clarity, commitment, and vulnerable honesty. Their forthrightness toward each other, sometimes verging on the testiness an exhausting and seemingly intractable argument can produce, models what dialogue can be like for those who can trust the shared commitment to the church's faithfulness and wholeness to bear the weight of disagreement. It is always disagreement in search of resolution, however, even if resolution does not yet come in this engagement.

"This book is nevertheless a courageous exercise in hope. All readers, regardless of strength of position or state of confusion will find much in this book to destabilize certainties that need to be rattled, much to shore up inadequately grounded convictions, and much to help understand those who think differently. That is no small gift."

—*Thomas R. Yoder Neufeld, author of* Ephesians, *Believers Church Bible Commentary*

REASONING
TOGETHER

REASONING TOGETHER
A CONVERSATION ON
HOMOSEXUALITY

TED GRIMSRUD
MARK THIESSEN NATION

FOREWORD BY TONY AND PEGGY CAMPOLO

Herald Press
Scottdale, Pennsylvania
Waterloo, Ontario

Library of Congress Cataloging-in-Publication Data

Grimsrud, Ted, 1954-
  Reasoning together : a conversation on homosexuality / Ted Grimsrud
and Mark Thiessen Nation.
      p. cm.
  Includes bibliographical references.
  ISBN 978-0-8361-9430-2 (pbk. : alk. paper)
  1. Homosexuality–Religious aspects–Mennonites. I. Nation, Mark.
II. Title.
  BX8128.H67G75 2008
  241'.66–dc22

                                              2008013316

REASONING TOGETHER
Copyright © 2008 by Herald Press, Scottdale, Pa. 15683
  Published simultaneously in Canada by Herald Press,
  Waterloo, Ont. N2L 6H7. All rights reserved
Library of Congress Catalog Card Number: 2008013316
International Standard Book Number: 978-0-8361-9430-2
Printed in the United States of America
Book design by Joshua Byler
Cover by Kevin Cook

13 12 11 10 09 08   10 9 8 7 6 5 4 3 2 1

To order or request information please call 1-800-245-7894
or visit www.heraldpress.com.

In memory of John Howard Yoder,
who taught us both to sustain conversation,
especially when we believe important issues are involved,
especially when agreement is difficult to obtain

Contents

Foreword

For years, we have carried on a dialogue on homosexuality that parallels what you are about to read in this book.

Peggy supports homosexual marriages and believes that such marriages offer gay and lesbian couples the possibility of the joyful fulfillment that God wills for all of us. Tony, on the other hand, is a conservative who tries to make the case that same-gender erotic behavior runs contrary to what the Bible teaches.

Both of us appreciate this book because the authors, Mark Thiessen Nation and Ted Grimsrud, deal with the same issues that play a big part in our ministries to homosexual people. We have a special place in our hearts for God's gay and lesbian children. Both of us have spent many hours trying to help gay and lesbian people deal with the pain of families and churches that have difficulties in accepting them. We try to show these sisters and brothers that there is nothing that can separate them from the love of God and help them see themselves as persons of infinite worth.

The mind, like a parachute, works best when it is open. Christians should always be open to learn those new things God wants to teach them.

God is still speaking. Jesus made that clear to his disciples when he told them that he had more truths for them to apprehend, but that he did not consider them able to handle them, given their present existential situation (see John 16:12).

In life, each of them was able to handle only so much truth at any given time. Sometimes what we are asked to accept proves to be too much for us to bear. That is because new truths can be comprehended only when we are socially, psychologically, and spiritually ready to accept them. Max Weber, a towering figure among sociologists, talked about "elective affinity" as a precondition for accepting radically new ideas and concepts. What he meant by this is that social factors highly condition what it is possible for us to integrate into our already established worldview (i.e., *weltenschung*).

There was a time when, because of social circumstances, accepting women as preachers was not possible. We lacked an elective affinity for ordaining women and we lived in a cultural milieu in which most Christians could not believe that women legitimately could be leaders of churches. There is, however, a dynamism to culture, and as culture changed so did our thinking. For most Christians the idea of women in church leadership roles became increasingly plausible. When Christians went back to Scripture, they found biblical justification for our new understanding of the places that women could occupy in the leadership of the church. Weber would say that society had changed so that what had been heretofore unthinkable had come to have an "elective affinity" in the new societal setting.

Another case that validates Weber's doctrine of elective affinity is that, nowadays, most Christians are willing to accept into the church persons who are divorced and remarried. This is quite a departure from what was ecclesiastically acceptable just seventy-five years ago. Back then, when persons were divorced and remarried, they became *persona non grata* so far as church membership was concerned. Clear biblical justification was cited for excommunicating such persons. But times have changed, and today it is a rare church that excludes divorced and remarried persons from the fellowship of believers.

All of this sets the stage for accepting the possibility that we may be moving into a new socio-cultural setting wherein acceptance of homosexual marriages in mainstream Christianity will be normative. Sociological surveys of church leaders certainly reveal a liberalizing shifting on this matter.

Those who, like Tony, hold traditional views that lead us to oppose homosexual marriages find it hard to accept such shifting. They argue that what we accept should be grounded on eternal, unchanging, and absolute truths and values. They contend that beliefs should not be subject to adaptation to cultural changes. However, they are all too aware that they are losing ground to the encroachment of liberal views on gay marriage.

The two of us writing this introduction hold opposing positions regarding homosexual marriage. Tony believes, in accord with two thousand years of church tradition in interpreting Scripture, that same-gender erotic lovemaking runs contrary to what the Bible says—especially what it tells us in Romans 1:21-27. Peggy believes that gay marriage can be a humanizing relationship wherein there is a mutual nurturing of spirituality. Citing numerous cases of gay and lesbian Christian couples that have maintained lifetime committed relationships, she argues that the meaningful spiritual and psychological gratification which has resulted from these partnerships makes condemnations of gay "marriages" unjustifiable.

Over the years, the two of us have carried on a public dialogue in which we express our differing views on homosexual marriage. We have done this at universities, denominational gatherings, and in local churches, motivated by our desire to show that it is possible to hold divergent beliefs on this "hot button" issue and not get a divorce. Unlike many mainline denominations that are presently facing schism, or have already experienced formally established divisions because of differing convictions regarding gay marriage, the two of us have demonstrated that we are able to maintain a loving, stable relationship in spite of our differences. We have been able to do this because we have established a basic rule; each of us is willing to entertain the possibility that he or she could be wrong.

As Christians, both of us hold to the doctrines spelled out in the Apostles' Creed. Both of us believe that Jesus is the Savior who can deliver us from sin and death. And we share a common conviction that, because the writers of Scripture were given guidance by the Holy Spirit, what they wrote became an infallible guide for faith and practice. But still, we differ in our interpretations of certain passages of Scripture, especially the first chapter of Romans.

While both of us are aware that there are bisexuals who have adopted a homosexual lifestyle, and might, at some point, choose to behave heterosexually and even enter into marriages, we are convinced that there is only a very slight possibility that gay and lesbian persons can change their orientations. Given this reality, as generally delineated by social scientists, we agree that the rest of the Christian community will have to come to terms with those gay and lesbian children of God who have tried to change, but have come to the conclusion that they cannot.

There is no question in our minds that it is the duty of Christians to stand up for justice on behalf of our gay brothers and lesbian sisters. We are convinced that God calls us to love them and that to love them is to advocate justice for them. Justice, when you stop to think about it, is nothing more than love translated into social policies. You cannot say to a homosexual, "I love you in the name of Christ," and then deny that person the same rights that you enjoy.

Tony and Peggy agree that, in our pluralistic society, homosexual couples who make lifetime monogamous commitments should be entitled to the same legal rights that heterosexual couples enjoy. However, whether homosexual couples should be able to legally deem their relationships marriages is a very controversial matter.

In this book, you will find a more sophisticated examination of the pros and cons regarding how Christians should deal with homosexuality than we have offered in our public dialogues. The authors make their respective cases with in-depth examinations of what the Scriptures teach about homosexuality and what the empirical evidence tells us about God's homosexual children. They also provide insights and information that will enlighten future discussions about homosexual people and help us to determine for ourselves where we will stand as Christians as we face up to the demands of gay and lesbian activists.

Most of us realize that the church has been hard on gays and lesbians. Too often, church people have made it clear that they despise them. From church pulpits, things have been said to make homosexual men and women feel dirty. Today, over and against such meanness there is a growing willingness among Christians to consider change. How much we are ready to change, just how we should change, and what we should expect in the way of change from other Christians are questions yet to be answered. This book will help us to answer such questions.

Tony Campolo
Peggy Campolo

Preface

The two of us first met each other in 1980 when we were students in the peace studies program at Associated Mennonite Biblical Seminary (AMBS) in Elkhart, Indiana. Our paths did not cross again for a number of years, but when they did we discovered a remarkable parallelism in our lives.

Both of us grew up outside the church and became Christians as teenagers. Later, in the mid-1970s, we each discovered the writings of John Howard Yoder. Yoder spoke to us both in language that as evangelical Christians we could understand, but pushed us beyond our received understandings to embrace the radical gospel message of following the way of Jesus.[1]

After college, in our mid-twenties, we each spent time at AMBS studying with Yoder and finding ourselves attracted to the Anabaptist-Mennonite tradition in general. Following seminary, we each spent time working in the peace movement, pastoring, and completing doctorates in theological ethics.[2] Both of us had James McClendon as a teacher, Ted at the Graduate Theological Union and Mark at Fuller Theological Seminary, where McClendon was his doctoral supervisor. We both ended up as teachers at Eastern Mennonite University (EMU), Mark at the seminary and Ted in the undergraduate program.

As would be expected from our common journeys, we find ourselves sharing many of the same convictions. We both see pacifism as integral to the biblical message of God's will for human life. We both believe Jesus is our savior and model, the embodiment of God in human life. We both understand the faith community as the locus of God's involvement in human history, the place where the message of peace needs first to be embodied and be the base for witness in the wider world. We both approach theology and ethics in light of the Bible, taking cues from writers such as Walter Brueggemann, John Howard Yoder, and Richard Hays.

However, we have discovered in recent years that we also have important areas of disagreement. One is our view of how churches best respond to gay and lesbian people in their midst. Ted takes a more inclusive or "welcoming and affirming" stance. Mark takes a "welcoming but not affirming" stance, which in certain ways lines up with traditional views.

EMU and Mennonite churches at large, like the rest of the North American Christian community and broader society, have faced intense debate and divisiveness over issues around homosexuality. Several years ago, our university formed a committee for the purpose of providing contexts for discussions and discernment among people with differing views. This committee asked us to participate in a series of public conversations that would voice some of the different opinions related to these issues.

In these conversations, we sought both to inform audiences of content relevant to the debate and, perhaps as important, to model a respectful and mutually edifying process of discussion in an arena all too often characterized by more heat than light, more polarization than enlightenment.

This book is an expanded version of our public conversations in the spring of 2006. We have sought to follow a genuinely open process. The book was written in the same order as the chapters.

Part 1 includes revisions of two previously published essays in which we each seek to provide some orientation to the theological debate up to this point. It intends to be largely descriptive.

Part 2 includes expanded versions of the basic presentations each of us prepared for our various conversations. Chapters three and four contain the basic constructive arguments we each have developed concerning homosexuality and the churches. Extensive responses to each other's main argument follow. We conclude this part of the discussion with shorter responses to each others' comments.

Part 3 contains a series of shorter point/counterpoint essays. Each of us poses two questions for further reflection. For each of the four questions we have four rounds of discussion: question, answer, follow up, and final comment.

Part 4 concludes the book with a short essay summarizing our central points of agreement. Then there are annotated reading lists from each of us, noting twenty books or essays that we have found helpful in our work.

We send this book forth hopefully. We have engaged in a conversation in which we address contentious issues with openness about our disagreements but also with sustained respect for one another and a commitment to keep talking. We each desire that we might actually grow in understanding. We have not sought a premature "consensus" but have believed it important to leave our raw edges visible.

We have certainly not resolved all the issues. Probably we have not even adequately identified our differences. But we hope that by persevering in our conversation we have at least provided a model for Christians trying to find their way through this oh-so-difficult terrain. And we believe it is significant that after our at times bruising exchange, we remain friends!

PART 1
GETTING ORIENTED

Chapter 1

The 'Homosexuality' Debate: Two Streams of Biblical Interpretation[1]

Ted Grimsrud

In seeking discernment concerning the controversy over intimate same-sex relationships among Christians, we must learn better to understand points of view different from our own. This essay represents my attempt to do that. I will be describing the main arguments of several recent scholars who, in general, may be seen as reflecting two different understanding of biblical teaching.

I use the terms restrictive and inclusive, which I hope are essentially value neutral, for each of these viewpoints. By restrictive, I mean views that support restricting the church participation of gay and lesbian Christians who are in intimate relationships. By inclusive, I refer to those who support church inclusion with no restrictions related to homosexuality per se.[2]

The Restrictive Case

1) Thomas E. Schmidt. Straight and Narrow? Compassion and Clarity in the Homosexuality Debate. *Downers Grove, IL: InterVarsity Press, 1995.*

In Thomas Schmidt's view, the basic message of the Bible stems from and elaborates on the teaching of the creation story in chapters 1 and 2 of Genesis. Our understanding of appropriate human sexual expression should follow from Genesis. The creation account makes four crucial points regarding sexuality: (1) Reproduction is good. (2) Sex is good. (3) Marriage is good. (4) Male and female are necessary sexual counterparts (43).[3]

Same-sex sexual relationships, according to Schmidt, are problematic in a fundamental way. They reflect an implicit rejection of the very order of creation—and in doing so they reflect a rejection of God. Same-sex sexual relationships undermine the sanctity of opposite-sex marriage. They declare that a different expression of sexuality outside of the God-created intent for human beings is good (48). Such a rejection of God's will has to be unacceptable for all Christians who accept the authority of the Bible.

The biblical teaching against same-sex sexual intimacy in the rest of the Bible all presupposes the Genesis portrayal of normative marriage and is consistent with that portrayal. The main reason the Bible speaks so clearly about sexual activity outside opposite-sex marriage is because illicit sexual activity is understood to be a threat to the very social foundations of the Bible's faith communities.

Leviticus 18:22 and 20:13 give us the most direct Old Testament teaching proscribing same-sex sexual relationships. These two verses have normative force, even though they are surrounded by other commands that present-day Christians no longer consider binding. The normativity of the anti-same-sex sexual intimacy verses follows from their rootage in the creation story. The sexuality commands have the force of abiding moral law, not simply temporal purity regulations that Christians understand to have been superseded in Jesus (90).

Paul's writings reflect the creation ordering of human sexuality. A key text is Romans 1:18-32. This passage begins with a reference to idolatry as the root cause of the immorality addressed in the verses that follow (53). Paul points here to an inherent connection between idolatry and homosexuality. He singles out same-sex sexual activity because he seeks a vivid image of humankind's primal rejection of the sovereignty of God the creator (67). Since God's intent for opposite-sex marriage as the only appropriate context for sexual relationships, the denials of the exclusivity of this context implicit in same-sex relationships means rejecting God.

Schmidt understands Paul to be teaching in Romans 1 that homosexuality is a paradigmatic case of human being's sense of their identity being distorted due to idolatry. Living in a same-sex relationship is to be in revolt against God. When people live in revolt against God, inevitably their lives will be corrupted, with the consequent consequences of alienation and brokenness (85).

Paul's teaching against same-sex sexual intimacy also found expression in 1 Corinthians 6:9 and 1 Timothy 1:10. Paul uses a term here that he likely coined himself in condemning same-sex sexual intimacy. The Greek word *arsenokoites* clearly comes from the Greek translation of Leviticus 18:22 that Paul would have used. The Leviticus verse uses two words (*arseno* = "men" and *koiten* = "lies with") that are combined by Paul, presumably to evoke memories of the teaching of Leviticus that forbids "a man laying with another man as he would with a woman" (95-96).

Schmidt concludes that the biblical teaching is being confirmed in our present day as we observe the self-destructiveness of same-sex sexual activity that Paul's teaching in Romans 1 would lead us to expect. Idolatrous behavior is invariably self-destructive as God "gives up" idolaters to the consequences of their rebellion versus God (100-30).

2) Richard B. Hays, The Moral Vision of the New Testament: A Contemporary Introduction to New Testament Ethics. *San Francisco: HarperSanFrancisco, 1996.*

Richard Hays admits that the Bible rarely refers directly to homosexual behavior; however, he asserts, we must recognize that each of these rare references is totally negative and needs to be taken seriously. The two references in the book of Leviticus

(18:23; 20:10) establish the basic tone. Their unambiguous prohibition of same-sex sexual intimacy founded the universal rejection of such relationships in Judaism (381).

Hays focuses most of his attention on pertinent New Testament texts, especially Romans 1:18-32. Romans 1 plays a special role in Christian sexual ethics because it is the only place in the New Testament that explains the Christian condemnation of homosexual behavior in an explicitly theological framework (383).

Underlying Paul's theology here is his reference to God as creator. This reference grounds Paul's discussion of sexuality in the story of creation in Genesis 1 and 2 (i.e., the portrayal of male/female sexuality as the norm, 386).

The practice of same-sex sex may be understood as a type of "sacrament" for the contra-faith of those who reject God as creator and ruler of the universe (386). Faith in God includes, by definition, an acceptance of the order God has created. Blatantly to deny the exclusive normativity of male/female sexuality, hence, is par excellence an expression of the refusal to honor God as God, which Paul sees as the core problem with pagan idolatry.

When Paul writes that same-sex sex is "against nature," he means it goes against the order of creation, as "nature" for Paul means the created order. Those who engage in sexual relations with people of the same sex are acting against nature in defiance of the Creator (387).

Why does Paul single out homosexual intercourse here? According to Hays, Paul does so because it so graphically reflects the way in which human rebellion against God is expressed in ways that blatantly distort the way God created things to be. When rebellious human beings "exchange" their created sexuality for same-sex intimacy, they manifestly show how sinful human beings have "exchanged the truth about God for a lie" (Romans 1:25, 388).

The created order, the "natural" pattern, points toward the

exclusivity of heterosexual marriage as the context for appropriate sexual intimacy. The entire Bible supports this understanding. This normativity of heterosexual marriage provides the context for the Bible's univocally negative explicit mentions of same-sex sexual activity (390).

The fact that some human beings might feel a strong sexual attraction toward people of the same sex is not to be understood as necessarily good and trustworthy. That these desires and impulses happen to be involuntary is not evidence that they are appropriately acted on. Due to the depth of the power of sin in the human heart, even our involuntary impulses may well be corrupted (390).

3) *Stanley J. Grenz.* Welcoming but Not Affirming: An Evangelical Response to Homosexuality. *Louisville: Westminster/John Knox Press, 1998.*

Stanley Grenz's position rests on his interpretation of biblical texts of two sorts, the handful of texts that he understands directly to address the issue of same-sex sexual intimacy and the overall understanding the Bible gives of marriage as rooted in the creative intent of God. He believes that the fundamental issue in the debate ultimately boils down to how much respect one is willing to give to the teaching of the Bible. For those who uphold the authority of the Bible in the church, Grenz asserts, rejecting the moral validity of all same-sex sexual intimacy is the only option (89).

Grenz understands Old Testament morality concerning sexual relationships to be reducible to one basic principle. The overarching focus of Old Testament sexual ethics is to defend family and married life. The holiness code in Leviticus 17–26 argues that any sexual activity outside of the context of heterosexual marriage is a threat to the institution of marriage and hence is an abomination (46).

The extremity of the punishment in Leviticus 20:13 for same-sex sex reflects the seriousness of such a violation of God's intent for human sexuality. Even if we no longer use the death penalty for such offenses, we nonetheless should recognize the seriousness of the violation that evokes it in Leviticus. The prohibition remains normative for us today, even if the punishment does not (47).

Turning to the New Testament, Grenz argues that in Romans 1 Paul echoes the concerns of the Levitical holiness code in rejecting same-sex sexual intimacy as contrary to God's intentions for human beings. For Paul, only the model of male/female marriage as the one legitimate context for sexual expression is natural and fits with the Creator's design. Sex outside of this context is "against nature" and brings upon itself God's anger (56).

In responding to claims by inclusivist thinkers, Grenz rejects the idea that understanding the core Christian ethical criterion to be love should lead the church to affirm same-sex covenant relationships as expressions of the ultimate Christian value—love. For Grenz, love must be understood in the context of the overall biblical message of God's intentions for human social life. If God's order is being violated, it is not a loving response to condone that violation.

The creation account in Genesis provides us with crucial information in relation to these questions. Our direction may be seen in the fact that God created human beings as male and female (Genesis 1:27, 103). Furthermore, Genesis 2:18 tells us that simply as male, the first human being was incomplete. To be complete, human living must include both sexes, different from one another yet complimentary.

Grenz understands the creation stories to provide the normative model for marriage—male and female, complimenting each other, completing each other. From this portrayal, he concludes that sexual intimacy is meant *only* for people in an opposite-sex marriage. Sexual intimacy is meant to address our incompleteness—the incompleteness that God resolved by creating women to join with men (104).

Sexual intercourse has profound symbolic meaning for Grenz. It is always a symbolic act, with three central messages at its core: (1) Sexual intercourse symbolizes the exclusive bond between husband and wife—reflecting the biblical confession that the person of faith has an exclusive bond with God. (2) Sexual intercourse symbolizes the mutuality of the marriage relationship—each partner finding pleasure in the intimacy and seeking to foster the other's pleasure. (3) Sexual intercourse symbolizes the married couple's openness to new life emerging from their relationship through the birth of children (108).

Grenz argues at length that same-sex covenant relationships simply cannot share in the richness of this symbolism. He believes that legitimate sexual intimacy must always be symbolic in these ways and that the institution of marriage is meant to foster such rich symbolism. In doing so, marriage serves as a crucial element in the life of the faith community.

For Grenz, probably the most fundamental reason same-sex covenant relationships among Christians should not be affirmed is that they devalue marriage (141). He understands monogamous, male-female marriage to be the foundation for Christian communal spirituality.

4) Willard Swartley. Homosexuality: Biblical Interpretation and Moral Discernment. *Scottdale, PA: Herald Press, 2003.*

In his introductory chapter, Swartley asserts that unlike his previous writing on issues such as war, male/female relationships, and slavery, there is clarity and uniformity in the biblical witness regarding homosexuality that does not allow for movement away from a more "status quo" view towards a more "liberative" view. "Homosexual practice is not related to grace-energized behavior in a single text," he writes (18).

The three main points Swartley draws from the Old Testament in developing his case for opposing same-sex sexual intimacy are: (1) Genesis 1 portrays God's intention toward creation by establishing sexuality as a good gift, one with great power and subject to misuse (27-28). The only appropriate context for sexual intercourse is male/female marriage.

(2) The story of Sodom and Gomorrah is rightly understood as focusing on threatened rape as an expression of inhospitality, not on "loving homosexual relations." Nonetheless, it is significant that in Genesis 19 and Judges 19, "it is precisely (homo)sexual lust that precludes hospitality" (31-32).

(3) Leviticus 18:22 and 20:13 regard same-sex relations as an abomination in the same category as idolatry and child-sacrifice (33). "The fact that same-sex male relations and Molech worship, which involved sacrificing offspring, are linked may be 'telling' of the seriousness of the same-sex offense" (35).

While acknowledging that Jesus did not overtly speak of homosexuality, Swartley draws a number of points from Jesus' teaching that are relevant for our ethical discernment. He believes that Jesus combines a commitment to holiness (e.g., a condemnation of *porneia* [fornication, defined by Swartley as "as sexual genital relations outside heterosexual marriage," 40]) with mercy (e.g., be loving toward even those you must critique for transgressing holiness requirements, 47).

In relation to Paul, Swartley focuses on Romans 1:24-27 and 1 Corinthians 6:9. He proposes that the Romans passage is particularly important because it links same-sex practices with idolatry—a rejection of the God-ordered normativity of heterosexuality. For people to turn to others of the same sex as sexual partners, according to Paul, reflects a substituting of worship of creation for worship of the creator (51-52).

Because Paul also condemns female-female sexual intimacy in Romans 1:26-27, he cannot have in mind only specific sexual practices peculiar to males (i.e., pederasty) but means to make a categorical judgment of all same-sex sexual intimacy (57). Paul grounds this general condemnation on the normativity of Genesis 1–2 and its portrayal of male/female sexual intimacy as the exclusive norm. All exceptions are "unnatural" (57).

Swartley understands 1 Corinthians 6:9 in the context of Paul's concern with sexual libertinism that is reflected in 1 Corinthians 5 and the critique of *porneia* (fornication). Because of the general level of unrestrained sexual behavior in Corinth, Paul and his readers likely knew of all kinds of same-sex relationships, including long-term stable partnerships. Hence, his writing against same-sex intimacy is to be seen as all-encompassing (70).

Paul is best understood, in Swartley's view, as being unalterably opposed to same-sex intimacy simply because it involved people of the same sex. Hence, it is misleading to focus on particularly "problematic" types of sexual expression as if that might make room for Paul accepting "less problematic expressions" (70).

4) Robert A. J. Gagnon in Dan O. Via and Robert A. J. Gagnon. The Bible and Homosexuality: Two Views. *Minneapolis: Fortress Press, 2004.*

Robert A. J. Gagnon has become the most prolific and arguably most influential writer supporting a restrictive view. His arguments are developed at the greatest length in his massive volume, *The Bible and Homosexual Practice.* A more concise and accessible summary is found in a book he co-authored with Dan Via, *Homosexuality and the Bible: Two Views,* from which I draw for this summary of Gagnon's argument.

Gagnon's opposition to the acceptance of homosexual practice stems from his sense of clarity concerning the thrust of the Bible's core values. These core values point unequivocally against homosexual practice (42). As Gagnon develops his argument, he draws on materials from throughout the Bible to support this assertion.

Most of the arguments in favor of the churches taking a welcoming stance toward gays and lesbians use to some degree various analogies that devalue explicit anti-homosexual practice texts. Gagnon discusses various of these (e.g., Gentile inclusion as reflected especially in the book of Acts; the Bible's apparent support for slavery, which is rejected by modern Christians; the recent acceptance of women's leadership in the church; and the acceptance of remarriage after divorce for church members). He argues that none of these analogies holds much weight (43-47).

By far the clearest moral analogy, in Gagnon's view, is the parallel between the Bible's perspective on incest and its perspective on homosexual practice. For Gagnon, just as the Bible's prohibition of incest remains normative for contemporary Christians, so too does the parallel prohibition of homosexual practice (48-50).

Contrary to the argument that Jesus, in his love command, provides warrant for the churches to practice toleration toward gays and lesbians, Gagnon asserts that Jesus' love command most certainly does not underwrite modern-day notions of tolerance (50-53). Jesus' call to love neighbor and God is fully consistent with ethically rigorous convictions concerning moral purity and practices of church discipline that challenge Christians to separate themselves from sinful behaviors.

Gagnon believes that the Bible as a whole clearly and explicitly condemns same-sex sexual intimacy. The Old Testament has a large web of texts that directly and indirectly indict same-sex intercourse as inherently unacceptable (56). One key part of this "web of texts" is the story of creation that portrays "one-fleshness" as requiring a male *and* a female (61). The core of the creation account, according to Gagnon, is to establish for all times the significance that God has created males and females for each other. This complementarity of the sexes establishes the exclusive normativeness of heterosexuality as the only morally acceptable context for sexual intimacy.

A second key part of the Old Testament's stance may be found in the Leviticus holiness code. Leviticus 18 and 20 single out male-male sexual intercourse as uniquely problematic and in direct violation of the complementarity of the sexes as the only acceptable context for sexual intimacy (65). The on-going significance of the Leviticus laws for Christians is seen in how Paul directly draws on Leviticus to articulate his own negative views about same-sex sexual intimacy (67).

Gagnon understands Jesus' "silence" on these issues not to be evidence in any way of him having an accepting or affirming view of such practice. To the contrary, that Jesus did not speak directly to this issue much more likely reflects his acceptance of the traditional view that judged all same-sex sexual intimacy as inherently wrong. The best explanation of Jesus' "silence" is that Jesus assumes the anti-homosex assumptions of his day and simply found no need to articulate those assumptions since they were so commonly shared. As support for this view, Gagnon mentions Jesus' general concern with sexual purity (68-74).

Unlike Jesus, the apostle Paul did directly address same-sex sexual intimacy. He articulates the normative New Testament view. In Romans 1, Paul links idolatry and same-sex intercourse. He asserts that each problem absurdly denies the clear and natural revelation that each leads a person away from authentic life and toward self-destruction. Paul widens the net by also condemning lesbianism, providing the basis for making the biblical condemnation of homosexual practice equally applicable to all same-sex relationships. Paul's comments reflect awareness on his part of all sorts of possible same-sex relationships; hence, his negative conclusions apply to all (75).

In 1 Corinthians 6, Paul links back to the judgments of Leviticus in a direct allusion to the language of the Levitical prohibition. Here Paul obviously has in mind the biblical presumption about the creation norm of heterosexuality (81).

A third text, 1 Timothy 1, while in Gagnon's view not necessarily written by Paul himself, does reinforce Paul's thinking concerning same-sex practice. This passage echoes the Ten Commandments in condemning every conceivable type of male-male intercourse (87).

As a consequence of the clear message of the Bible—and the centrality that biblical ethics should have for Christians—Gagnon concludes that the church must explicitly oppose homoerotic acts in order to remain faithful to its Lord (91).

The Inclusive Case

1) Letha Scanzoni and Virginia Mollenkott. Is the Homosexual My Neighbor? A Positive Christian Response, *2nd ed. San Francisco: HarperCollins, 1994.*

According to Letha Scanzoni and Virginia Mollenkott, the core message of the Bible is the command from Jesus to love one's neighbor as oneself. With the love command as central, we are then going to be impressed with a passage such as Acts 10–11, the story of the change in which the early Christians began to welcome non-Jewish Christians as full members of the church. With Acts 10–11 as our model, they assert, we will realize that we may be called to transcend rules and simplistic readings of Scripture in order consistently to live in light of the love command (17).

Scanzoni and Mollenkott believe the gospel calls upon Jesus' followers to be partisans and advocates of marginalized people (39). When the love command is the starting point in approaching the Bible, we will place the highest priority on biblical texts that call upon us to welcome the lowly and outcasts. This benefit of the doubt toward compassion for the outcast challenges followers of Jesus to overcome the social gap between themselves as heterosexual Christians and homosexuals. This gulf is necessary for objectifying and excluding (51).

Scanzoni and Mollenkott do turn to the traditional texts that overtly refer to same-sex sex. They begin, however, by emphasizing that the context for the mention of same-sex sexual activity in Scripture is always that of other negative acts—for example, adultery, failure to propagate, promiscuity, violence, and idolatrous worship. The sexual acts themselves are not condemned in isolation from the other problems (56).

For example, the story of Sodom in Genesis 19 tells not about same-sex sexual orientation and intimate loving relationships. The story there is about heterosexual males who were bent on gang rape (58). A second example, Leviticus 18–20, reflects a deep concern for ritual purity as a means of showing Israel's distinctiveness as a people set apart for God. Activities that reflected conformity with surrounding cultures, particularly their religious practices understood by Israelites to be idolatrous, were strictly forbidden. It appears that Israelites associated male/male sex with such practices.

A third example of the Bible's references to same-sex sexual activity being connected with other problems is seen in Romans. In chapter 1, Paul says nothing about homosexual *love*; rather, the focus is on sexual activity in the context of lust and idolatry (68).

The final examples of the Bible's mention of same-sex sexual activity come in 1 Corinthians and 1 Timothy. In both of these cases, Scanzoni and Mollenkott argue, the writer is referring to particular types of sexual abuse, not homosexual orientation in general (76).

Another central issue in discussions from the Bible, according to Scanzoni and Mollenkott, is the argument that the story of creation establishes male/female sex as the only acceptable type of sexual expression. However, they argue that the core concern in Genesis 1–2 is to tell us how we got here (hence, the allusion to procreation)—not to indicate that this is the only valid type of sexual expression. To say that procreative sex is the only morally legitimate form would not only condemn same-sex sex but also any opposite-sex sex from which procreation is known ahead of time not to be a possibility (81).

2) Daniel A. Helminiak. What the Bible Really Says About Homosexuality. *San Francisco: Alamo Square Press, 1994.*

Daniel Helminiak argues that we must not draw strong conclusions about the applicability of biblical texts to present-day issues when we do not have adequate historical background to determine what the texts meant to their writers and first readers (32). This uncertainty applies to all the small handful of biblical texts that appear to address issues of same-sex sexuality.

As well, Helminiak argues, from what we can tell about the biblical teachings concerning same-sex sexuality, it appears that the Bible was not addressing the same types of relations that are under scrutiny in today's context. The Bible did not know of homosexuality as a sexual orientation; only of homogenital acts. Hence, it gives no answer "about spontaneous affection for people of the same sex and about the ethical possibility of expressing that affection in loving, sexual relationships" (33).

In Helminiak's view, an action is not wrong simply because a Bible verse seems to label it as such. "A thing is wrong for a reason. If the reason no longer holds and no other reason is given, how can a thing still be judged wrong?" (33).

Genesis 19, the story of the judgment of Sodom, tells of a violation of hospitality expectations—not of a society that is judged because of its tolerance of loving same-sex intimacy (40). The second Old Testament passage commonly referred to in discussions of sexuality, Leviticus's double mention of the prohibition of "men laying with men as with women" (18:23; 20:10), stemmed from concerns about idolatry—not from scruples about sex per se (45).

The prohibitions in the holiness code include a wide variety of actions with the common theme being actions that were characteristic of those outside of Israel. Many of these actions were not understood to be wrong in and of themselves, but because they were connected with Gentile, and not Jewish, identity. Hence, Helminiak asserts, "no thought is given [in Leviticus] to whether the sex *in itself* is right or wrong" (46-47).

Male/male sex is called an "abomination" in Leviticus 20:13. By abomination is meant "impurity," Helminiak argues, or the violation of a taboo. It is *not* called something wrong in itself, a "sin." It is a ritual violation (52). Helminiak concludes that the focus in Leviticus is on practical, historically-particular concerns. The prohibition against male/male sex here must not be seen as a timeless, absolute prohibition. Rather, it is time and context bound.

Helminiak argues that Paul's concern in Romans 1 centered on people engaging in sexual practices of the type that was not normal for them—that is, people who normally were heterosex-ually oriented having sex with people of their own sex. He refers to Paul's use of "against nature" in Romans 11:24 (cf. it is "against nature" for Gentile "branches" to be grafted on to the "tree" of Israel) to support the argument that when Paul uses that phrase in Romans 1 he has in mind simply that which is *unexpected* (65).

In Romans 1:27, Paul is concerned not with same-sex sex as the key issue but with idolatry, people worshipping that which is not God. Paul is making a point about various idolatrous prac-tices among Gentiles, including people having "unexpected" sex—sex of a sort that they do not normally practice (77). If this is an accurate reading of Paul's intent, then the thrust of Romans one is not to provide a basis for present-day rejection of the moral legitimacy of loving, mutual, committed same-sex inti-mate relationships. Rather, Paul's words apply more to people engaging in sexual practices that are obsessive, out-of-control, promiscuous, and directly refuting godly values of commitment, mutuality, and respect.

Helminiak understands the other brief references to same-sex sexuality in Paul's writings (1 Corinthians 6:9 and 1 Timothy 1:10) to be similar in meaning. The key term, used in both verses, is the Greek word *arsenokoitai*. According to Helminiak, Paul uses this term (translated "sodomites" in the NRSV) to indicate a type of male/male sexual activity that is wanton, lewd, and irresponsi-ble. Paul is not meaning to focus on the fact that this activity hap-pens between people of the same sex so much as on its nature as exploitative and obsessive (85). That is, Paul is concerned about the harm done to people when they are out of control sexually, not about mutually edifying intimate relationships.

3) Martti Nissinen. Homoeroticism in the Biblical World. *Minneapolis: Fortress Press, 1998.*

Martti Nissinen argues that the Levitical holiness code reflects a perspective on sexual activity that understood regulations in terms of strengthening the identity of society, its integrity and growth. For the ancient Israelites, social cohesion was linked with strong sex roles and protection of family relationships. Anything that challenged sex roles or family relationships would have been seen as a terrible threat to the viability of the Israelite community. Taboos related to sex roles and sexual expression arose to protect this identity (41-42). The regulations on sexuality, including the prohibitions of male/male sex, must be understood in light of this quest of community survival.

Nissinen links sex roles with the prohibition of male/male sex. The code focuses exclusively on males because it would have been impossible for female/female sex to challenge male domination (the domination being symbolized by the active, penetrating role males played in sex). What made male/male sex an "abomination" was one of the males taking the female role (being penetrated), thereby transgressing sex boundaries and confusing sex roles (43-44).

The holiness code prohibits such sexual activity because of a desire to maintain clearly distinct sex roles and because of a specific concern about rejecting non-Israelite religious practices. Neither of these concerns applies to modern-day Christians; hence, the prohibition has no direct application for us, Nissinen writes.

In Genesis 19, the story of Sodom is basically a story of inhospitality, not a story of sexual behavior. The story makes this point by presenting two positive examples of hospitality, Abraham (18:1-5) and Lot (19:1-3), that contrast with the inhospitality of the Sodomites.

The story of the murdered concubine in Judges 19 parallels the Sodom story in important respects and reinforces the point that the mob's concern was the expression of dominance and inhospitality, not same-sex sexual desire (51).

Moving to 1 Samuel, Nissinen calls the relationship between David and Jonathan "homosocial" (a close friendship between men that may or may not have erotic expressions, 17). He suggests that their kind of friendship, based as it as on love and equality, may be "more comparable with modern homosexual people's experiences of themselves than those texts that explicitly speak of homosexual acts that are aggressive, violent expressions of domination and subjugation" (56).

In addressing Paul's writings, Nissinen states initially that in the Hellenistic world of Paul's day, same-sex sex was considered "against nature" for two reasons: first, it did not lead to procreation, and, second, it signaled a violation of sex roles in which the male always was "active" and the female always "passive" (88).

Paul himself uses the phrase "against nature" several times in his letters as "a matter of the common order of things as Paul had learned it." For Paul, "unnatural" or "against nature" means something beyond normal experience—good or bad. When he uses the term in Romans 1:19-32, he is not using it as a technical term with specifically Christian content. "Against nature" here simply means "unusual" or "not what one would expect" (105). Paul does not have "the created order" in mind when he uses "against nature." He is not alluding to Genesis 1–3. He is simply reflecting the Hellenistic sense that these people he's speaking of in Romans 1 are not practicing the kind of sex one would expect (106-7).

Paul's central concern in Romans one is not sexuality at all. Paul uses the references to idolatrous sexual activity in order to raise the ire of his readers and to gain their approval of his condemnation of what his readers would have seen as typical Gentile sinfulness. Paul does this, though, not in order to add to the sense of righteousness that his readers may have had in reading these words but actually to turn the tables. Paul's use of Romans 1:18–32, as it turns out, is to drive home his point about the problematic self-righteousness of his readers. Paul, in the end, is challenging his readers not to be judgmental (111).

The specific meaning of the terms used in 1 Corinthians 6:9 and 1 Timothy 1:10 that are often translated as referring to same-sex sexuality is actually quite obscure. In both passages, though, the context makes it clear that both *arsenokoites* and *malakos* are examples, along with numerous other terms used in these verses, of the exploitation of persons. Paul is concerned with the wrong that people do to others, not with non-harmful intimate relationships (118).

4) David G. Myers and Letha Dawson Scanzoni. What God Has Joined Together? A Christian Case for Gay Marriage. *HarperSanFrancisco, 2005.*

David Myers and Letha Scanzoni address as their fundamental concern the issue of marriage among gay and lesbian Christians. Human beings thrive best in life-giving intimate relationships, as our most basic human drive is for loving connections with other people (11). Human happiness tends to be linked with the possibilities of covenanted attachments in marriage partnerships. Married people tend to be happier than unmarried people (16-17).

Myers and Scanzoni assert that we do not yet know *why* people end up attracted to others of their same sex; we do know, though, that for some people this attraction is irreversibly fixed. Hence, to forbid people with such attraction to enter into possibility of marriage is highly problematic. In doing so, we may be consigning a significant number to people to lives that will be less fulfilling and fruitful than they could be. We face, in the authors' perspective, a major benefit of the doubt against so limiting the options of our gay and lesbian brothers and sisters.

So, Myers and Scanzoni ask, do we have clear bases in Scripture for taking a stance that seems, in face of the life-enhancing possibilities of marriage, to be morally problematic? They do not think so. The Bible does not use the actual word homosexuality. The few references to same-sex sexual acts all seem to have in mind other kinds of problems as well—e.g., idolatry, violent rape, lust, exploitation, promiscuity. The Bible seems to have no awareness of our contemporary understandings of homosexual orientation or the possibility of covenanted same-sex partnerships (84-85).

In regard to the New Testament, Myers and Scanzoni point to the story in the book of Acts about how Peter gave up his long-held assumptions and came to a more open view concerning Gentiles. Peter's change of heart stemmed in part from his personal contact with Cornelius and recognition that Cornelius truly was a person of faith. Peter ultimately stated, "I truly understand that God shows no partiality, but in every nation anyone who fears him and does what is right is acceptable to him" (Acts 10:34-35). This experience of Peter's sheds light on how Christians today might approach issues related to homosexuality. As heterosexual people get to know devout gay and lesbian people of faith, they may well be "forced to reconsider long-held assumptions and interpretations of Scripture" and come to see God as showing "no partiality" (102-3).

Jesus himself did not directly speak to homosexuality. However, Myers and Scanzoni believe that Jesus' general orientation of compassion and care should mark the churches' approach to same-sex relationships (103-4).

They reject the argument that Jesus established an exclusive norm for heterosexual marriage in his comments about marriage in Mark 10:6-9. He was responding to a direct question about the permanence of marriage, not making a philosophical statement about sexual differences and about the idea that human wholeness requires the merging of two incomplete halves. As did Paul, Jesus spoke positively about singleness with no hint that single people were not whole human beings (109).

The notion of innate sexual differences and the need for heterosexual marriage to provide the context for a needed "complementarity" that uniquely allows for human wholeness fosters a continued dependence of women on men for their completeness. According to Myers and Scanzoni, such an approach hinders everyone's call to "be whole persons who can develop both their active and affective sides" (111).

They cite Hosea 2 characterization of the marriage covenant

as including "justice, fairness, love, kindness, faithfulness, and a revelation of God's personhood," asserting that these characteristics can just as likely be part of a same-sex marriage as a heterosexual marriage (113).

5. Jack Rogers. Jesus, the Bible, and Homosexuality: Explode the Myths, Heal the Church. *Louisville: Westminster John Knox, 2006.*

Jack Rogers starts with an affirmation that discriminating unjustly against anyone in the church is a terrible problem. He develops the argument that discrimination against gays and lesbians in the churches is an important example of such unjust discrimination.

Rogers links the present-day movement to secure full inclusion of gay and lesbian Christians with earlier movements in which the church, "guided by the Holy Spirit in understanding the Scriptures," came to affirm the full inclusion, including ordination, of African-Americans, women, and divorced and remarried Christians. In each case, he argues, Christians moved from a more literalistic reading of the Bible to one that centered on the life and teaching of Jesus (15-16).

Following the way of Jesus should empower Christians to show love for all, including especially the "outcasts of society." Rogers believes it is unthinkable that Jesus would turn away people who had been treated harshly by society, including those whose treatment had pushed them to attempt suicide (56-57).

If we read the Bible in light of Jesus' compassion toward those labeled as outside of the boundary lines of "pure religion," we will seriously question the applicability of biblical statements that in their context spoke against same-sex sexual behavior as expressions of idolatry and unbridled lust to present-day instances of monogamous, covenanted intimate partnerships among Christians whose lives reflect fruitful relationships with God. That is to say, the "plain sense" of the "anti-gay" texts requires consideration of the contexts of those texts—and such consideration will make it clear how different the biblical contexts are from the present context of twenty-first century North American churches (58).

According to Rogers, the Bible's condemnation of sexual contact between two men reflects cultural assumptions that saw such conduct as a confusion of sex roles—assumptions totally ignorant of what we understand today to be the innate sexual orientation of many who are attracted to those of the their same sex (65). The cultural embeddedness of these assumptions renders them non-normative for present-day Christian ethical discernment.

The Bible's strongest prohibitions of male/male sexual relationship statements are found in Leviticus. The cultural context for those statements is the Israelites' need for strong cohesiveness as a means of sustaining their identity as a people in relation to the Egyptians and Canaanites. A key aspect of maintaining this separation was to avoid mixing in any way with Canaanites and their social and religious practices. This priority on the avoidance of mixing came to apply to a wide range of behaviors, not having more than one kind of seed in a field and not having more than one kind of fabric in one's clothing. For two men to have sex would be to mix sex roles, one taking on the role of a woman, thus crossing a cultural boundary in intolerable ways (72). Thus, the condemnation of male/male sex in Leviticus applied to a specific cultural context. It was not a timeless, absolute directive.

Rogers also does not believe that the texts in Paul's writings that are often cited actually support exclusionary approaches to gays and lesbians in the church. Partly, this view is based on his understanding of the meaning of the words Paul uses, *arsenokoitai* and *malakos*. He concludes that *arsenokoites* is best understood as alluding to economic exploitation, likely related to sexual activity—not as a general condemnation of all same-sex sexual intimacy (73-74). *Malakos* likely refers to effeminacy and/or general lack of self-control (74). In both cases, to accurately understand Paul's meaning we must think in terms of specific cultural contexts and not general, meant-for-all-time ethical prescriptions (75).

In discussing Romans 1:18-32, Rogers again emphasizes reading the text in its cultural context, arguing once more that the meaning of the text does not have direct relevance to present-day same-sex intimate partnerships. Paul's main concerns here are with idolatry as expressed in excessive, lustful sexual behavior. When Paul uses the idea of the behavior he is referring to being "unnatural," he is not speaking about "homosexuality" versus "heterosexuality." Rather, he means to be saying that the excessive, lustful aspects of the behavior are "unnatural" (that is, unconventional, out of the ordinary, contrary to social expectations). Hence, his point does not speak same sex relationships per se (77-78).

Finally, Rogers also rejects the argument that the biblical understanding of creation (male and female as the exclusive norm for covenanted partnerships) provides a basis for discriminating against gays and lesbians in the churches. He points out that nowhere in the Bible is creation used as a supporting motif in the formulation of norms for sexual relations and marriage. Genesis 1–2 are not about homosexuality or marriage; that passage is not intended to speak to present-day questions concerning homosexuality (85).

What Are the Key Issues?

In this essay I have summarized diverse theological and biblical perspectives on the issues related to homosexuality. In conclusion, I will simply identify some of the key questions that arise from this comparative report.

Applicability of biblical materials. Our two groups seem clearly to differ on how we should apply biblical materials, though not necessarily on the authority of the Bible per se. One of the basic issues here is how clear do we understand the Bible to be? Is it possible categorically to equate the biblical teaching with a certain present-day position? One side seems fairly comfortable with such an equation, the other seems more to be saying that when studied carefully, the Bible does not yield a clear position. These latter writers do not dismiss the Bible out of hand but rather come to a different understanding from what is found in the Bible.

Another issue concerning the applicability of the biblical materials may be framed as a question of how directly these materials should be applied to the present day. How seriously must we take the great distance in time, geography, language, and culture between Bible times and ours? What are the implications of this distance?

One crucial text where this issue is central is the one overt biblical prohibition of male/male sex, the holiness code in Leviticus. One side understands that, even carefully considering the distance, the Levitical prohibition does provide us with a clear and directly applicable directive; the other side tends to understand Leviticus as part of an entirely foreign context that at most has general relevance for Christians.

Meaning of core references. The handful of biblical texts that speak directly of same-sex sex lend themselves to a variety of interpretations. A central difference can be seen in opinions about whether these texts are referring to relationships that are analogous to present-day same-sex intimate relationships. The differences in relation to this question may be the most substantial in this controversy—certainly at least among the writers I have summarized here.

For progress toward rapprochement in the controversy, it is crucial to focus some serious energy on the extent to which legitimate analogies may be drawn between biblical cases and present-day cases. I actually believe that some progress could be made, but that progress requires careful work in constructing criteria for what constitute legitimate analogies—followed by applying those analogies to the biblical materials.

Differences related to specific texts are also obvious. Four of my restrictive writers do not draw upon the Sodom story in Genesis 19 as central to their arguments, though certainly others do, including Robert Gagnon.[4] The inclusive writers all reject such an application.

The three texts whose interpretations are the most conflicted are Leviticus 18–20, Romans 1, and 1 Corinthians 6. Is Leviticus reflecting an underlying, universal, creation-based principle as the basis for the prohibition of male/male sex, or is it reflecting instead time-bound contextual concerns that no longer are directly relevant for Christians? Is Romans 1 relevant to all same-sex relationships or only same-sex sex that is practiced by people who are heterosexual in orientation? Does its critique of the sex "against nature" rest on an understanding of a God-ordained created order in which male/female sex is the exclusive norm or does it rest on a more practical view that this is sexual activity that is "unexpected"? How certain may we be about the meaning of the Greek terms in 1 Corinthians 6:9, which in recent years have been translated in English as "homosexuals" and similar terms? Are these terms referring to same-sex sex per se or rather to exploitation and moral laxity?

Creation and marriage. The restrictive writers understand the creation account of Genesis 1–2 and its later use by Jesus as crucial to establishing the exclusive normativeness of male/female marital sex. People on the other side reject that interpretation and application.

What is the significance of human beings being portrayed as male and female? Is this simply a descriptive statement centered on saying that we come from procreative sex without the implication that such sex is the only morally legitimate type? Or is it more a normative statement meant to establish that male/female marital sex is all that God endorses?

How should we apply Jesus' use of the creation story in a passage such as Matthew 19? Is he echoing a normative portrayal of the only appropriate type of sexual intimacy? Or is he merely focusing on male and female relations because that was specific concern he was addressing in speaking on divorce?

Even if one understands the Bible to affirm the centrality of male/female marriage to human community lived before God, does it follow that same-sex intimate relationships must be rejected as morally inappropriate? Does seeing male/female marriage as the norm mean that any alternative to that is a threat to the norm? Or are these actually two separate issues, with a small minority of Christians living in same-sex intimate relationships no more a threat to male/female marriage and procreation than are singleness and childless male/female marriages?

Sin and purity. The basic question under the rubric of sin is how one interprets the basic biblical moral thrust. Are the sins that Christians should be most concerned about threats to the purity of the community and direct violations of biblical law codes? Or is the sin problem understood to be centered on mistreatment of marginalized and vulnerable people? That is, should the church be focused on the sin of the alleged misbehavior of homosexual people—or should the church be focused on the sin of the alleged misbehavior toward homosexual people?

Concluding thoughts. To the extent that the controversy over sexuality lends itself to rational resolution, we would do well to devote more energy to trying to find common ground in relation to biblical interpretation. I do not believe the differences are so much based on different understandings of biblical authority as they are simply on different people finding different meanings in the texts. Hence, in theory we should be able to progress toward some common ground.

To do so, we need to take each other's good faith attempts to grapple with the Bible seriously. Perhaps our biggest challenge is to make the effort to understand one another before launching into our critique. Rather than treating this controversy as an argument to win or lose, we would do much better to think more in terms of a puzzle to solve—and that we all have a contribution to make to such a solution. No one is benefiting from the acrimony of the current impasses in which the churches find themselves.

Chapter 2

The Fruit of the Spirit or Works of the Flesh?
Come Let Us Reason Together[1]

Mark Thiessen Nation

"There was once an art critic, I have been told, who had a sure way of identifying ancient Maltese art objects: he found himself crying before them."[2] So begins the moving and wonderful story of Magda and André Trocmé and the parish of Le Chambon in southern France, and how, amid the terrors of World War II, these three thousand or so people, led by a pacifist pastor, saved the lives of thousands of Jews from the Nazis who wanted to kill them. This opening sentence reflects Philip Hallie's own response when he first read the story of Le Chambon: he found tears streaming down his cheeks.

By opening his book this way Hallie intends to suggest that there are emotions that are appropriate for certain experiences, certain realities. Here those emotions relate to the excellence and moral goodness embodied in Le Chambon. Today many emotions are connected with the varied realities surrounding homosexuality: anger, fear, disgust. Amid such feelings, I do not know how we can approach this subject in the church without considerable pain. As I approach the issue I am reminded of

Walter Brueggemann's statement that "theology that is 'pre-pain' must be treated with suspicion."[3]

In relation to this issue, there must be pain because there are still "ministers" of the gospel who attend the funerals of prominent gay people carrying placards reading "God hates fags." Pain because adult children tell wrenching stories of being disowned by their families when they come out, reporting that they have been gay or lesbian for as long as they can remember. Pain because of sitting in the presence of someone who has repeatedly wished he were dead due to living in a world that tells him he must be straight—yet, after years of yearning to be, of seeking help to be, he isn't. Pain because those who claim to be brothers and sisters within the church want to know why they cannot be fully a part of this church that is as much a part of their lives as anyone else's. Pain because this issue continually threatens to divide denominations. Pain because in fact the church (including the Mennonite Church) through more than two decades of struggle, has still not really moved forward on this complicated and only partly understood issue.

One of the reasons we cannot move forward is that we are polarized, which is not uncommon with this sort of emotionally charged subject. Many of us, after some period of agonizing, believe we cannot live in mid-air forever. Therefore, with considerable discomfort, and aware of remaining questions and areas of ambiguity, we take positions. We are, when all is said and done, for or against homoerotic relations.[4] From that point forward we are mostly identified by our public stance.

This chapter is, in part, an attempt to do in essay form what practitioners of conflict resolution do in relation to such polarized issues. It attempts to help people realize that, although many of us have taken positions on homoerotic relations, that does not mean we are at polar opposite places. In point of fact, most of us, even after having taken positions, are somewhere along a spectrum. We agree with many others on a variety of issues, even when we have finally taken a different stand on homoerotic relations.

I will attempt to display this spectrum and name what continues to separate us through four steps. First, I will delineate a number of issues about which I believe most of us in the church agree. Second, I will name a few issues I believe cause some in this debate to reach for strong rhetoric. Third, I will provide glosses or annotations on what I have named in the first step. These glosses are an invitation to people who disagree to hear the potential inadequacies in their own positions as well as to hear the views of others. Finally, I will offer some thoughts to keep in mind which, I hope, will help us to move forward in ways that are potentially helpful for the church.

In all of this discussion I am not pretending to be neutral. I have attempted to read widely and listen carefully to many voices in this debate over the last twenty-five years or so. I am aware of my own views. However, throughout most of this essay I am attempting to keep my views in the background.

What Can We Agree On? Naming the Spectrum

I am under no illusions that *all* of us agree on the following matters. Some of us are at opposite ends of the spectrum. However, we should not assume that the majority are at opposite extremes simply because activists, who are most vocal, tend to represent the extremes. I suggest that most people within Mennonite churches—and also the larger church—would agree on the following:

(1) The social and biological sciences have raised complicated questions about how people come to be gay and lesbian, questions that present puzzles we do not pretend fully to understand.

(2) We affirm that the Bible is centrally authoritative in defining the Christian faith and thus, among other things, provides instruction in what it means to live morally.

(3) There are only a handful of biblical texts that speak directly to the issue of homoerotic relations. Those texts which do address the subject, taken at face value, speak negatively.

(4) Any discussion of biblical teachings on homoerotic relations must include a more comprehensive biblical framework that would contain not only other texts related to sexuality but also a broader understanding of Christian theology and ethics. Furthermore, this discussion should be placed within an overall framework of what it means to be Christian.

(5) As we wrestle with these matters, we have something to learn from the various ways the church throughout history has dealt both with sexuality in general and homoerotic relations in particular.

(6) We believe Christians are commanded to love their neighbors as themselves. This would include repudiating any cruel behavior toward people (certainly including friends, family members, and co-workers) who are engaged in homoerotic relationships. Moreover, it would also include being loving toward people who believe homoerotic behaviors to be wrong.

(7) We believe it is important to support and nurture heterosexual married couples (and their children). Moreover, if the church were to shift positions on homosexual relationships, what is being suggested for adoption is a parallel monogamous arrangement for gays and lesbians.

(8) Homoerotic behavior is really the issue we are wrestling with. Of course this issue can neither be separated from the lives of the people who are in homoerotic relationships nor disconnected from broader issues related to sexuality.

It is important that we not pass lightly over this list, and perhaps there are other things that should be added. If I am right that most of us would agree on these things, then it is important to note this common ground, perhaps more common ground than sometimes appears to be the case, amid the strong polarizing rhetoric. If I am right that most of us agree about this much, then why do we not only disagree on the issue of homoerotic relations but even have substantial disagreements sometimes connected to oppositional rhetoric? Let me name, in the next section, three possible reasons.

Supercharging the Rhetoric

(1) The first reason that may help explain the strong rhetoric connected with homoerotic relations is that this is not just an "issue" but is connected to people. We are talking about family, friends, and brothers and sisters in Christ—in short, relationships. If anyone fails to understand why parents of gay or lesbian children, even parents who are theologically very conservative, come to have strong feelings about this issue, then they have a failure of imagination—or compassion.[5]

In fact, I would guess that this debate may be more painful within a context like the Mennonite Church than in some other denominations (not to minimize the intensity in other churches) precisely because we are in some ways (including literally) an extended family. Families have a commitment to one another and, of course, have closer relationships to each other than to those outside their families. It is also the case that because they trust each other and have granted power to the other family members, they can cause each other more pain than anyone else can. As Philip Yancey has said, "Troublesome issues like divorce and homosexuality take on a different cast when you confront them not in a state legislature but in a family reunion."[6]

The next two reasons are mirror images of each other and are related to what George Lakoff identifies in his book, *Moral Politics: What Conservatives Know That Liberals Don't*.[7] Lakoff examines the way in which such issues as gun control, feminism, and abortion are connected to worldviews. Therefore, the issues are symbolically related to larger concerns, convictions, and moral commitments. In times of significant cultural shifts and transitions, worldviews can be under significant challenge, whether perceived or actual. In such contentious times, specific issues assume important symbolic roles. Fears and heightened concerns become attached to these issues. They become plugs in the dike. If the plugs do not remain, who knows? The whole dam that is presently holding back a flood of evil may come

crashing down. So, how does this specifically relate to homoerotic relations?

(2) Some who affirm homoerotic relations have fears about
those on the conservative side. Within the church they fear fundamentalists may take over. Something like what has happened
among Southern Baptists could happen in the Mennonite
Church. A rigidly defined orthodoxy would be enforced. Pastors
and teachers in colleges and seminaries would have to be constantly looking over their shoulders worrying about whether
someone was going to haul them before a disciplinary body for
not believing and teaching the right thing. Or perhaps the fear is
of a more specific Mennonite variety: we will return to our own
earlier days (not that terribly long ago) when a set of beliefs and
practices was rigidly enforced.

Furthermore, some who affirm changing the church's position
on homoerotic relations fear that the Religious Right is already too
powerful in North American society. We do not want them taking
over more and more of society.[8] In fact, matters of sexual (including homosexual) behavior should be a private matter, not something the state should monitor and enforce.

Finally, often the affirming folk perceive that the traditional
folk have the bulk of the power. They are in the majority of the
positions of power within the church and society. This makes the
affirming folk feel rather powerless.

(3) On the other hand, those who endorse the church's traditional stance believe the debates over this issue demonstrate
that there is reason for concern about moral decline. Within the
church, there is cause for concern about moral and theological
confusion and spiritual sickness. Homosexuality issues are not
the first sign of such confusion. However, as a presenting issue,
it provides an opportunity. They are merely indicative of a more
wide-ranging confusion, and if properly resolved, might provide
a beginning point to rectify the spiritual deterioration.

Many would argue that in the larger society there is also more moral confusion than there needs to be. And although it is true that it is inappropriate for the state to monitor what are quite appropriately private sexual acts, nonetheless it is acceptable to have certain laws that serve not only to restrain but also to educate. Society, with its diversity, can decide it is appropriate, for instance, only to sanction heterosexual marriages or to forbid curricular materials for schools, intended for young children, that affirm homoerotic relationships.[9]

Glosses on Areas of Agreement

In this section I offer some glosses on the things about which most of us agree, which I named earlier. In doing this I hope to help us name the differences within the agreement so that, once identified, they can perhaps be more accessible as points of discussion and debate. Also I want to call for greater honesty about the nature of disagreements.

(1) *Social and biological sciences.* I list and discuss this first not because I think it most important. I do not. But in many formal and informal discussions, the science related to how people become gay and lesbian assumes a significant role. In fact it often becomes a trump card, preventing honest conversations about difficult issues.

My central point here is simple: questions about how people become gay and lesbian present puzzles no one has really solved.[10] The questions make it clear that sexual identity is complex and includes the interaction of biological makeup and the organism within which it resides, familial relations, and the social environment beyond the family. Exactly how these factors interact is complicated, different for different individuals, and, I believe, not fully understood by anyone.

It has been intriguing to me to notice that many who affirm acceptance of homoerotic relations within the church seem to presume an essentialist view of sexual identity, assuming rather simply "they have no choice," "that is just who they are." On the other hand, many who affirm the traditional Christian approach to homoerotic relations often assume a social constructionist view of sexual identity. That is to say, they presume a substantial plasticity to our sexual identity. Otherwise, why worry that your children might become gay or lesbian if their social world communicates in multiple ways that homoerotic relations are every bit as legitimate as heteroerotic relations?[11] Much of the public rhetoric that has pulled at heart strings has also been essentialist: How could you raise moral questions when they *cannot* be any other way?[12] Yet the recent trend in much secular writing about gays and lesbians is social constructionist in orientation.[13]

What in my view is disingenuous—or reflective of inadequate reading—is to suggest that science provides clear data that make it impossible for us to raise moral questions about homoerotic relations.[14] Or, similarly, that we know enough about homosexuality today, through what science has taught us, that we can be confident that what the Bible is talking about in Leviticus or Romans is not what *we* are talking about. It goes without saying that the writers of the Bible did not use modern scientific models to study sexual identity or behavior. However, it does not follow that this silences the Bible's voice on the subject. Furthermore, we need to be a little more circumspect about our own "clear" knowledge. Science does not provide those in the know with a trump card in these discussions (which is not the same as saying that it is not a part of the conversation).

(2) (3) (4) *The Bible and Christian theology and ethics.* First let me speak to those in the church who are not biblical scholars or theologians. It is important for us all to be honest about the complexities surrounding this issue. There are the scientific complexities I discussed above. There is also the complexity of interpreting some of the relevant texts.[15] It is true that Leviticus 18:22 is straightforward in what it says, "You shall not lie with a male as with a woman; it is an abomination." But then Leviticus is also straightforward when it says, "You shall not let your animals

breed with a different kind; you shall not sow your field with two kinds of seed; nor shall you put on a garment made of two different materials" (19:19).

Why is it that one text matters a great deal to us and the other not at all? There are quite legitimately complex matters of interpretation here.[16] We should not invoke the complexity simply as a way to dismiss or relativize the texts, but rather be honest about the need for those who study such matters to help us know how to interpret such texts.[17]

Furthermore, we should be honest in asking why the question of homoerotic relations has assumed such importance. Money—and our temptations to serve it—has a much larger role in the Scriptures (and in the wealthy United States this has considerable relevance). Why is that not exercising us as much if what we care about is the authority of the Scriptures?

Now a word to us biblical scholars and theologians. It is important that we not, directly or indirectly, communicate contempt for sincere Christians who seek to take the Bible and the call of Christ to discipleship seriously. We cannot expect most Christians to read the Scriptures in the way scholars would. I am grateful for those Mennonites who have refused to kill enemies during America's wars because of their commitment to take the Bible seriously and faithfully to live out Jesus' teaching to love enemies. That these same people do not understand the complexities of biblical interpretation related to the wars in Joshua or the violent imagery in Revelation is not something for which they are blameworthy (as if any of the rest of us fully understood these complicated matters). They are called to be faithful Christians. It is our job as teachers and pastors to provide adequate instruction for members of our churches, even as we accept that they need never be scholars.

Furthermore, it is imperative that we be honest about the complexities and diversity of opinions regarding the issues around homoerotic relations and biblical teaching. I have often heard it implied by theologians (Mennonite and otherwise) that no serious Scripture scholarship supports the traditional view (or that only fundamentalists do). That is simply not true.[18] It is true that for a while in the 1980s many were under the sway of the readings of the Bible provided by John Boswell.[19] However, beginning in the mid-1980s and continuing today, there are serious scholars who come to various conclusions.[20]

Moreover, since there are various academically respectable views, it is important that we as scholars not overestimate our role. I believe we do have a crucial role in these conversations. But it will not do to imagine that we can invoke the word *scholarship* as a trump card to short circuit full conversations with contributions by various people, including biblical scholars and theologians.

(5) *Church history.* More than a few believe that our central learning from the church on this topic, as with sexuality generally, is a negative learning. That is to say, the church has so often gotten it wrong, been overly negative about the body and preoccupied with sexual behavior, that—except for learning what not to do and say—we can largely ignore much of what has been done and said in relation to sexual behavior throughout church history. There is some truth in this. We can find numerous quotations and incidents to support the claim. There is much we need to learn by looking at mistakes of the past.

However, I believe we also have some important positive things to learn from the church on this subject. The stereotype of Christian sexual repressiveness from the outset is at best an exaggeration.[21] As renowned classicist Paul Veyne has said, "If any aspect of ancient life has been distorted by legend, this is it. It is widely but mistakenly believed that antiquity was a Garden of Eden from which repression was banished, Christianity having yet to insinuate the worm of sin into the forbidden fruit. Actually, the pagans were paralyzed by prohibitions."[22]

Similar things could be said about other periods of church

history.[23] Again, this is not to say one could not find writings and actions regarding sexual relations by church leaders that would be objectionable (though such texts should be read contextually, not anachronistically). This is simply to say that other voices from the history of the church can provide guidance that is much needed in our time.

I believe Linda Woodhead has it just right in saying that "When 'Christianity' and 'the Christian tradition' come under attack, it often seems that what detractors have in their targets is not two thousand years of Christian history, but the Christianity of their youth and of the previous generation."[24] For Mennonites this is relevant to much more than sexuality. Many currently living have memories of overzealous church leaders seeking to enforce codes of conduct on a whole church or an area conference in ways that were experienced as oppressive and may often have been unwise.[25] These memories should provide a caution. And they should counsel us to desire wisdom. But the caution and counsel should not equal moral or doctrinal neutrality. Nor do they negate either the authority of Scripture or the riches that can be gained from drawing on Christian history.

(6) *Love of neighbors*. I believe it should be obvious to any Christians that—as people called to love our neighbors as ourselves—we are not to be cruel to anyone. This "anyone" certainly includes those engaged in homoerotic relationships. Moreover, our love should express itself in tangible, positive ways toward our neighbors. However, it is more than that, is it not? Mennonites as a group believe that following Jesus entails, among other things, being peacemakers—being committed to peace, justice, inclusion, welcoming the marginalized as Jesus did. Does this not exclude rejecting those who are engaged in homoerotic relationships?

This question deserves brief exploration. Some have made much of the fact that Jesus said nothing about homosexuality. However, there are many issues to which Jesus never spoke. If, as Martti Nissinen and others have said, the Judaism Jesus knew was

rather unequivocally negative on the matter of homoerotic relations, then Jesus had no reason to say anything if he agreed with
the consensus.[26] In fact, given the consensus, it might be significant that Jesus didn't challenge convictions and practices firmly in
place that denied the legitimacy of homoerotic relationships.

At a more abstract and principled level, one might argue that
Jesus welcomed the marginalized; he was inclusive. But stating it
this way begs the question. Adulterers, especially women, were
marginalized in the world of Jesus, and although Jesus in John 8
prevented the stoning of a woman caught in adultery, he nonetheless asked her to "go and sin no more." As Croatian theologian
Miroslav Volf has put it, "Jesus was no prophet of 'inclusion'. . . for
whom the chief virtue was acceptance and the cardinal vice intolerance. [He did scandalously include many who were normally
excluded, but he also] made the 'intolerant' demand of repentance
and the 'condescending' offer of forgiveness."[27] In short, an argument either from Jesus' teaching on peacemaking or his silence on
the specific issue of homoerotic relationships in no way provides an
endorsement of homoerotic relations.

(7) *Support for heterosexual married couples*. I do think it is
important to note that most of those who want the church to affirm
homoerotic relationships do not intend to undermine heterosexual
relationships or families. Quite the contrary, they wish them well.
However, whether or not the formal affirmation of homoerotic
relationships does in fact in some ways undermine the future of heterosexual identities and relationships is an open question.[28] It
depends on how gays and lesbians come to be gay and lesbian or,
put differently, how their gay and lesbian identities are formed
(about which, I believe, we are still unsure). And it depends on what
specific proposals for affirmation are suggested and accepted.[29]

Moreover, there are two other complicating issues. First, the
debate about homosexuality is happening at a time when there
is hardly a consensus within society, church, or the theological
world about sexual relationships and monogamous marriages.[30]

Second, many who write theological books or essays about homoerotic relations argue for non-traditional ways of structuring relationships, to put it most neutrally.[31] It is not clear to me that most of the relevant parties to these conversations distance themselves from, say, non-monogamous relationships. If that is indeed the case, then it needs to be stated.

(8) *Homoerotic relations and broader issues of sexuality.* I am certainly in agreement with those who say that it is inappropriate to reflect on homoerotic relations without dealing with the contexts within which we discuss such relations, including broader issues related to sexuality. We need to discuss cultural and social contexts within which we live our lives, contexts that cannot help but shape our understandings of sexuality and our concepts regarding appropriate and inappropriate sexual attitudes and behavior. As Christians we also need to name biblical teachings and Christian convictions rooted in the Scriptures that serve to shape our lives, leading us to embody our convictions faithfully, including the ways in which we conduct ourselves sexually. And in fact contexts and convictions are interrelated for us. But what are the contexts to be named? And what are the convictions?

In 1991 a committee of the Presbyterian Church USA produced a document on human sexuality.[32] Early within this document the relevant contexts related to human sexuality were named as "patriarchy, heterosexism, and homophobia." It is important to name abusive patterns of authority and structured forms of injustice. Likewise, it is vital that we acknowledge stereotypes of and hateful attitudes and behaviors toward gays and lesbians. However, only to name this one set of contexts ignores too many other relevant elements of our context. For instance, Walter Brueggemann, hardly conservative, at the beginning of an insightful essay says that "we may as well concede at the outset that we live, all of us, in a promiscuous, self-indulgent society that prizes autonomy."[33] Might these elements of our context not also be relevant for our deliberations about sexuality?

It is not particularly surprising that, when "patriarchy, hetero-sexism, and homophobia" are the only contexts named, then the only substantive moral guidance given by the Presbyterian document is a commitment "to an inclusive, egalitarian ethic of common decency," or what is elsewhere referred to as the criterion of "justice-love."[34] Our Scriptures certainly implore us to pursue justice and to embody love. However, there are also admonitions regarding sexual immorality, lust, passions, the works of the flesh, and self-control—concerns more at home with Brueggemann's reminders.

I worry that many of us, because of our reticence to be morally clear about sexuality, have been unwilling to take seriously this latter set of concerns that respond to other dimensions of our context. We have, for instance, allowed the conversations about sexuality to be hostage to the public rhetoric about "safe sex." But as Kari Jenson Gold has said, "Surely the words are ludicrously contradictory! Sex can be many things: dark, mysterious, passionate, wild, gentle, even reassuring, but it is not safe. If it is, it's not likely to be very sexy."[35]

Camille Paglia, an ex-Catholic, offers some devastating and insightful criticisms of the Presbyterian document just mentioned that I think can instruct us all as we approach sexuality.[36] She—herself approving of all manner of dissident sexual conduct—does not want Christians to be naive about the realities of sexuality. As she puts it, the document

> reduces the complexities and mysteries of eroticism to a clumsy, outmoded social-welfare ideology. The old-style Protestant suppression of the passions, torments, and untidy physicalities of the body is in fact still abundantly evident in the report, which, in its opening premise of "the basic goodness of sexuality," projects a happy, bouncy vision of human life that would have made Doris Day and Debbie Reynolds—those '50s blond divas—proud. . . . "Eros," says the report's glos-

sary, is "a zest for life." Is this a soap commercial? Eros, like Dionysus, is a great and dangerous god. The report gives us vanilla sex, smothered with artificial butterscotch syrup. In its liberal zeal to understand, to accept, to heal, it reduces the grand tragicomedy of love and lust to a Hallmark card. Its unctuous normalizing of dissident sex is imperialistic and oppressive. The gay world is stripped of its outlaw adventures in toilets, alleyways, trucks, and orgy rooms. There are no leathermen, hustlers, or drag queens. Gay love is reduced to a nice, neat, middle-class couple moving in next door on "Father Knows Best". . . .This is censorship in the name of liberal benevolence.[37]

Moreover, given the complex, powerful realities of sexuality, Paglia thinks Christians make a serious mistake when we strip ourselves of our own best resources:

The report assails the "influential tradition of radical asceticism" in "Western Christianity." . . . It assumes that eremites and monks were not contemplatives but killjoys, neurotics, and misogynists, scowling while the rest of the world caroused, footloose and fancy free. The report complains of "our cultural captivity to a patriarchal model of sexuality and its ethic of sexual control," as if sexual rules and taboos were not prevalent in every culture. . . . The institutional religions, Catholic and Protestant, carry with them the majesty of history. Their theology is impressive and coherent. Efforts to revise or dilute that theology for present convenience seem to me misguided.[38]

Is there something "impressive" and "coherent" about our theological traditions—even in relation to sexuality and homosexuality—that we ignore at our peril? Are there cautions here that we should heed?

Revision for Present Convenience?

I believe it is reasonable for Christians—simple believers or academics—to ask, with Paglia, whether revisions regarding our approach to homosexuality (and sexuality), currently underway in many circles, are "for present convenience."[39] Moreover, it seems reasonable to argue that the burden of proof is on the shoulders of those who would challenge the historical consensus within the church that the plain sense of Scripture on this issue is right, namely, that homoerotic behavior is not to be formally affirmed within the church.

However, that is not the same as saying that anyone should approach this subject without humility. Rather, for many of us it seems quite appropriate to approach it with an openness to learn and with significant pain. I sense this, for instance, in the recent words of Kathryn Greene-McCreight: "Let me say for the record that I am among those who wish they could be convinced that Scripture and tradition could be read to support the revisionist position, which would argue for the theological and religious appropriateness of homoerotic relationships for Christians who feel drawn to them. . . . While I have not yet been convinced by the revisionist position, I keep listening in hopes that someone will come up with something new."[40]

Furthermore, though I hope that people at various places along the spectrum hear each other, I nonetheless think it is a mistake to minimize the potential importance of the issues at stake in relation to this matter. No less a voice than that of the major German Protestant theologian, Wolfhart Pannenberg, has said that "if a church were to let itself be pushed to the point where it ceased to treat homosexual activity as a departure from the biblical norm, and recognized homosexual unions as a personal partnership of love equivalent to marriage, such a church would stand no longer on biblical ground but against the unequivocal witness of Scripture. A church that took this step would cease to be the one, holy, catholic, and apostolic Church."[41]

Lest someone imagine that strong theological claims are made only by theologians who affirm the tradition which stands against homoerotic relations, we should listen to Eugene Rogers, Jr., another theologian. Rogers argues that if straight Christians do not move to affirm monogamous gay and lesbian marriages, then they are in danger of losing their salvation! In *Sexuality and the Christian Body*, Rogers makes the argument, offered also by others in recent years, that homosexuals are analogous to Gentiles in the New Testament.[42]

If there is anything that is centrally linked to many of Paul's theological arguments, it is that in Christ, Jews and Gentiles have been made one. Paul went to great effort and used strong rhetoric to indicate that Gentiles, which now includes almost all of us, are in Christ equal members of the people of God. Paul proclaimed this despite how offensive this was to many of those who, like himself, were Jews. In fact, to deny the inclusion of the Gentiles, said Paul, is to deny the gospel and the work of the Holy Spirit. Likewise, so this argument runs, in Christ, gay and straight have been made one.[43] If this is right, says Rogers, then "failing to accept faithful, monogamous gay and lesbian marriages may deny the work of the Spirit and put Gentile Christians [who are in the present denying what some Jews were then denying] in danger of their salvation."[44]

I think we do no one any favors if we forget that more than a few share the views of either Pannenberg or Rogers. Each side can claim that profound theological issues are at stake—that the gospel and the future of the church are in the balance. And even if the theological stakes are not this high, we are still left with what seem irresolvable issues. We still need help moving forward when many tell us the stakes are this high. Thus this discussion should be taken seriously. We err if we take the questions related to homoerotic relationships with less seriousness than they deserve.

Whether Rogers' argument is convincing or not, he is at least attempting to do what needs to be done. That is to say, he is attempting to give solid, compelling theological reasons for his position, a position that seeks to overturn the consensus within the church.[45] Kathryn Greene-McCreight contends that "for traditional readers to be convinced of the righteousness before God of homoerotic relationships, they would need to be convinced on 'traditionalist' grounds. . . . Or the revisionist side must convincingly show how and why the rules must be changed."[46] It will not do simply to invoke words like tolerance, inclusion, or "our commitment to peace and justice." Properly understood, all of these are a part of the discussion. However, they must be situated in a broader theological framework that includes the centrality of Jesus, the teachings of the Scriptures on homosexuality, sexuality, and what it means to be embodied persons while being faithfully Christian.[47]

As we continue to wrestle with these matters, we need to listen to each other. We need to speak honestly and humbly, with an openness to learn.[48] And we would do well to live with the apostle Paul's admonitions regarding "the works of the flesh" and "the fruit of the spirit" (Galatians 5:16-26).[49] We should not allow categorizations like liberal or conservative to prevent any of us from taking seriously Paul's admonitions regarding fornication, impurity, licentiousness, carousing, faithfulness, self-control, and "things like these." Nor, if we need to remind ourselves, should we allow these categorizations to prevent any of us from hearing Paul's admonitions regarding enmities, strife, anger, quarrels, dissensions, factions, love, patience, kindness, and gentleness.[50]

PART 2:
THE MAIN STATEMENTS

'Teacher, Which Commandment in the Law Is the Greatest?' On Commandments, Compassion and Fundamentalism

Mark Thiessen Nation

The first time I spoke publicly on the subject of homosexuality, in 1993, I invited a lesbian friend of mine to attend my lecture. I wanted to be held accountable. I wanted to speak with integrity and compassion. Six years ago, in my first published essay about homosexuality, I attempted to name what it is that many of us Christians have in common on this subject even in the midst of our differences, as well as what continues to separate us and why.[1]

I cannot speak abstractly about this issue. I've known and continue to know gay and lesbian people—people with names and faces, pain and suffering. I never want to forget that when we speak about same-sex erotic relations, we are still speaking about people, many of whom simply desire deep, meaningful relationships. Even as I remember names and faces, however, I know I am called to be a teacher in the church. I am to carry out this calling with responsibility, with faithfulness to God—all in the midst of my profound limitations.

I write this essay with great reluctance. In what follows, I have tried to refuse to be held hostage to pre-established categories. More than anything else, I want to help us move forward on this difficult and painful issue. I hope the reader can at least sense the effort.

Our Greatest Commandment(s)

I do not want to mislead anyone. Given my theological orientation I do not begin my approach to this subject primarily by focusing on the experiences of gays and lesbians nor on my experience or impressions of them. I want my—and, as Christians, our—approach to this subject to be Christian, meaning richly biblical and theological.[2] Therefore I must focus first of all on the Bible. It seems to me that the starting place on this subject is in the Old Testament—Leviticus and Deuteronomy, to be specific. I begin there because Jesus, our Lord, leads us there. The Gospel of Matthew records an occasion in which a Sadducee asks Jesus:

> "Teacher, which commandment in the law is the greatest?" [Jesus] said to him, "'You shall love the Lord your God with all your heart, and with all your soul, and with all your mind.' This is the greatest and first commandment. And a second is like it: 'You shall love your neighbor as yourself.' On these two commandments hang all the law and prophets." (Matthew 22:36-40; cf. Mark 12:28-34; Luke 10:25-37)[3]

Jesus takes the first half of his response from Deuteronomy 6:4-5, the second half from Leviticus 19:18.

On one level Jesus' response to this Sadducee says it all. Jesus began by affirming what every Jew knew by heart: the Shema (i.e., Deuteronomy 6:4-5). At the time of Jesus, Jews recited this passage twice daily. It reminded them that there was only one God, the Lord God of Abraham and Sarah, the Lord who delivered them from the bondage of slavery and the Lord who spoke to them from Sinai. Jews regularly heard the call to "love the Lord your God with all your heart." Such love called them to specific faithfulness, to "keep these words that I am commanding you today in your heart." That the Hebrew word (Shema) that means "hear" also means "obey" rooted them in the firm conviction that once they had *heard* God they were to obey God.

The exhortations preceding the Shema in Deuteronomy 6 reminded Jews that they were to fear the Lord. They were to be singularly committed to the Lord their God. Eugene Peterson suggests that we need a reminder of the significance of these words today. He writes:

> We need a common and comprehensive term for referring to the way we live the spiritual life. . . . The biblical word of choice for the term we need is "fear-of-the-Lord". . . . "Fear-of-the-Lord," as we notice the way our biblical writers use it, turns out to be a term that is plain without being reductive, clear without being over-simplified, and accurate without dissolving the mystery inherent in all dealings with God and his world. It also has the considerable advantage of evading the precise definition or "control" that we could use to locate ourselves along a spectrum of piety or goodness that would feed our instincts for coziness with God. . . . "Fear-of-the-Lord" is the best term we have to point to this way of life we cultivate as Christians.

Peterson goes on to open our imaginations further concerning these currently uncommon words: "fear the Lord."

> The Christian life consists mostly of what God—Father, Son, and Holy Spirit—is and does. But we also are part of it. Not the largest part, but still part. A world has been opened up to us by revelation in which we find ourselves walking on holy ground and living in sacred time. The moment we realize this, we feel shy, cautious. We slow down, we look around, ears and eyes alert. Like lost children happening on a clearing in the woods and

finding elves and fairies singing and dancing in a circle around a prancing two-foot-high unicorn, we stop in awed silence to accommodate to this wonderful but unguessed-at revelation. But for us it isn't a unicorn and elves; it is Sinai and Tabor and Golgotha.[4]

Most of us do not hear "fear of the Lord" from the pulpit these days. I refer to it here partly because it figures significantly in the passage to which Jesus referred, and, as Peterson says, it is a prominent term in the Old Testament.[5] I also mention it because its starkness reminds us of the singularity of God's claim upon our lives. Walter Brueggemann proves helpful here:

> The terse prohibition of Sinai has become the love commandment that sets God alone above all else, to be regarded with the loyalty of our entire being. The command to love God may be taken, as may be inevitable in our society, as an affective matter, to be "in love" with God. . . . Or alternatively, the command may be taken, as Old Testament scholars mostly think, in political idiom, as treaty language concerning a pledge to the policies of Yahweh. Either way, as affective or as political, the terse command of Yahweh bespeaks radical, singular, undivided attentiveness to the one who miraculously orders and reorders life in wholeness and well-being.
>
> Israel in every generation and circumstance is invited to other loyalties—political, economic, religious, and moral. And of course it is not different in every circumstance and generation of the church. And in every such circumstance, we are drawn by memory and instruction and liturgy and exegesis back to Sinai, to the vision of the holiness that dwells at the center of our peculiar imagination.[6]

"You shall love the Lord your God with all your heart, and with all your soul, and with all your mind."[7] This "greatest and first commandment" must remain with us always. Knowing the love of this God reminds us that the commandment must remain attached to our gracious Lord who uttered the command—to the Lord who redeems us, is present with us and calls us to give the whole of our being to Him. This is perhaps another way of saying that many of us have been reminded by Dietrich Bonhoeffer to embrace a "costly grace." "It is costly, because it calls to discipleship; it is grace, because it calls us to follow *Jesus Christ*. It is costly, because it costs people their lives; it is grace, because it thereby makes them live."[8]

Yet we must not forget that the young man asked Jesus which was *the* greatest commandment. One would have expected a single response. However, Jesus felt compelled to add: "And a second is like it: 'You shall love your neighbor as yourself.'" On the one hand we must remind ourselves that the first commandment cannot be collapsed into the second—as if loving our neighbors equals loving God. As Frederick Dale Bruner observes:

> Jesus belongs squarely within a certain humanist tradition, as all four Gospels provocatively teach. But Jesus' humanism is always rooted in his prior theism, a God-centeredness that cannot be erased from Jesus' portrait. Love for God is not *independently* sovereign above love for others—Jesus' "first" *and* "second" prevents this independence. But love for God is the best place for believers to *begin* love for others. This first responsibility exhilarates believers because it continually refers them back to their reason for living and loving at all.[9]

Bruner demonstrates how the biblical narratives help us to sustain this interdependence:

> The Anointing-Bethany text, preserved in three Gospels (Matthew 26:6-13; Mark 14:3-9; John 12:1-8), is the other great text in the Jesus Tradition that protects divine worship from a progressive people-centered usurpation, a constant temptation in church history precisely because Jesus himself is so outstandingly social,

progressive, and people-centered. . . . In the Gospel neither the Anointing-at-Bethany paragraph nor the
Double-Love-Command will allow the substitution of
love *for* God by love *for others.* Remember the Death of
God theology.[10]

In the midst of Bruner's vital reminders, we nonetheless
cannot forget that Jesus deliberately answered a question about
a single commandment with a two-fold response. Moreover, he
specifically named *this* particular second commandment. Bruner
suggests that Jesus seems to have been saying that "the greatest
kind of commandment in the whole Bible is broken down into
two kinds and into two commands: *Love the God who loves you,
and cherish the person who meets you.*"[11] It is vital as we seek to love
God, as we reflect on what such love means in terms of daily faithfulness, to understand that love of God cannot be divorced from
the second command that is "like" the first one. Bruner offers that
"like" might be translated, "just like it." He observes:

> "Just like it" (*homoia*), according to a majority of the
> commentators, equates the second command with the
> first *in importance*—the second is *just as important* as the
> first—but without a secularizing absorption of the first
> by the second. . . . The first is first and second is second,
> but is *equally as important* as the first. Only *together* in a
> nurturing mutuality is either love kept pure. A neigh-
> bor-minimizing love of God is as reprehensible to the
> prophetic Jesus as a God-minimizing love of neighbor is
> impossible to the pastoral Jesus.[12]

These two intertwined commands are also the commandments on which "hang all the law and the prophets." Bruner
continues:

> Not just the law, but "the *whole law*" dangles from these
> twin pegs. This is Matthew's Jesus' way of saying that the
> *purpose* of God's law in Genesis, Exodus, Leviticus,
> Numbers, and Deuteronomy is not so much multiform

as it is duplex. The law wants the adoration of God and the cherishing of people. This simplification does not by any means wish to dispense with the rest of Scripture as so much dead wood; it wants believers to read Scripture with the bifocal of Jesus' Double-Love Command. With these lenses they will dependably interpret the rest of Scripture. Jesus' love *command for action* is also Jesus' love *canon for interpretation*. . . . We need the full witness of all the rest of Scripture to teach us exactly what love for God and love for neighbor look like in practice.[13]

The centrality of the "double-love command" prepares us to do the hard, even painful, work of discerning together the particular texture of contemporary faithfulness in regards to difficult issues like same-sex erotic relations. We do this work by engaging "the full witness of all the rest of Scripture to teach us exactly what love for God and love for neighbor look like in practice" within our current contexts. We need to ask critical questions about contemporary temptations to evade the fullness of this two-fold challenge in the face of the issues surrounding same-sex erotic relations. Only within faithfulness to this double-love command can we claim to be biblical and true to the full witness of the Scriptures.

On Compassion and Ethics

How might we practice faithfulness to the biblical witness, to the double-love command in our current contexts? Philip Yancey provides some startling reflections that we need to hear as we begin to wrestle with this question. He relates:

> Visiting another city a few months ago, I met with three gay men who consider themselves Christians, attend church regularly, and take their faith seriously. . . . "We feel like we're in the same situation as the Jews in the early days of Hitler's regime," said one. "We're trying to discern whether it's 1933 or 1939. Should we flee to

Canada now? It's obvious the country doesn't want us, and I believe most evangelicals would like to see us exterminated."[14]

Some of us may need to hear Yancey's initial response to his friend: "How can you think such a thing! Homosexuals have more rights in this country than ever. And I don't know a single Christian who wants to have you exterminated."[15] Yet all of us need to heed Yancey's further reflections on his friends' alarm. "I went away from that discussion with my head spinning. . . . [W]hat have we evangelicals done to make Good News—the very meaning of the word *evangelical*—sound like such a threat?"[16]

It needs to be said clearly that Christians who continue to affirm the traditional view on this subject should not imagine that these convictions allow us to join forces with people whose actions express something other than love for our gay and lesbian (bisexual and transsexual) neighbors. We must seek ways actively to love such neighbors. If we are unwilling to love gay and lesbian people then we should simply keep our mouths closed. Moreover, our rhetoric should not undermine our stated commitment to love these neighbors, especially when they are in need, especially if we find them along the road because they "fell among thieves."[17] And God forbid that we do any of this for the sake of mere public perceptions. We love because this is who we know we are to be as followers of Jesus.

I believe it is partly because the perceptions Yancey named are real, and because compassionate deeds have too often been lacking on the part of those committed to the church's traditional views on this topic, that many on the affirming side have responded by reaching for substitutes to a holistic gospel. This is understandable and a challenge to the church. Nonetheless, we also must name responses that tend to undermine a fuller, holistic biblical response.

Words like tolerance,[18] inclusiveness,[19] compassion,[20] justice,[21] freedom,[22] grace,[23] non-judgmentalism[24] and diversity[25] name concerns to which we ought to attend. However, when we invoke them as centrally defining, comprehensive terms calling for a shift from the traditional stance, the terms undermine a holistic Christian response. In order for these words to function as more than pale substitutes for a full-orbed theological approach, we must nestle them within a robust understanding of the gospel, a gospel that is connected to our embodied, faithful and communal existence across time—in light of the whole biblical witness.

Far too often I have seen these partial substitutes joined to views about sex that partake more of the contemporary climate than any rich theological understanding of sexual fidelity. We do well to recognize that our current cultural climate regarding sexual ethics—which, for instance, makes fun of a *40 Year Old Virgin*—is fundamentally at odds with traditional Christian views and practices.[26] Walter Brueggemann provides a needed warning as we reflect on these issues: "We may as well concede at the outset that we live, all of us, in a promiscuous, self-indulgent society that prizes autonomy." Brueggemann continues: "It is only slightly reductive to say that the two great accents of Freud and Marx, sexuality and economics, are the two great arenas for evangelical obedience. . . . It follows that sexuality and economics, zones of great power, are also the most likely candidates for distortion and loss of the very communion for which we so yearn."[27]

As an example, consider the word "compassion." Paul uses the word when he admonishes the Colossian church: "As God's chosen ones, holy and beloved, clothe yourselves with compassion, kindness, humility, meekness, and patience" (Colossians 3:12). Especially when we approach difficult topics such as homosexuality we must be so clothed. However, we must also remember that for Paul this requisite clothing in no way mutes the call to be faithful with the whole of our embodied lives. Within this same chapter, for instance, he says, "put to death, therefore, whatever belongs to your earthly nature: sexual immorality, impurity, lust, evil desires and greed, which is idolatry" (Colossians 3:5, TNIV).[28]

Paul joins his call to compassion with a call to faithfulness—and in specific terms. This takes us back to the double-love command. Biblically we cannot collapse the call to love God, which includes a commitment to faithfulness, into the call to love our neighbor.[29] However difficult it may sometimes seem, we must attempt to hold these inseparable commands together. And we must heed the warnings concerning our failure to do so.

In an earlier climate Karl Barth suggested: "throughout the world, the Church is concerned today with the problem of the secularization of the modern [person]. It would perhaps be more profitable if the Church were at least to begin to become concerned with the problem of its own secularization."[30] As it concerns the current crisis plaguing the church in relation to sexual ethics we should heed the warning of Methodist theologian Stephen Long:

> The true crisis United Methodism faces at this present moment is only secondarily related to questions of sexuality. The true crisis is that, given the arguments presented for holy unions and the strategies of protest used to force the Church one way or another, our leaders are evacuating the Church of its tradition and replacing it with the tradition of liberalism and its forms of cultural exchange. We have produced an ecclesiology that fits well with the tradition of liberal exchanges that so thoroughly defines our lives.[31]

If we as Christians desire to avoid reducing our ethic to an adherence to a vague, liberal tenet such as tolerance, we must recapture a holistic biblical theology and ethic. One way to name such an ethic is to engage the central emphases of two major current writers on this subject, Richard Hays and Eric Osborn.

Drawing on stories, images and teachings from the New Testament, Hays names Christian community, cross and new creation as the central focal images of New Testament ethics. Specifically in relation to community Hays observes: *"The church is a countercultural community of discipleship, and this community is the primary addressee of God's imperatives.* The biblical story focuses on God's design for forming a covenant people. Thus, the primary sphere of moral concern is not the character of the individual but the corporate character and obedience of the church."[32]

When dealing with the cross Hays says, "Jesus' death is consistently interpreted in the New Testament as an act of self-giving love, and the community is consistently called to take up the cross and follow in the way that his death defines."[33] Furthermore, the "new creation" image points to New Testament eschatology. That is to say, the New Testament claims both that we are made new in Christ—we are new creatures, including in our capacity to be faithful—and that we await the fullness, the perfection, that evidences the completion of God's redemptive work.[34]

Osborn frames his approach differently. He too attempts to name the central moral language of the New Testament. He claims that what it means to be Christian is to live in the rich intersection and intermingling of righteousness, discipleship, love, and a dialectical relationship between faith and freedom. This richly textured account of New Testament ethics—naming the necessity of our dependence on God while linking that to a clear call to specific acts of faithfulness—avoids the twin temptations of legalism and the emotional evasion of concrete ethics.[35] I believe a combination of what both of these authors offer can provide us a substantive and holistic ethic for living faithfully.

To repeat again the call in the previous section: our life together as Christians is fundamentally about obeying the double-love command:" We are to "love the Lord our God with all our heart, soul, mind and strength" "and [our] neighbor as [our self]." The perennial temptation is that we will keep this wonderfully comprehensive command vague and free of any substantive claims on our lives. This section has attempted to begin clearing a path so that we might hear some of the specifics related to God's claims on our sexual lives.

How Should We Then Live?

Later in this chapter I look at the specific biblical texts dealing with same-sex erotic relationships. I do this because of my conviction that "we need the full witness of all the rest of Scripture to teach us exactly what love for God and love for neighbor look like in practice."[36] Before I proceed with that work, however, I want to highlight where the double-love command and the full-orbed gospel have led me in practice and convictions concerning same-sex relations. Recognizing that these are complex issues I mostly make assertions, giving hints or raising questions in order to generate needed discussion and discernment.

(1) I believe that, in the midst of our needed conversations and debates around this issue, it is vital not to lose sight of proclaiming the gospel, the good news, with our lives and our lips. We cannot forget the perspective offered by N. T. Wright, namely, "to think through and live out the attractive, outgoing life of love and service which was, for Paul, what being a Christian was all about."[37] This needs to be said because I believe Yancey is right to remind evangelicals (and others of us) that many gays and lesbians and those on the affirming side of this issue believe that traditionalists are motivated by hate. Not only must we not be motivated by hate, we must embody love for our neighbors—in ways that matter and are experienced as love by our neighbors.

Specifically, if we are to continue to say that marriage is reserved for heterosexuals and sex outside of marriage is wrong, then we have to ask how we care for people—gays and lesbians as well as heterosexual single people—who feel lonely, isolated and alienated. Are we loving our gay and lesbian neighbors? Do we need to listen to the challenge Jesus issued to the scribes and Pharisees: "They tie up heavy burdens, hard to bear, and lay them on the shoulders of others; but they themselves are unwilling to lift a finger to move them" (Matthew 23:4)?[38] We cannot imagine that we are being faithful to God if we do not care for and have compassion for gay and lesbian people.

(2) Why this issue? I don't know how many times I have had people say one of two things to me. Either they have said this is not a very important issue. Or similarly they have asked why I would give this much attention to this (relatively unimportant) issue. I believe this is an important question that requires a couple of serious responses. On the one hand I want to make it clear that I do not believe this issue, in itself, is of singular importance.[39] Nonetheless, I believe it is important to focus on it for several reasons. First, in the Mennonite Church, and other churches, I see many who are shifting positions on this issue for very inadequate reasons. This is partly because not many, especially academics who hold the traditional position, have addressed themselves to this issue within our church. Second, this set of issues needs serious attention in our time. There are certainly issues I believe to be of more fundamental and general importance—our relationship to money, for instance. However, I know of no one who is directly arguing for the moral legitimacy of greed. The importance of these other issues does not minimize the significance of the issue of homosexuality.

I believe, as several authors have indicated, that money, sex, and power are perennial moral issues that every generation needs to revisit and take seriously. I have also come to believe that those who argue that shifting on the issue of homosexuality is related to shifting on sexuality in general are, in some significant ways, right. Thus this issue has more importance than is sometimes acknowledged.

(3) However, having said what I just said, it is vital to speak on the other side. It is imperative that we not make gays and lesbians scapegoats on which to focus our anxiety about significant changes in sexual mores in our culture and within the church. In fact I would suggest that if we are genuinely not making gays and lesbians scapegoats, we should have a desire to be honest and consistent in how we approach *this* moral issue in relation to other issues.

Let me offer some reflections on how to begin to think about this. The prohibition against same-sex behavior appears in three different vice lists within Paul's letters (in Romans 1:26-32; 1 Corinthians 6:9-10; 1 Timothy 1:8-11). This is one vice listed among the eighteen or so lists scattered throughout the New Testament, lists that together include more than fifty vices—from abusive language to wickedness.[40] Paul routinely issues a warning at the end of these lists much like the warning at the end of his "works of the flesh" list in Galatians 5: "I am warning you, as I warned you before: those who do such things will not inherit the kingdom of God" (v. 21).

If we were to examine the lists we would notice many things. We would notice, for example, that some of the vices are very specific (murder); others are clearly important and yet difficult to attach to specific behaviors (mischief maker). We might notice that sexual immorality is listed more frequently than any other vice. If we were not only to do a statistical study but also notice emphasis we would identify the importance of money in the New Testament. Paul says that greed is idolatry (Colossians 3:5). Money is the only object that Jesus personified as a god—Mammon—indicating that it is a competitor for our ultimate loyalty (Matthew 6:24; Luke 16:13). In order to underscore the point, 1 Timothy names the love of money as "the root of all kinds of evil"![41] And yet I wonder: How many congregations have been expelled from conferences because they are turning a blind eye to sexual intercourse before marriage or because they tolerate the love of money?[42]

I have not written the preceding paragraph to undermine a call to serious discipleship. God forbid! I want us to care about greed, selfishness, sexual immorality, drunkenness, gossip, strife, arrogance, etc. I want us to take Paul's warnings and calls to faithfulness seriously. And I want us to be known as Christians who seek—with all of our failings and inadequacies, with our need to forgive and be forgiven—to be faithful to the God and Father of our Lord Jesus Christ. I simply want us to be honest and consistent in how we are holding one another accountable. If we agree that money, sex, and power are three very important issues in our life together then let us be honest, transparent, and consistent in how we hold one another accountable in relation to all of these issues.

Moreover, let us be honest and consistent in our employment of pastoral forbearance and patience within the life of our churches. Let me report a story I was recently told by a pastor friend:

> Just the other day, I drove an elderly couple from our congregation to visit their gay son's former partner who has HIV and is in declining health. On the drive down, this couple told me their story—about how they found out about their son's relationship, how they reacted, etc. This couple told me that they made it clear to their son and his partner how they felt about what they were doing. But they also told me that they decided early on that they must express love for both their son AND his partner—because that's what Jesus would do. They told me that the sexual relationship between the two ended. Regardless, what I find so powerful is that now their son's friend considers them as his mother and father. He also says that they led him to a deeper faith in Christ. To me, this couple has embodied the double love command that you described. I am moved just writing about it again.[43]

More than a few of us with "traditional" views resonate at a deep level with this story. Some of us believe that such a story poses questions to the church, questions with which we and the church must wrestle. How can the church *as church* embody this sort of love in the midst of not affirming behavior we believe to be immoral? Put differently, how can we be genuinely, deeply welcoming and loving while recognizing the need to retain our identity as Christians with a commitment to particular forms of faithfulness?[44] And finally, how do we, in general, continue to affirm clear moral commitments on the part of the Christian community while knowing that one of those commitments is precisely to love those who have not joined us in certain commitments or fail when they have?[45]

(4) Not long after I had published my earlier essay on homosexuality (see chapter 2) a Mennonite pastor announced to me rather proudly that he had helped his congregation to leave the Mennonite Church USA because it was too liberal, too open, especially on the issue of homosexuality. He was, at least implicitly, claiming that he and his church were more biblical than the Mennonite Church USA. I can't remember whether I asked him or simply thought of asking him if he had read Galatians 5:6-26 recently—thinking, in this instance, of dissension and faction being works of the flesh; and peace, patience and gentleness being fruit of the Spirit. Later I thought of Romans 14:19: "Let us then pursue what makes for peace and for mutual up-building"; and Colossians 3:14: "Above all, clothe yourselves with love, which binds everything together in perfect harmony." None of these passages are simply proof texts. Working for unity, peace and mutual up-building seem to be quite important in the New Testament. They must be important for us as well. Concerns for unity ought not to mute concerns for truth or faithful living. What we must do is the hard work of attempting to hold these concerns together— as difficult as this is.

(5) I believe we need to remind ourselves that our first task as Christians is to be Christian. Thus we discuss this set of issues first and foremost for ourselves. This means that we primarily use Christian and theological categories among ourselves, and are aware that we are first discussing norms that apply to those who are a part of the church, to those whose self-identity is Christian.[46] Then, being as clear as we can about our own identity as Christians, we ask how we relate to and communicate our convictions and our moral practices to the larger society—or even, with due consideration and careful reflection, commend

our moral practices. I believe we can and should do that. I also believe it is important to realize that task is different from speaking to ourselves.[47] These are deeply complicated issues. I have believed for some time that however I am to relate Christian convictions regarding sexual issues to the larger society, I ought to be consistent with how I have thought about relating my Christian convictions about peace and justice to the larger society. Not to do so is illegitimate. Although I also have to recognize appropriate differences among varying issues (e.g., the realization that sexual relations are in some ways appropriately private and yet also affect society in multiple ways).[48]

On Fundamentalism?

I have used the heading "On Fundamentalism?" for this section because I have repeatedly sensed that *many* relatively educated people believe that only those who are fundamentalists or who are unaware of the complex issues of hermeneutics could possibly continue to hold to the traditional view on same-sex erotic relations. This assumption needs to be challenged. But let me also say that just as there are multiple views that are "non-traditional" or revisionist, so there are multiple views that might be labeled as "traditional." My position can probably broadly be labeled as traditional in the sense that (a) I believe it is imperative that we seek to take the Scriptures seriously in what they say specifically—directly and indirectly—on this topic; (b) I believe it is important that we take seriously the Christian tradition on moral and theological subjects, knowing that we have to read the tradition critically in light of biblical teachings; and, (c) I believe that on this issue the Scriptures are clear and the tradition has mostly affirmed this clarity: God created us as male and female and intends for us to have sexual intercourse within the context of marriage between a man and a woman.

If I have to give a name to my way of reading the Bible, I would say that I read the Bible post-critically. I am keenly aware in general of questions posed to biblical texts, specifically in relation to this issue. However, I also ask critical questions of the critical theories—thus post-critical.[49] Moreover, I do not consider the specifics on this set of issues or study these Scripture texts apart from the double-love command. This appropriately complicates matters.

As I begin this section concerning specific Scriptures related to same-sex relationships, I want to quote Kathryn Greene-McCreight as I did in chapter 2: "Let me say for the record that I am among those who wish they could be convinced that Scripture and tradition could be read to support the revisionist position, which would argue for the theological and religious appropriateness of homoerotic relationships for Christians who feel drawn to them."[50]

A part of me identifies with this quote. This is largely, for me, because I cannot help but be moved by gays and lesbians I've known who desperately want the church to change positions on this issue. For me this is not insignificant. However, I cannot ignore the fact that, as far as we know from written documents, until roughly thirty years ago, there was more or less a consensus within the church that heterosexual marriage was the norm and context for sexual intercourse. Same-sex erotic relations were therefore considered a violation not only of specific biblical texts but also of the way in which we are created as males and females. For me this is crucial. Again I will let Kathryn Greene-McCreight articulate what is also my view:

> When a new convention or interpretation is offered within the community of Christian theological discourse which contradicts an interpretation or set of interpretations traditionally held, its warrants need to be presented in order for the proponents to argue for its validity. Furthermore, its warrants must be coherent within the structure of Christian theological discourse. That is, we cannot demand change for the sake of change, or even change for the sake of a noble goal, without coherent rea-

sons, or without reasons that cohere with the way we give reasons for anything else. On this basis, I would reject the assertion that the burden of proof (regarding the failing of homoerotic activity to attain covenant righteousness) rests on the church, even while I affirm the clear obligation of the church to repent for any and all participation in hostility and cruelty toward homosexuals throughout the ages. My point here is that the "burden of proof" always rests on those who propose something novel. In order for traditional readers to be convinced of the righteousness before God of homoerotic relationships, they would need to be convinced on "traditional" grounds. This will mean that if we are to offer a revisionist interpretation of Scripture, either the revisionist interpretation must follow the same "rules" as the traditional interpretation or the revisionist side must convincingly show how and why the rules must be changed.[51]

◆◆◆

Around 1983 I helped to start an ecumenical study group in Urbana, Illinois. At first it primarily looked at issues related to peace, an issue very much related to my work at the time. However, not long into the existence of this group we decided to look at homosexuality, partly because we had people who differed on this issue within the group. Some of us were members of a church that had specifically stated it was wrong to have homoerotic relations while others were members of an affirming Presbyterian church. (I believe this was before such churches used the label, "More Light Presbyterians.") I led these discussions. At that time I read the then-current books by John Boswell and Robin Scroggs.[52] I had previously read the less academic book by Letha Scanzoni and Virginia Ramey Mollenkott.[53] I was recently reminded of the general drift of most of these writings through a quote from Robin Scroggs: "Not only is the New Testament church uninterested in the topic [that we call 'homosexuality'] . . . Biblical judgments . . . are not relevant to today's debate."[54] And thus, it is supposed, current debates need not reference New Testament (or biblical) specifics on this topic. We make our decisions based upon other considerations (usually current moral sensibilities).[55]

From roughly 1983 until the late '80s I lived with significant questions about the traditional position on the issue, largely because of the reading I had done at that time. It is my impression that very many continue to live with questions—or even have settled revisionist positions—largely because of such reading. However, since the late '80s and especially beginning in the mid-90s the scholarly weight has tilted considerably.

Much of the most considerable recent work has confirmed the traditional Christian view. Let me mention only some of the more significant works. First, Richard Hays, now of Duke Divinity School, published a technical, scholarly article on Romans 1 in the mid-80s and a popular-style overview several years later.[56] In the mid-90s he included an overview essay on the New Testament in his large and highly respected work, *The Moral Vision of the New Testament.*[57] In 1995 Thomas Schmidt, a Presbyterian New Testament scholar, wrote a popular-style yet sophisticated book on the subject.[58] Anthony Thiselton, arguably the foremost Christian expert on hermeneutics, has written a long essay on hermeneutics and an excursus on the subject. The latter appears at the appropriate place in his massive commentary on 1 Corinthians.[59] Stanton Jones, in conjunction with other scholars, has provided quite adept surveys of biological and social scientific data relevant to the subject.[60] Willard Swartley, a Mennonite New Testament scholar, has written a competent book intended for a general readership.[61] But without question Robert Gagnon has written what is the most sophisticated and thorough book, aptly titled *The Bible and Homosexual Practice.*[62]

None of this proves that any of these people are correct. What it does establish is that sophisticated readers of biblical texts—who also reflect on the related issues of hermeneutics, ethics, biology, and social science—can with due consideration of the complex issues, affirm the traditional view regarding homosexual practice.

I will not attempt to give detailed exegetical discussions of the relevant biblical texts here. Such studies are readily available.[63] Instead, I will simply provide some basic guidance and offer relevant reflections for dealing with this subject in relation to the biblical texts. For the sake of simplicity I will primarily reflect on the five biblical texts that are most obviously related to same-sex erotic relations: Leviticus 18:22 and 20:13; Romans 1:26-27; 1 Corinthians 6:9; and 1 Timothy 1:10.[64]

The first two texts appear in Leviticus: "You shall not lie with a male as with a woman: it is an abomination" (18:22); and "If a man lies with a male as with a woman, both of them have committed an abomination; they shall be put to death; their blood is upon them" (20:13).[65] These texts themselves are straightforward in terms of what they prohibit. The questions arise because of the nature of the book of Leviticus. It is a book that is foreign to us in many ways. If texts from it are to be normative for us we need some hermeneutical reflections to suggest why.

To begin with, aren't these two passages within what is often referred to as "the holiness code" of Leviticus? Aren't these teachings irrelevant to Christians? Yes, the passages are within chapters 17–26, which scholars often refer to as the holiness code. But I would argue that we have to be more discerning than simply to say that such teachings are thereby irrelevant for Christians. It is important to note that: (a) Jesus' teaching about "loving your neighbor as yourself" is drawn from these chapters (19:18); (b) specific provisions for the poor, the call to "judge your neighbor with justice," and the reminder to "love the alien as yourself, for you were aliens in the land of Egypt" are within these teachings (19:9-10, 15, 33-34); and, (c) some of the Ten Commandments are reiterated here as well (19:11-14). These are some of the more obvious teachings that the New Testament—and most of us—perceive to have ongoing relevance. Thus, it requires careful and mature exegetical and hermeneutical work, not simplistic dismissal, to know what it might mean that nestled among these teachings we also find such admonitions as: "You shall not sow your field with two kinds of seed; nor shall you put on a garment made of two different materials" (19:19); and, "You shall not round off the hair on your temples or mar the edges of your beard" (19:27). How do we discern which admonitions apply today?

One of the primary purposes of the holiness code was to issue a call for Israelites to be holy. This call had specific terms. As the opening of Leviticus 18 states: "You shall not do as they do in the land of Egypt, where you lived, and you shall not do as they do in the land of Canaan, to which I am bringing you. You shall not follow their statutes. My ordinances you shall observe and my statutes you keep, following them: I am the *Lord* your God" (vv. 3-4; cf. 20:26). That Israel was to be a peculiar people should not surprise us nor should we see it as peculiar to sexual ethics. For example, those of us who have focused much on the issue of violence in the Old Testament are aware that God did not want Israel to have a king to rule over them because he was to be their king. In this way they were not to be like other nations (1 Samuel 8–12). Moreover, it is a repeated refrain within the Old Testament that the Israelites are to be holy because their God is holy. This identity will often make them different from the other nations.

This call to be a peculiar people is carried over into the New Testament. One of the classic passages concerning this identity is found in the opening of Romans 12: "I appeal to you, therefore, brothers and sisters, by the mercies of God, to present your bodies as a living sacrifice, holy and acceptable to God, which is your spiritual worship. Do not be conformed to this world, but be transformed by the renewing of your minds, so that you may discern what is the will of God—what is good and acceptable and perfect" (vv. 1-2). The book of 1 Peter issues one of the clearest statements in the New Testament of the call to be "resident aliens" wherever we live. The New Testament is full of the twin claims: we are to be faithful to God *and* this will often set us apart from the surrounding world.

Returning then to the chapters in Leviticus, most of chapter 18 is given to teachings about sexual holiness. Numerous elements of the text remind us that this is a text from a culture that is both ancient and somewhat foreign to us. For example, the teaching regarding abstaining from sex during a woman's menstrual cycle (18:19) is not generally considered morally normative for us. However, what is intriguing is that most of the teaching within the chapter—prohibiting adultery, incest, and bestiality—seem to most of us to have ongoing relevance. Until roughly thirty years ago the same could easily have been said for the prohibition against same-sex erotic relations. In fact within the context of Leviticus, the strength of the prohibition against same-sex relations is underscored within chapter 18 by specifically naming male same-sex erotic relations as "an abomination" and in chapter 20 by both naming it "an abomination" and prescribing death for such behavior.[66] As with the holiness codes generally, these passages call for careful exegetical and hermeneutical work in order to attempt to understand what is being said as it relates to our current debates.[67]

One way to interpret Leviticus 18 and 20 is to say that the writer of Leviticus names the parameters for moral order within the people of God. He defines the difference between moral purity and impurity. We need moral order for our lives. Anthropologist Mary Douglas helped to name this many years ago.[68] As the fine recent book by Jonathan Klawans helps to articulate in detail, one of the lasting legacies of Douglas's work is that she helps us to see that concerns about moral purity and impurity (or order) are not merely concerns of "ancient" religions but are simply a part of human, including religious, communities.[69] We are always in need of moral order, including in regard to sexual relations.[70] The prohibition against incest is one clear example of this.

Though the concern for moral purity is articulated in certain ways in Leviticus, it is also reiterated in the New Testament.[71] Given that one of the time-honored traditions for discerning the normativity of Old Testament teachings for Christians is whether or not they are reaffirmed in the New Testament, this would seem to have considerable significance. On two occasions Paul lists same-sex relations as prohibited by verbally echoing the language of Leviticus (see 1 Corinthians 6:9 and 1 Timothy 1:10).[72] Paul poses a rhetorical question at the beginning of 1 Corinthians 6:9: "Do you not know that wrongdoers will not inherit the kingdom of God?" He then proceeds to list nine categories of people who "will not inherit the kingdom of God." One such category is *arseno-koitai*. This is a word that Paul coined, specifically drawing from the words used for men lying with men in Leviticus 18:22 and 20:13 (*arsen*-male + *koite*-bed/lie).[73]

Likewise, hear the words that introduce the list in 1 Timothy: "Now we know that the law is good, if one uses it legitimately. This means understanding that the law is laid down not for the innocent but for the lawless and disobedient, for the godless and sinful, for the unholy and profane" (1:8-9a). This opening is followed by a list of seven categories of people, ending with "and whatever else is contrary to the sound teaching that conforms to the glorious gospel of the blessed God, which he entrusted to me" (1:10b-11). Among the categories of people who are listed among the "godless and sinful" are again *arseno-koitai*.

Romans 1 is often pointed to as the most significant New Testament passage bearing on the subject of same-sex erotic relations. Unlike the two passages just named, this passage has a fuller theological context—both the immediate context of Romans 1 and the context of the opening chapters of Romans.[74] Let me quote enough of the immediate context to convey what it says about same-sex erotic relations.

> For the wrath of God is revealed from heaven against all ungodliness and wickedness of those who by their

wickedness suppress the truth. For what can be known about God is plain to them, because God has shown it to them. Ever since the creation of the world his eternal power and divine nature, invisible though they are, have been understood and seen through the things he has made. So they are without excuse; for though they knew God, they did not honor him as God or give thanks to him, but they became futile in their thinking, and their senseless minds were darkened. Claiming to be wise, they became fools; and they exchanged the glory of the immortal God for images resembling a mortal human being or birds or four-footed animals or reptiles.

Therefore God gave them up in the lusts of their hearts to impurity, to the degrading of their bodies among themselves, because they exchanged the truth about God for a lie and worshiped and served the creature rather than the Creator, who is blessed forever! Amen.

For this reason God gave them up to degrading passions. Their women exchanged natural intercourse for unnatural, and in the same way also the men, giving up natural intercourse with women, were consumed with passion for one another. Men committed shameless acts with men and received in their own persons the due penalty for their error." (Romans. 1:18-27)[75]

I would suggest that Paul's belief that same-sex erotic relations are wrong is clear within the context of this passage. But a number of comments need to be made about the passage. (1) The admonition appears within the context of a general description of Gentile/pagan wickedness. (2) We need to keep in mind that in 1:28-32 more than fifteen additional expressions of Gentile evil are mentioned. (3) These descriptions are not of individuals but rather of Gentiles in general. (4) There is no reason to believe that any of the last three points calls into question or qualifies Paul's condemnation of these behaviors. (5) There are a number of allusions to the creation accounts within this passage; Paul uses terms like "the creation of the world" and "the Creator" as well as the expression, "images in the likeness of." Historically the Christian tradition has seen this passage, like Leviticus, against the backdrop of God creating humans as male and female (see Genesis 1:27-28; 2:18, 21-25), of Jesus affirming this (Matthew 19:4-6; Mark 10:6-9), and of the significance this implies for sexual differentiation and a theology of heterosexual marriage.[76] (6) It is important to notice, as Richard Hays does, that Paul performs a sting operation: he immediately challenges self-righteousness. (See the larger context of Romans 1–3.) Paul wrote this letter to Roman Christians, some of whom were Jewish—and, like himself, now followers of Jesus—and others of whom were Gentiles. The passage just quoted would resonate quickly with the Jews within the congregation. They might be tempted to say: "Yes, aren't those Gentiles/pagans just the most sinful lot." Paul wants to make sure that this does not simply create an us (Jew/righteous) versus them (Gentile/unrighteous) mentality. Thus the first part of chapter 2:

> Therefore you have no excuse, whoever you are, when you judge others; for in passing judgment on another you condemn yourself, because you, the judge, are doing the very same things. You say, "We know that God's judgment on those who do such things is in accordance with truth." Do you imagine, whoever you are, that when you judge those who do such things and yet do them yourself, you will escape the judgment of God? Or do you despise the riches of his kindness and forbearance and patience? Do you not realize that God's kindness is meant to lead you to repentance? But by your hard and impenitent heart you are storing up wrath for yourself on the day of wrath, when God's righteous judgment will be revealed. For he will repay according to each one's deeds: to those who by patiently doing good seek for glory and honor and immortality, he will give eternal life; while for those who are self-seeking and who obey not the truth but wickedness, there will be wrath and fury. There will

be anguish and distress for everyone who does evil, the
Jew first and also the Greek, but glory and honor and
peace for everyone who does good, the Jew first and also
the Greek. For God shows no partiality (vv. 1-11).

After this transitional paragraph, Paul speaks of Jews in such
a way that they should have no illusions that they have any inherent righteousness apart from the faithfulness of God, especially
as revealed through Jesus Christ. Jews may have "the law" but
that did not and does not make them righteous. Jews will be
judged with the law and Gentiles will be judged apart from the
law: both Jews and Gentiles by the righteous, holy, and gracious
God known through Jesus Christ.

But let me make several comments about the passage just
quoted: Paul does engage in a sting operation, but of a particular
kind. The particulars have to be named. Certainly these verses are
a warning to avoid self-righteousness, as a people and as individuals. We need to be honest about our need for God and our own
temptations and sins. However, we cannot stop there. Consistent
with all of Paul's letters, having placed everyone on a level playing
field before God, he says we are all called to be faithful. Nothing
he says in chapters two and three cancels either his call (positively)
to faithfulness or (negatively) to avoid wicked conduct. He is clear
in verses 6-8: "For [God] will repay according to each one's deeds:
to those who by patiently doing good seek for glory and honor and
immortality, he will give eternal life; while for those who are self-
seeking and who obey not the truth but wickedness, there will be
wrath and fury." The letter of Romans continues this pattern of
thought through chapter eight. In various and creative ways Paul
reiterates: Jews and Gentiles both depend on God's graciousness
and must trust in him. Furthermore, Jews and Gentiles should not
be slaves of sin but rather slaves of righteousness in the way they
live their daily lives (see Romans 6:15-19).[77]

I have not engaged in debate with alternative views on these
passages in these reflections. However, I am well aware of many

of them.[78] I will address some of them briefly here. Some writers make much of the fact that the word *homosexuality* did not exist until the nineteenth-century, thus the Bible does not speak about the same realities we speak about. This is true if one is referring to the truism that the Bible was written in various ancient periods and thus does not utilize modern thought forms. If we imagine that such knowledge necessarily renders the Bible mute on any topic about which we (as moderns/postmoderns) think differently, then we as Christians invite huge problems. Yet I am intrigued by the fact that few people mention that the word *sexuality* did not exist until the nineteenth-century either.[79] Do we really imagine that Jesus or the apostle Paul cannot be instructive to us on sexual immorality because, given that they did not use the word *sexuality*, they could not have understood what we mean when we use the word?[80]

Other critiques of the traditional view include the following: (1) Paul only knew of sex between men and boys, thus he does not criticize same-sex relations in general but abusive pederastic relationships. (2) Paul only knew of promiscuous relationships among gays and lesbians, thus he does not have in mind committed gay and lesbian relationships. (3) Paul only thought of same-sex relationships as pertaining to heterosexuals who are oversexed and have turned to same-sex relations even though they are "naturally" heterosexual. Thus his critique in Romans 1 is not relevant to those who are "naturally" homosexual. (4) Paul had no concept of "orientation," of those who were gay or lesbian "by nature." (5) Paul's disdain for gay relationships is related to his general low, even misogynist, views of women. (6) Specifically in the vocabulary of 1 Corinthians and 1 Timothy the term (*arseno-koitai*) is a new word and we really cannot know what it means; it probably has a more narrow meaning than simply male same-sex relations in general. (7) Similarly in relation to the apparently clear prohibition in Leviticus (or 1 Corinthians), the prohibitions are only to do with cultic/religious/temple same-sex prostitution.

These are the sorts of arguments that are often given to challenge the "plain sense" of these texts. Many scholars who affirm the traditional stance have worked hard over the last twenty years to address these claims—and I believe quite successfully.[81] Therefore, thoughtful, reflective Christians should not be embarrassed to affirm the traditional understanding of these texts in the face of the questions raised by critics of the traditional view. Which is not to say that we should close our eyes to potentially legitimate questions, especially when they raise important issues we must face.

I end with a few comments about the "silence" of Jesus on the issue of same-sex relationships. Some ask rhetorically: "If this was such an important issue, why didn't Jesus say something about it?" Let me highlight several points: the Gospels portray Jesus as mostly, with some notable exceptions, circulating among and addressing Jews. As far as we know the Jewish teaching at the time of Jesus was clear: same-sex erotic relationships were considered wrong. Thus, there is no reason to assume that Jesus, a Jewish rabbi, disagreed with the Jewish teachings and practices at the time. Moreover, had he wanted to challenge the consensus why did he not speak up as he did on other subjects? Jesus did speak specifically, and in strong terms, against sexual immorality—which in that time would probably implicitly have included same-sex erotic relations (Matthew 15:19; Mark 7:21-23).

Jesus often embraced those on the margins, and we should follow his example. Too often in the church we do not. But this embrace did not prevent Jesus from naming sin and calling for its cessation (John 7:53–8:11). Jesus repeatedly and forcefully called upon those who would follow him to love their neighbors and even their enemies. We fail if we forget this. We also fail if we forget that God's call upon our lives requires that we live faithful, righteous and just lives.

It is important as we end this section to hear a reminder from the English bishop and New Testament scholar N. T. Wright. It

is a reminder about the context of the verses I referred to in
1 Timothy 1. It is an important reminder; a much-needed perspective in relation to this whole discussion:

> The point of it all [i.e., 1 Timothy 1:8-11] seems to be,
> not so much to list various types of bad behavior for their
> own sake, but to say: the law is fine, if you want a map
> of where all the dangers lie. There are indeed dangerous
> types of behavior out there, and the gospel message of
> Jesus, through which God's glory is truly revealed (verse
> 11), is just as much opposed to them as the Jewish law
> is. But don't imagine that by teaching the Jewish law you
> will do more than put up some more signposts warning
> people about these dangers. What's far more important
> is to explore the gospel itself, the message which was
> entrusted to Paul and the other apostles....
>
> [The law] won't tell you what you *should* do; by itself,
> it won't encourage you to think through and live out the
> attractive, outgoing life of love and service which was, for
> Paul, what being a Christian was all about.[82]

Wright has named this very well—reminding us in the midst
of this necessary, particular focus to keep things in perspective. We
mustn't forget that proclaiming and living the gospel with gratitude to God and service to others is central. And on sexual issues
we certainly should learn from some of the errors and sins of the
past. We fail if we focus mostly on sexual prohibitions. We must
continue to work to display and articulate what is righteous and
commendable about sexual relations within the context of loving
and committed marriages. But knowing what is most important
does not mean that the "warning signs" related to unrighteous or
unjust behavior, can be taken lightly.

On Being a Member of the Flat Earth Society

I initially placed the following comments into an appendix,
as I did not want them to disrupt the flow of my essay.

Additionally, I did not want their insertion into the middle of my essay to give the wrong impression. I believe that Christians should hold the position they do on moral issues fundamentally for biblical and theological reasons. Thus I did not want to give a discussion of "facts" related to this subject an overly prominent place. Having noted that, I do not want to give the impression that I believe it is somehow virtuous to "believe six impossible things before breakfast" every morning.[83]

I sometimes get the impression that many who have embraced a "revisionist" or affirming position on this subject imagine that people like me must be unaware of issues related to orientation and recent biological studies. On this issue, traditionalists are some-times viewed as the equivalent of those who we imagine in earlier times continued steadfastly to believe that the earth was flat despite clear evidence to the contrary. I have been asked: Are you not aware that the American Psychiatric Association removed homo-sexuality from the *Diagnostic and Statistical Manual of Psychiatric Disorders* already in 1974? I am indeed both aware of that decision and I am aware of the fact that this change did not happen because of any major findings but rather because of heavy lobbying on the part of gays and lesbians.[84]

I have read widely on the subject of same-sex relations, and I have come to several tentative conclusions. First, these are gen-uinely complicated matters. Second, the experts who study these matters are themselves, in many ways, not clear; on some issues they make educated guesses. Third, though of course the data can be interpreted differently, reasonable, intelligent people interpret the data to confirm traditional understandings of heterosexual marriage. And finally, it seems to me that there are many ques-tions that at least should be a part of this discussion—and often are not.

I will proceed with this portion of the essay in two steps. First, I will provide my own brief summary of what I believe to be a more or less "traditional" Christian view of heterosexual marriage.[85]

Thus even in this section regarding "facts" I present a theological norm, placing before us the norm that many have in mind when they reflect on the facts to which I am alluding. Second, I will provide a series of questions or assertions, with brief reflections, related to facts about same-sex relationships. I believe these are relevant to the traditional view. I will suggest that the facts involved can be understood to support the traditional view.

A Traditional Christian View of Heterosexual Marriage.[86] God created human beings as male and female—not wanting either gender to be alone—and made them both in the image of God. As the images of God, the Lord gave them dominion over the earth. They were created as sexual beings—and are not to be ashamed of that. A man and a woman leave their parents' households in order to join together as husband and wife and become one flesh in a covenant for life. As husband and wife God blesses them and tells them to "be fruitful and multiply."

The New Testament clarifies that the central purpose for all of us who are in a covenant relationship with God is to witness to the God revealed in Jesus Christ. This leads to three sometimes offensive conclusions. First, though family is important, we should not idolize the family. Second, a corollary of the first: whether situated within families or not, our lives are to be given to praise of God, including service and hospitality in his name. Third, we should also honor a life of celibate singleness as a worthy way to serve God.

Our covenants of sexual faithfulness (to God and others) are fragile according to the New Testament. Many passages strongly emphasize various sexual temptations often subsumed under warnings against sexual immorality. In the midst of these warnings the New Testament reaffirms that the vitality of marriage bonds depends upon the sexual differentiation of male and female. The New Testament does not view sexual intercourse as essential for a healthy fulfilled life: sex is less important than we make it today. On the other hand, these passages make sex more important than the view of "casual sex" often does. Instead, sexual intercourse is a gift intended to bond the married couple—a gift effective enough that when it is divorced from this union it becomes the sins of lust and sexual immorality.

While there are other ways to name a traditional account of heterosexual marriage based upon Scripture and the Christian tradition, I trust that the one I have given is at least not idiosyncratic. Something like this account serves as the basis for questions about a general affirmation of same-sex erotic relationships, even through marriage.

Some Factual Evidence Supporting a Traditional View. I will proceed now to list a set of issues, related to facts, that I believe indicate that one does not have to be a latter-day member of the "flat-earth society" to continue to believe that the traditional view not only has relevance but should be normative for Christians.

(1) The concept of "sexual orientation" often functions as a trump card against a traditional view. Is it true, as some suggest, that gays and lesbians as a group have no choice in the matter—they just are the way they are? That homosexuals have their orientation and heterosexuals have theirs? If orientation language is intended to challenge anyone who might speak as if a sexual or gender identity is in a simplistic way something one chooses one day, as one might choose to go to college, then it might serve a purpose.[87] However, when it becomes a simplistic and generalized theory about sexual identity it becomes more obfuscating than clarifying.[88]

Three realities seem clear. First, sexual identity is formed within each of us in a complicated way. Second, and closely related, is the reality that gays and lesbians become gays and lesbians for a variety of reasons. Third, if we are to speak about biological makeup and its bearing on sexual identity, much of the research indicates that there is a complicated way in which the biological makeup of a person interacts with both the environment provided by the organism and the larger social environments within which the organism exists. Speaking of genes, for instance, one biologist refers to the interaction through the metaphor of light switches. The environments, at various points, switch certain switches on or off within the genes, thus allowing traits within genes to be expressed by the organism. Of course this means that the traits had to have been present within the genes, but it also indicates that certain conditions must have been present within the environment for the traits to be expressed.[89]

All of this suggests some plasticity in our sexual identity that our social environments affect. Therefore there are genuine and realistic concerns—rather than homophobia—about how a general affirmation of gay and lesbian sex might affect our future generations. Though, of course, these concerns also indicate that many of us are not neutral about whether we want our children to be heterosexual.

My own story confirms this finding. I had a sexual relationship, off and on, with one of my best friends from approximately age three to age twelve. My very first memory is my sexual experience with him at age three. I have vivid memories of some of our sexual interactions. Sometime around age twelve I jumped up from the back seat of the car we were in, saying (or thinking) something like: "This is wrong." Why did I say this? I did not grow up in church. I never heard anyone speak about homosexuality. The explanation that seems most obvious to me is that my whole social world said to me that the way males and females relate sexually is as male with female—not male with male or female with female. I decided at age twelve that that is what I would do. I never had any desire to have relationships with boys or men from that point forward.[90]

(2) Interestingly, despite the reality that many "mainstream" Christians who affirm gay and lesbian relations have an essentialist understanding of sexual orientation, they nonetheless often affirm activist denominational organizations working with gays and lesbians. I know of no such groups which do not include within their general affirmations "gays, lesbians, bisexuals and transsexuals." And yet clearly bisexuals by definition do not have the "no

choice" problem that is presumed to be the fate of gays and lesbians. [91] And transsexuals present different questions altogether.[92] In fact, it seems to me that this very typical grouping gives away some of the agenda and visions for groups that are designed to support gay and lesbian people.

(3) Is it possible that some of the recent writings on parenting and its relationship both to healthy gender and sexual identity should be taken seriously? Mary Stewart Van Leeuwen puts it this way in her book, *My Brother's Keeper*: "So, the bottom line appears to be this: children of both sexes need to grow up with stable, nurturant adult role models of both sexes to better develop a secure gender identity that then—paradoxically—allows them to relate to each other primarily as human beings, rather than as gender-role caricatures."[93]

(4) Is it irrelevant that gay men as a group are by far the most sexually promiscuous group? Some would want to say that this is because the state does not allow them to marry, thus denying them structures for stability. But if this were the central reason then the second most or equally promiscuous group should be lesbians. But such is decidedly not the case. Heterosexual men are by far the second most promiscuous group, though far behind gay men.[94] Some evidence suggests that male sexuality, typically, needs domestication, which seems to be better provided by women and the rearing of children than by bonds with other men.[95]

(5) Again, is it irrelevant that the preferred form of sex by gay men is inherently dangerous, even aside from HIV/AIDS? The health risks for the general gay population are well reported in medical journals. How is it compassionate to grant a generic blessing to relationships that more often than not involve sexual behavior that is inherently harmful? I fully understand the gut response that personal behaviors are far too private and personal to discuss. But I also wonder if the relatively common medical problems connected to typical gay sexual expression serve to affirm the traditional notion that bodies are designed the way they are for a reason.[96]

(6) Is it the case that the significantly higher incidence of emotional and psychological disorders among gays and lesbians is mostly because of the fact that they have had to exist in a homophobic world for so long? Or are these disorders rather mostly because their gay and lesbian identities in fact reflect some flaw in their identity, a "disability" that manifests itself in various ways, including, not unusually, psychological disorders?[97]

I derive no pleasure from writing what I have written in this section. I have written what I have for several reasons. First, these matters are often not discussed honestly when dealing with the issues surrounding same-sex relations. But they matter. Second, taken together I believe the data related to these questions appear to affirm the wisdom of the traditional convictions about same-sex erotic relations. Third, taken together they would suggest that we are doing no one any favors by offering blanket affirmations of gay and lesbian sexual relationships. I often get the impression from many discussions about these issues that we are Gnostics or docetics when it comes to discussions of sex.[98] That is to say, it is as if the particularities of our embodiedness, our social existence, and our existence across time are irrelevant. But they are not.

Having said this, however, I cringe when I write a comment like "some flaw in their identity." I honestly do not know of a better way to put it; nonetheless I cringe. My wife has a flaw in her hearing. Life is certainly rendered more difficult for her. Sometimes those with hearing losses are probably ignored, not treated kindly, or even treated rudely. That should not be the case. A disability is not an excuse for others to treat those with disabilities with anything but love and compassion. However, because some people are insensitive is not a reason to "celebrate" the disability, as if having a hearing loss is the way my wife was intended to be.[99]

If I understand Paul in Romans 1 he is, following Genesis and Jesus, critiquing those who would ignore the good and wonderful designs of God's creation—those who would celebrate those things which violate God's creation. I believe we need to hear Paul in this. But then, as many of us have learned the hard way, we still have to live with tough questions.

What does it mean to live with a "disability" that in some ways forms a substantial part of one's identity and yet also gives one a propensity for behavior that flies in the face of God's intention and thus is wrong? And how do we, who love such a person, live with the challenges posed by these realities?[100]

A couple of years ago I sat with a good friend, a Christian, who confessed that he had multiple addictions, naming his "gateway" addiction as heterosexual sex. I know this man and his family background very well. To understand his sexual life adequately, one has to contextualize it in a much larger set of contexts—including who he is as a whole person. Knowing those contexts, knowing him, I can't help but ache for him and empathize with him regarding the apparently irresolvable challenges with which he lives. He has been married five times and has had who knows how many casual sexual encounters. I have no idea how his biological makeup has interacted with a difficult home life, including the loss of his father at a young age and a harsh and domineering mother. What I believe is that, in some sense, his sexual identity is something he has received more than chosen. This means that certain choices, though possible for him, are anything but easy. If they were to ask my advice, I would want leaders in any congregation of which he was a part to listen to his story, relate to him as a person, and be gracious and patient, while calling him to be faithful to the God he claims to worship and serve. Can we do any less with the gays and lesbians who are among us?

If we are to begin to have integrity in this regard, we must enlarge our concept of sin, acknowledging the traditional Christian notion of the fall and the similarly useful concept of brokenness. The truth in the notion of orientation language is that it seems that for many gays and lesbians their homosexuality is something that is received, not chosen. But I believe, following the lead of Romans 1, that British ethicist John Colwell is right when he says that when it is received, it is received not as male and female identities are received—through God's created intention—but more the way loss of hearing is received, as a disability. As Colwell has put it:

> We rightly respect those who strive to accept their disability as the context in which life must be lived. But attempts to redefine disability as something other than disability lack conviction: overwhelmingly those who are blind would prefer to see; those who are deaf would prefer to hear; those who are lame would prefer to walk. To attempt to redefine disability as something good in itself is to deny the ultimate goodness of creation by denying its present fallenness. The failure to admit the reality of present fallenness is a refusal to believe in the future liberation defined in the Gospel. Disability may be given but it is not given in the same manner that maleness and femaleness are given; it is dissonant; it is not given as an aspect of creation's goodness but as an aspect of creation's fallenness, distortion and corruption. . . .
>
> If it is understandable that those who are disabled protest against dehumanizing effects of patronizing pity it ought similarly to be understandable that some pronounce themselves "proud to be gay." Sexual identity, like disability and like maleness and femaleness, is [sometimes] an aspect of received identity. For this reason it is not something to be apologized for. Without prejudice to a doctrine of original sin I [may be] no more directly culpable for my sexual [identity] than the man born blind was culpable for his blindness. But I am accountable for what I do with my sexual [identity], just as I am accountable for the way I live with my masculinity and the man born blind was accountable for the way in which he lived with his blindness.[101]

Yes, indeed. As I end these reflections, I—one last time—want to reiterate the challenge with which I began the essay.

Concluding Comments

I end this chapter not with any grand conclusions but with what I hope are some helpful reminders. First, I want to remind the reader that one of my desires is to help us live with Jesus' response to the question posed by the title of the chapter: "Teacher, which commandment in the law is the greatest?" Our lives and teachings should communicate that we know Jesus' response: "You shall love the Lord your God with all your heart, and with all your soul, and with all your mind" and "You shall love your neighbor as yourself" (Matthew 22:37-39). And they should convey that we know that this twin teaching always summarizes the particulars of faithful lives.

One way to heed the call to attend to particulars in our own day is to live with the challenges posed by a brief article on the subject of homosexuality by British Old Testament scholar Walter Moberly:

> Why bother with the Bible at all? In a culture impatient of traditional authorities, why should Christians go through the complicated rigmarole of biblical interpretation? Is it not a prime case of "If you will believe outdated nonsense, then you must expect the consequences"? Why not abandon the Bible and be free? To such siren voices the Christian response is, in essence, simple. When you have found the pearl of great price, the one thing needful, then you are foolish to let it go. There is—in the God revealed in Jesus Christ, to whom Scriptures bears witness—a reality, a love, a truth which is worth holding on to, come what may. What is at stake is not petty rules and restrictions on puzzles about contemporary sexuality, but one's whole understanding of life and death.[102]

Earlier in the same article Moberly commented:

> What one does with these texts [specifically on homo-
> sexuality] is bound up with deciding which are the best
> questions to ask. If the question is simply, "Do these
> biblical writers disapprove of those same-sex activities to
> which they refer?" the answer is a straightforward and
> uncontroversial "Yes." Yet if one asks the further ques-
> tion "So what?" there is instantly a debate which is ardu-
> ous and anguished. The complicating factor is always, in
> one way or other, what is entailed by the responsible use
> of Scripture.[103]

I believe it is imperative that we be deeply and richly biblical
and theological in our approach to this subject. Moreover, I
believe, with Moberly, that "what is at stake is not petty rules and
restrictions on puzzles about contemporary sexuality, but one's
whole understanding of life and death."

As John Yoder used to say about the call to love enemies: if
one does not see the vital importance of the Bible for our
Christian life, what is needed are not more essays or books on the
subject but perhaps a call to conversion, or at least some reading
on biblical authority. Despite all the attempts to obscure the texts,
I cannot help but agree with Moberly that the biblical texts speak
clearly on this subject. Then, as he says, the question begs to be
asked: So what? In response, as a community of followers of
Christ, we are called to engage in a "responsible use of Scripture."
I have attempted, in my small way, to help in that process. But I
have no illusions that I have asked all of the questions that should
have been asked. Nor do I have any illusions that the process of
living with this—loving the Lord our God with our whole being
and loving our neighbors as we love ourselves—is easy. May our
gracious Lord be with us as we wrestle and engage together with
careful and loving discernment.[104]

Ted's Response: Where's the Sin?

First, I want to express my gratitude to Mark for his willingness to engage in this conversation. As will be clear in what follows, I disagree with him on numerous important issues. However, I greatly appreciate his friendship, his commitment to respectful conversation, his irenic spirit, and his engaging writing style. And I deeply respect his commitment to the way of Jesus, to the truthfulness of scripture, and to seeking the truth through engagement in mutually enlightening conversation with differing perspectives.

As will be developed in a later chapter in this book, Mark and I do share significant points of agreement—including placing high value on the Bible as our basic source for theology and ethics, affirming the sanctity of marriage and believing that sexual intimacy should be reserved for couples in covenanted relationships, and opposing the special hostility Christian churches have shown toward gay and lesbian Christians and their supporters. However, in this response, I will be focusing my energies on the key areas of disagreement that I have with Mark's first two essays. I will spend most of my time on the second essay, "'Teacher, Which Commandment of the Law is the Greatest?'" I will start, though, with a couple of comments related to the first essay, "The Fruit of the Spirit or The Works of the Flesh?"

Does Mark Understand His Opponents?

In chapter 2, "The Fruit of the Spirit or Works of the Flesh?" Mark does not demonstrate awareness of the perspective of those on the "affirming" side in the current *Mennonite* milieu. This is understandable to some degree given the lack of safety Mennonite pastors and theologians have had in relation to expressing their views on these issues. However, there is one document that has been widely circulated, the "Welcoming Letter" published in the *Mennonite Weekly Review* (February 17, 2000) and available on the Welcoming Committee website (http://www.welcome-committee.info/openletter.html). As well, the Welcome Committee has published eight booklets addressing various issues related to homosexuality (also available on the website).

Several times, Mark's essay presents the affirming position in ways that do not correspond with Mennonites on the affirming side, if the Welcoming Letter is to be considered representative of this position within the Mennonite churches. This point is important if this essay's intent is to foster better understandings for the Mennonite "conversation."

A couple of examples: Footnote 31 cites several sources that affirm non-monogamy. However, the Welcoming Letter does affirm monogamy, as do (as a rule) arguments made in "Letters to the Editor" in Mennonite publications and in the Welcome Committee's booklets.

It may be that some unnamed "Mennonite theologians" imply that "no serious Scripture scholarship supports the traditional view" but this is not a representative perspective—even less representative is the view mentioned several paragraphs earlier that science "silences the Bible's voice on the subject."

Finally, the essay implies that the affirming people do not take promiscuity seriously. This is actually precisely an issue the Welcoming Letter does take seriously—arguing that the Mennonite churches would help *reduce* promiscuity among gay and lesbian Christians were it to bless monogamous, committed partnerships.

What is the core issue that we are conversing about? This is really the crucial question, and it is here that I have my most serious concerns about Mark's essay. Is the issue predominantly about sexual practices or is it predominantly about social justice?

The essay's fourth paragraph identifies the issue: "We are, when all is said and done, for or against homoerotic relations." In fact, though, for many who signed the Welcoming Letter the issue would be phrased otherwise: "We are, when all is said and done, for or against continued emotional violence against gay and lesbian people."

My main point here is not to argue about who is more accurate in identifying the issue, but to suggest that an essay attempting to situate the conversation in a useful way should probably start by recognizing this fundamental difference. The point of such an article then, it seems to me, would be to struggle with how there could be a meeting of minds in identifying the core issue—with a call to people on all sides to seek better to understand what those with other views of feeling so passionate about.

Later on, the final one of the eight points of agreement discussed in the essay reflects this same misperception: "It is homoerotic behavior that is really the issue we are wrestling with." Then, much later, the essay acknowledges that addressing "injustice" is important as "a part of the background of our discussions," but then immediately marginalizes that point. Perhaps Mark thinks making injustice too central is a problem in seeking for the truth; however, if he hopes to have fruitful interaction with those who disagree he needs to do a better job of indicating that he takes their concerns seriously.

Are Same-Sex Intimate Relationships *Inherently* Wrong?

In responding to Mark's longer essay, I will comment on three general areas of concern. First, we have the basic issue of whether or not same-sex sexually intimate relationships are *inherently* wrong or not. When we take away the various elements of sexually intimate relationships that are also problematic for heterosexual people (e.g., promiscuity, coercion, physically harmful practices) is there still something about same-sex sexual intimacy in a covenanted relationship that makes it wrong? Mark clearly assumes that there is; I will suggest that he has not made a case for supporting this assumption.

Second, I am concerned with Mark's reading of the Bible—both how he privileges the "direct texts" in his ethical reflection and with how he actually interprets those texts.

Third, I am concerned with Mark's discussion of "issues

related to facts" and his use of moral analogies in relation to same-sex intimate relationships. I will question the factuality of Mark's facts and the appropriateness of his analogies.

First, the question of inherent wrongness. I see this as the most fundamental question in this conversation. People on what I call the restrictive side seem to assume inherent wrongness, that there is something about the same-sexness of these relationships itself that makes these relationships inherently immoral. People on the inclusive side, on the other hand, tend to assume that the same-sexness is morally neutral. If particular expressions of sexual intimacy are immoral in the inclusive view, they are this way due to other factors than simply that the partners are both male or both female.

In considering the morality of heterosexual sexual intimacy, most Christians would agree that we have various "heterosexualities;" some are morally good and others are morally problematic. The morally problematic expressions may include, as examples, sexual intimacy outside of marriage, promiscuity, coercive or abusive sexual behavior, sexual behavior that is economically exploitative, or lustful sexual behavior linked with idolatrous religious activities.

The inclusive perspective, as I present it, would agree that same-sex sexual activity that fits in this list of morally problematic expressions should be opposed by the churches. But what about sexual intimacy between partners of the same sex that do not encompass any of those aspects? This is where we would like to see the discussion focused. Don't focus on same-sex behavior that would also be morally problematic when engaged in by heterosexuals. We agree that that is to be opposed. However, just as no one would say all heterosexual sexual intimacy is wrong because many of expressions of it are, we would say not all same-sex sexual intimacy is wrong just because many expressions of it are.

Unfortunately, Mark does not engage the discussion on this level. Essentially, he simply assumes that each possible expression of same-sex sexual intimacy is immoral. Throughout, he presents the issue being whether Christians should tolerate "immorality" or not—with the assumption that this is the basic issue dividing the restrictive from the inclusive perspectives.

However, I am arguing that the issue is not whether we tolerate immorality but where we draw the line in making a distinction between moral and immoral sexual expression. Is it between monogamous sex in the context of covenanted relationships (marriage) and sex outside of such relationships? Or is it between heterosexual monogamous sex and all other expressions (including same-sex monogamous, covenanted relationships)?

Mark clearly concludes that the latter is the key distinction, but he does not make a case for it. He fails to address the arguments for making the former distinction.[105] Throughout his essay, Mark alludes to the immorality of same-sex relationships.

These are just a few examples:

Mark implicitly draws a connection between the inclusive perspective and "directly arguing for the moral legitimacy of greed." Then, Mark repeats as an established fact that "as far as we know the Jewish teaching at the time of Jesus was clear: same-sex erotic relationships were considered wrong." But such a generalization is based on scanty evidence; we know little about what Jewish teaching on this subject was since there is virtually no record of any such teaching. Also, this term "same-sex erotic relationships" is used in an all-encompassing way, again implying that all such relationships are morally on the same level. Then, Mark asserts that Jesus spoke, "in strong terms, against sexual immorality" and that this opposition "would probably implicitly have included same-sex erotic relations"—presumably because they are all obviously immoral.

Mark suggests that "the significantly higher incidence of emotional and psychological disorders among gays and lesbians" might well occur "mostly because their gay and lesbian identities in fact reflect some flaw in their identity, a 'disability' that manifests itself in various ways, including, not unusually, psychological disorders."

As an example of a person with a problematic sexual identity, Mark tells the story of a heterosexual friend with a sexual addiction, with the implication that this problem is morally on the same level as any possible same-sex intimate relationship. He urges church leaders to call his friend "to be faithful to the God he claims to worship and serve. Can we do any less with the gays and lesbians who are among us?"

Amidst all these statements implying that all same-sex intimate relationships are equally wrong morally, Mark never explains *why* the same-sexness of such relationships is itself always a problem.

Mark does not acknowledge the reality of healthy, genuinely committed same-sex relationships between two Christians. He does have one reference in a footnote to one of Roberta Showalter Krieder's three books telling stories of gay and lesbian Mennonites, but he shows no evidence of reflecting on the stories told in these books.

In the past twenty some years, I have learned to know a fair number of gay and lesbian Christians across the United States. They are a diverse group, just like my heterosexual friends. However, most are part of long-term relationships that show clear evidence of being just as healthy and life giving as the relationships of my other friends—and just as permanent. I think of two couples I learned to know when I was in graduate school in the mid-1980s, one a male couple, the other a lesbian couple. Both couples are still together and flourishing. And I could name numerous others who have or will soon celebrate ten years and more together.

Though such evidence is anecdotal, these relationships are real. And they are plentiful enough for me to assert quite confidently that it is indeed possible for same-sex, covenanted relationships to flourish. This reality does not prove my case theologically, for sure. However, it does lead me to believe that the phenomenon of these healthy relationships challenges people arguing the restrictive case to explain why these relationships are morally wrong.

It is not enough to refer, as Mark does—echoing most of the theological literature I am aware of from the restrictive perspective—only to same-sex practices that would also be wrong for heterosexuals. For Mark persuasively to make his case, he would have to address the good relationships—and explain why those particular relationships are wrong.

How Do We Best Apply the Bible?

I am concerned with Mark's reading of the Bible—both with the way he privileges the "direct texts" in his ethical reflection and with the way he actually interprets those texts.

In my main chapter below, I ask for clear biblical evidence to override a benefit of the doubt in *favor* of vulnerable people. I suggest that because gay people are vulnerable in similar ways to people with which the Bible was concerned (e.g., widows, orphans, poor people, resident aliens, lepers, people labeled as "sinners" in Jesus' time), people of faith should be inclined to include them in our fellowship—unless we have strong bases for restricting their participation.

What clear biblical evidence do we have to support Mark's implication that even the life-giving, faith-filled, morally rigorous same-sex covenanted relationships I allude to are wrong? If we assume, based on the fruitfulness of such relationships in any observable sense, that these relationships should be affirmed, what bases do we have for overruling this assumption? Specifically, what clear biblical evidence do we have for same-sexness per se being wrong?

My reading of the texts commonly cited as speaking most directly to our issues concludes that none of these texts, when read contextually, speak to all "homosexualities." None of these texts condemn my friends' partnerships because they do not address the possibility of covenanted same-sex intimate relationships.

They all have other concerns in mind and, at most, express moral critiques of behaviors that would also be problematic for heterosexual people. In my reading, each of these texts seems clearly to be raising their critiques for contextual reasons that do not apply to the type of homosexuality my friends are embodying (e.g., coercive rape in Genesis, fertility cults in Leviticus, unbridled lust in Romans, and economic exploitation in 1 Corinthians).

Hence, I turn to Mark's treatment of the biblical passages asking how strong of a case he provides challenging the perspective I am advocating. Even though Mark concludes "the biblical texts speak clearly on this subject," in the essay he does not give us a careful consideration of the best arguments from inclusively-inclined writers on which to base his conclusion. He lists the writings from those arguing for a restrictive perspective that he believes indicate "the scholarly weight has tilted considerably" in the direction of "the traditional Christian view." However, he does not interact with any writings from the other side.

Mark gives no sense that he has entertained the possibility that someone could read the Bible with an approach similar to what he takes, giving it a "plain reading" and drawing different conclusions on these issues. Instead, he hints several times that one of the basic issues dividing Christians on this issue is whether we give the Bible adequate authority or not.

Certainly Mark is entitled to his conclusions regarding the Bible's message. And he clearly has strong support in the scholarly community for his readings. But by not engaging the strongest of the arguments of those on the other side, by not indicating that someone could share his high view of biblical authority and still disagree with his conclusions, by not *showing* how his readings are better than his opponents' readings, Mark does not engender much confidence that his easy dismissal of views differing from his own is warranted.[106]

For each of the texts Mark discusses ("the five biblical texts most obviously related to same-sex erotic relations"—Leviticus

18:22 and 20:13; Romans 1; 1 Corinthians 6:9; 1 Timothy 1:10), he focuses on the specific verses and pays little attention to the wider contexts of the passages.

So, with Leviticus, he simply quotes the few directly applicable words and states categorically "the texts themselves are straightforward in terms of what they prohibit." Unfortunately, Mark does not explain what is prohibited. Is it only sex between two *males* (since that is all that is mentioned) or a blanket prohibition against all possible same-sex intimacy? Since the verses only mention men, it certainly seems possible that the bases for the prohibition have to do with contextual factors that apply only to men. If that were the case, though, the Leviticus verses can't simply stand as absolute, for-all-time, prohibitions for women as well as men.

Mark does comment on the location of these verses in the holiness code in Leviticus 17–26. He cites Leviticus 18:3-4 stating that the context for these holiness teachings is Israel's call to be an alternative to the ways of life they left behind in Egypt and were to be surrounded by in Canaan. However, Mark presents the thrust of the holiness teaching being more to sustain the moral order by maintaining sexual purity than a calling to subvert the moral order of their surrounding societies by embodying a social transformation that centers on empowerment for the most vulnerable members of their society (widows, orphans, resident aliens—Leviticus 19). I tend to believe that the present-day relevance of the holiness code lies in its vision for the community of faith finding ways to empower its most vulnerable members, which in our setting would include gays in covenanted relationships who are treated with hostility in our wider culture.

Mark points to a link between male/male sex and "adultery, incest, and bestiality" while ignoring menstrual sex and masturbation. If we include all the examples given in Leviticus 18, we cannot say the list should be understood as once-for-all-time prohibitions, since these latter two are no longer prohibited by most Christians, nor is there any present-life basis for doing so. But if being on this list is not basis enough for permanent prohibition, we must return to the question Mark fails to answer—what is there about the male/male sex per se that supports making a permanent, all-encompassing prohibition?

Mark goes on to discuss how the "prohibition of same sex relations" in Leviticus 18 and 20 (notice the assumption that one can obviously move from the male/male specificity of Leviticus to an all-encompassing prohibition that includes women) is reaffirmed in the New Testament in 1 Corinthians 6:9 and 1 Timothy 1:10.

Mark writes as if it were a fact that Paul's word *arsenokoitai* was one he "coined, specifically drawing from words used for men lying with men in Leviticus 18:22 and 20:13." We simply do not and cannot know that Paul coined this word nor that it is specifically drawn from Leviticus. All we know is that we have no record of this word being used other than in Paul's writings, but we have no further evidence of where it came from or even what Paul meant by it, since his only use is as part of a list that includes no explanation of his meaning.

In relation to Romans 1, Mark treats Paul's discussion of men and women being consumed by lustful actions as direct ethical admonition to Christians. He disregards the clear context of the passage that presents the problematic behavior here as an example of what idolatrous people outside the community of faith do as a consequence of refusing to worship God. To the extent these examples are directed to Paul's Christian readers, they have to do with lulling those readers into a sense of self-righteousness that they do not do these things—as if their "purity" in some sense in itself establishes them as righteous before God. Paul disabuses them of that notion, making the point that all people rely equally on God's mercy.

That Paul is talking about extreme behavior that clearly reflects a rejection of trust in God makes it clear that his point is not speaking to the kinds of same-sex intimate relationships among Christians that inclusive writers are supporting. A careful consideration of the broader context of Romans 1–3 and the role of 1:18-32 in that argument should make this apparent.

Mark makes a point of criticizing inclusive writers for failing to follow a method of reading the Bible in the "plain sense" of the texts, though without giving specific examples of such writers. He assumes that the traditional understanding of these texts reflects such a plain sense reading. He does not really explain what he means by plain sense, but I will assume that it has to do with following the most obvious and direct meanings of the texts and not explaining those meanings away in terms of cultural blind spots.

My main article below attempts to interpret these texts in their plain sense. I have tried to show that such as interpretative strategy can indeed lead to inclusive conclusions. Here I want to question whether Mark's interpretations do indeed obviously reflect a plain sense reading.

Is it a plain sense reading of Romans 1 and 1 Corinthians 6:9 to interpret them as providing direct ethical exhortation for Christians? In both cases Mark pays no attention to the intent of Paul in his naming problematic ethical behavior. In Romans 1, Paul's intent is to illustrate unjust behavior by idolatrous non-Christians in order to exhort his Christian readers to refrain from being self-righteous and judgmental and thereby implicitly denying their own sinfulness and need for God's mercy. In 1 Corinthians 6, Paul's intent is to illustrate unjust behavior by non-Christians in order to exhort his Christian readers not to take their fellow church members to secular courts.

To note these points about Paul's intent is not to say that the ways he chooses to illustrate these problems are insignificant. These texts do provide important content concerning the homosexuality issue, especially since they are the only places where the issue comes up in any direct way in the New Testament (along with 1 Timothy 1:10, which is clearly derivative from 1 Corinthians 6:9). However, it would seem that the plain sense of these texts is not that they explicitly provide normative and timeless all-encompassing ethical directives for Christians concerning homosexuality. Rather, their plain sense seems to be to address Christian judgmentalism and Christian lawsuits.

Is it a plain sense reading of Jesus' teaching to assume that he must have condemned all possible same-sex relationships even though he never speaks of them? Certainly, that we have no record of Jesus speaking to this topic is not evidence that he would have taken an inclusive stance. We should let the silence remain and recognize that we have no proof texts from Jesus that can settle our debate.

Is Gagnon a Reliable Guide?

Throughout his chapter Mark cites Robert A. J. Gagnon's book, *The Bible and Homosexual Practice: Texts and Hermeneutics*, as the crucial resource on this topic. Numerous times, Mark mentions a point of contention and simply cites Gagnon as having resolved the point as if this settles the matter.

However, Gagnon's work is problematic on several levels. I don't have the space here to develop a lengthy critique, but I do want to note several problems and question whether Gagnon is actually a reliable guide for our interpretation of biblical materials.

From the start of his massive book, Gagnon juxtaposes two general approaches he sees being followed by people writing on "the Bible and homosexual practice." Not once, in the entire book, does he grant any validity to any pro-gay arguments.

He seems to set up the two-approach polarity for the purpose of utterly refuting pro-gay viewpoints. Throughout the book, Gagnon understands the approach of the restrictive writers to be based on solid methods and the approach of the inclusive writers to be based on faulty methods. There is no sense of what problems there might be with restrictive assumptions and methods—nor of what validity might be found in inclusive assumptions and methods. Thus Gagnon "proves too much." The lack of even-handedness undermines the reader's trust in Gagnon's objectivity.

Gagnon's hostility toward gay Christians and their supporters emerges often throughout the book. He describes Paul's cryptic statements said to be speaking to "same-sex intercourse" in Romans 1 as "deep visceral feelings . . . of disgust toward same-sex intercourse" seeing such as "the zenith of detestable behavior" (page 269).

How warranted is Gagnon in attributing to *Paul* feelings of "disgust toward same-sex intercourse"? We do not actually have much evidence of Paul's "deep visceral feelings of disgust" here, especially since it seems clear from the passage Romans 1–3 as a whole that Paul's concern is not nearly so much the behavior to which he refers in Romans 1 as it is the self-righteous attitudes of the religious people he challenges in Romans 2.

When Gagnon turns to the Sodom and Gomorrah story, we see his methodology illustrated. Rather than considering the evidence for why Sodom and Gomorrah were destroyed, thereby acknowledging that this is an issue over which people disagree, Gagnon *starts* with the assertion that only something as heinous as attempted homosexual rape could explain why God would wipe the cities out. His logic seems to run, we all know that "homosexual practice" is extraordinarily evil and thus when these cities are punished it must be because of their homosexuality.

From the start, Gagnon seems to assume the worst about same-sex intimate relationships, taking it for granted that homosexuality must have been terrible and extraordinarily repulsive to the biblical characters. Yet beyond the cryptic commands in Leviticus, we have next to no clear evidence of this repulsion in the texts themselves. We have no stories comparable to David's adultery with Bathsheba or Amnon's rape of Tamar to illustrate what is so problematic about such behavior. On the other hand, the Old Testament is quite clear about the problematic nature of mistreatment of vulnerable people.

Gagnon's treatment of New Testament materials is equally tendentious. Overall, he has produced an extraordinarily fearful book. His inflexible refusal to allow for ambiguity and complexity and for the possibility that his opponents might be at least partially correct reflects this fearfulness. So does Gagnon's constant approach of making absolute and all-encompassing statements based on what turns out to be, upon examination, tenuous evidence. Consequently, I am troubled by Mark's uncritical use of Gagnon's arguments.

Are Mark's 'Facts' Factual?

In the section, "On Being a Member of the Flat Earth Society," Mark reflects on "a set of issues" related to present-day expressions of same-sex sexual intimacy. These reflections are presented as "related to facts." However, I am not quite clear what the facts are that Mark has in mind—or even why he would make a point of using this term *facts*. It would seem that what follows is mostly reflecting various opinions (how could it not?).

It is notable that for some of the key points Mark makes he cites numerous writings in support that come from writers who clearly are aligned with the anti-gay side. In these discussions of problems with same-sex intimacy, he once more chooses not to engage the other side at its strongest, not grappling with the possibility that some gay relationships are healthy and life-giving.

Many of Mark's facts could be valid in the sense that many gays do engage in harmful sexual practices. However, these negative consequences also may be seen in heterosexual practices that are problematic. Mark's arguments do not have much relevance to people in same-sex intimate relationships that are healthy and committed. If we suspect that there is something about same-sexness that is intrinsically harmful, we should examine the best and most healthy same-sex relationships and show that even they manifest the kinds of harmful consequences Mark discusses.

Mark's inclination to assume the worst about same-sex rela-

tionships, that they are immoral even though he has not established why the same-sexness itself is wrong, may also be seen in
his brief comments about analogies for same-sex relationships.
This is a very small part of his essay, but I think it illustrates a
general problem. That is, as discussed above, Mark does not take
on his opponents at their strongest.

All Mark's analogies are negative. He does not reflect on the
analogy of left-handedness, which we all now see as a neutral
condition, and explain why it is not as useful an analogy as hearing loss, alcoholism, bi-polar conditions, sexual addictions, and
Down syndrome. Perhaps Mark would have good reasons for
preferring these other analogies to left-handedness, but that he
does not even consider this possible analogy seems to me to a
further indication that his argument is founded on many unar-
ticulated assumptions.

Consider ways that left-handedness is analogous with same-
sex affectional orientation. In both cases, the origins of the condition remain mysterious. Probably 5 to 10 percent of the population is strictly left-handed, some are ambidextrous, and the
large majority is right-handed—similar to some estimations of
the breakdown of people's primary affection attractions.

Despite intense attempts to change handedness, it has proved
to be unchangeable in many cases. In the past, before social mores
changed, many left-handed people were able to pass as right-
handed even though they remained strictly left-handed in their
basic orientation.

In many cultures left-handedness has been seen as shameful.
It has often been associated with inherent impurity, even with
the powers of evil. Even in the Bible, the left side is associated
with being condemned by God and the right side with being
blessed by God (e.g., the judgment scene in Matthew 25).

In recent years, though, cultural mores have changed and,
more and more, left-handed people are welcomed as left-handers
with no stigma attached. Such acceptance has not resulted in any

negative effects on the wider culture. In North America, nonetheless, there are people still alive who have felt traumatized by the opposition they have faced for their left-handedness and their failed attempts to change.

A clear cultural consensus has emerged in North America by now that left-handedness is neutral morally. It is accepted that it is "normal" for our society to have a small percentage of people who are "abnormal" in their handedness, and that this abnormality does not threaten the right-handedness of the vast majority. In our culture, now, the basic goal with regard to left-handedness seems to be to accept left-handers as they are and to adapt to their needs.

In fact, it is accepted now by at least some people in our culture that it is appropriate to celebrate some of the unique attributes that left-handed people have.

Of course, no analogy is perfect, but the case for the similarities between left-handedness and same-sex affectional orientation does seem to have some merit, especially in comparison to all of the analogies that Mark suggests.

Mark returns to Jesus' love command in his conclusion. I wonder whether gay Christians, his neighbors, would feel he has shown love to them. His tone has generally been respectful. However, by not giving more credence to their own testimonies of their faith-filled lives and by not better explaining how his argument takes into account those testimonies, I wonder if Mark can be said to have gone the second mile in assuming the best of his opponents.

Mark ends his essay with a challenge to affirm biblical authority and engage in "responsible use of scripture." I have sought to meet this challenge—and to show that in doing so one may or should still draw inclusive conclusions. I am grateful for this opportunity of mutual give and take in which Mark has shared.

Mark's Response: Some of My Best Friends

In this brief response, I will organize my thoughts into three categories: knowledge of gays and lesbians and those who affirm committed gay and lesbian relationships; dealing with the biblical texts; and a few reflections on "direct texts" and what "the issue" is.

So, first I will offer a few comments on my awareness of gays and lesbians and affirming Mennonites. Ted says in several ways that I am not fair to those who are affirming within the Mennonite Church. To begin with, I think Ted missed something crucial in chapter 2, "The Fruit of the Spirit." Did he read the "What Can We Agree On?" section? Given the way I began this section I would have thought it obvious that I am pointing to affirming as well as non-affirming people within the church when I named the eight points of agreement, saying that most people in our churches are somewhere in the middle, not at opposite ends of the spectrum. Very specifically I said, under point seven, that "if the church were to shift positions on homosexual relationships, what is being suggested for adoption is a parallel monogamous arrangement for gays and lesbians."[107] Thus I was indeed suggesting, contrary to what Ted claimed in his response, that *most* affirming people in our churches do not want to encourage promiscuity.[108]

Ted, in the accusation I just referred to, is drawing from my section, "Glosses on Areas of Agreement." Ted would like for me simply to postulate that "the Welcoming Letter" speaks for the majority of affirming Mennonites and let things rest there. Out of honesty I can't do that. It is partly because of my knowledge of the Brethren Mennonite Council for Lesbian, Gay, Bisexual and Transgender Interests, partly because of many conversations, partly because of wide reading and partly because of what Ted has said and importantly *not said* that I would stand by my claim that "many who write theological books or essays about homo-

erotic relations argue for non-traditional ways of structuring relationships, to put it most neutrally"[109]

Ted himself has done what is more common among mod-
erates. That is to say, he has not affirmed "non-traditional ways
of structuring relationships." But interestingly, as I note in my
response to his longer essay, his only lengthy, substantive comments on marriage were of a deconstructive nature. I would have
no idea how he would even begin to write a whole essay that
would both argue for marriage (traditional, except for including
gays and lesbians) *and* specifically against sexual intercourse outside of marriage. Whether he could or would write such an essay,
it almost never happens among those with his position.[110]

I won't engage in a contest with Ted regarding who has known
a greater number of gays and lesbians or known them better. I
could discuss at some length several very different men I have
known. Or the lesbian I mentioned at the beginning of chapter 3.
When I was first introduced to her, I quite deliberately invited her
to a very long lunch, in which I asked her to share her story and
offer her own theological reflections on being a lesbian, which she
was happy to do. I met her partner, attended her wedding, met
some gay friends of hers, she twice attended lectures I gave, and we
exchanged letters. "Some of my best friends are 'fill in the blank'"
always sounds like special pleading. Let's just say I have had
enough gay and lesbian friends and acquaintances over the years
that I in no way imagine they are all alike or that all of them have
the same sorts of relationships. Simply because I have believed for
my whole Christian life that having sexual intercourse outside of
marriage is wrong does not mean I can't distinguish the difference
between a one night stand and a forty-five year relationship that
has never been affirmed publicly through an act of marriage.

Telling stories or using analogies is always difficult and filled
with potential misunderstandings. Maybe Ted misunderstood
the brief tale of my friend who is sexually addicted because of
my inadequate writing; maybe it was something else. In any

event, since it seemed not to be clear to Ted, let me explicitly state why I used this story. I was attempting to humanize someone who engages in what most of us would see as sexual sin. Put differently, I was trying to have the reader empathize with this man, even given that he has engaged in behavior that was wrong. And the direct analogy I was drawing with gays and lesbians is this: I am convinced that our sexual identity is integrated into who we are as a whole, an identity that is formed in complex ways and received more than chosen. I very specifically meant to complexify our conversations around these issues by using this story to point to questions regarding many typical understandings of sin in relation to sexual identity—thus following this story with a return to Romans 1, following leads from John Colwell.

Now for a few comments on biblical texts. To begin with, I should make it clear, if it isn't already, that I was convinced of my current position before Robert Gagnon published a word on this issue. I could make my argument without one reference to him. I know there are those who don't like the tone of Gagnon's writings. Ted seems to be one of them; in a short essay he tries to marginalize Gagnon's work. Despite Ted's attempts in this regard, it would be irresponsible to ignore Gagnon's writings. He is not only the most knowledgeable and prolific contemporary Christian writer on this topic, he is clearly a very bright and capable biblical scholar.[111]

I'm not sure my brief forays into biblical interpretation pay "little attention to the wider contexts of the passages," as Ted suggests. Granted, my comments were brief and emphasized different dimensions of the contexts than Ted, but I did try especially to situate the texts in Leviticus 18 and 20 and Romans 1 in their respective contexts. Let me simply add a few comments, with some references. First, I would reaffirm the difficulty of coming to grips with Leviticus 18 and 20—though I am somewhat stunned by Ted's misreading of what I actually said.[112] I won't repeat the several pages of comments I offered on Leviticus. I will simply ask people to read them again in light of Ted's response.

It is telling that Ted is troubled that I privilege the "direct texts" in dealing with this issue. Yes, it is a habit I've developed that when I want to know what the Bible says about something I look at the specifics of the texts that deal directly with that topic. For example, in relation to Leviticus, I named the complexities of the text, the context, and the issues it deals with in chapters 18–20, calling for honesty in this regard. Ted apparently doesn't allow the direct texts (the details of the text) to challenge or re-form his current ideology. He places his heavy interpretive grid over the details, thus making sure that no untidy teachings are allowed to seep through. Thus he can say: "I tend to believe that the present-day relevance of the holiness code lies in its vision for the community of faith finding ways to empower its most vulnerable members." Is it just coincidental that the "present-day relevance" matches Ted's ideology of inclusion more than the overall teaching of chapters 18–20—or the whole of the holiness code— of Leviticus?

I've already suggested my disagreement with Ted on Romans 1. Ted's arguments here mostly depend on certain understandings regarding homosexuality at the time of Paul rather than anything in the text. But these interpretations have been convincingly challenged.[113] When we turn to Ted's interpretation of 1 Corinthians 6:9-10, we see the great lengths he will go to sustain his argument. It is really quite extraordinary that he would claim that the overall message of 1 Corinthians 6:1-10 is a call to justice or the avoidance of injustice. In the name of taking the context seriously Ted has muted the rich texture of the specifics. Richard Hays is more on the mark when he says of this passage that: "Paul emphasizes that those who are baptized into the community of faith have been transferred out of one mode of existence into another. . . . Now—washed, sanctified, justified—baptized Christians are set into a new reality, not by some act of will or commitment but by the gracious action of a loving God."[114] Those Christians who are washed and sanctified are specifically being reminded in verses 9 and 10 of who many of them were before and now are not. (And again, reading over the list in these verses, it is astounding to me that Ted can imagine that this list can simply be subsumed under what he means by justice.) Many biblical scholars see the overall context here as being chapters 5–7. And in discussing these texts, many have noted the intermingling of various topics in chapters 5–7 of 1 Corinthians, sex being a topic off and on throughout.[115]

Finally, in relation to the Scriptures, it seems to be a truism among many scholars that Judaism at the time of Jesus was basically of one mind about the immorality of homosexual practice (contra Ted). I quoted two affirming biblical scholars to this affect in my "The Fruit of the Spirit" chapter.[116] If in fact this is true, then it is not such a stretch to imagine that when Jesus mentioned "sexual immorality" he would also have had homosexuality in mind. All one has to do is think of a church leader in the United States in, say, 1940. If such a person mentioned sexual immorality, the odds are very good that, if asked, that person would immediately respond that homosexuality was included within what they meant.

Now, finally, a few reflections on "direct texts" and "the issue." Early in his response Ted says: "What is the core issue that we are conversing about? This is really the crucial question, and it is here that I have my most serious concerns about Mark's essay." Elsewhere, Ted twice expresses concern about my reading of the Bible and the way in which I privilege direct texts in my ethical reflections on the issue of homosexuality. The issue for Ted, apparently, is justice or, put negatively, challenging injustice and "emotional violence" to gays and lesbians. Moreover, I suppose, for Ted, since he doesn't want to privilege direct texts (i.e., texts that deal directly with same-sex relations) he wants to privilege the texts that fit in with his ideology of inclusion, as I said at the end of my response to his chapter. On this issue as well as some others, what this seems to equal is that Ted doesn't need to attend to the specifics of the Scriptures at all. By his hermeneutical decision anything that falls foul of his understanding of inclusion is defined out of the canon. So, really, all of the apparent attempts to "take the text seriously" through engaging in "sophisticated" interpretive moves are unnecessary. He knows ahead of time what the conclusions will be. I must say, this approach has its advantages; it certainly makes things easier.

—— Chapter 4 ——

Toward a Theology of Welcome: Developing a Perspective on the 'Homosexuality' Issue

Ted Grimsrud

Present-day North Americans, including Mennonites,[1] are struggling bitterly over sexuality issues. At the heart of the struggle stands the question of how our culture will relate to gay and lesbian people in their midst. Certainly, many other elements of the "homosexuality"[2] issue require attention, but I will focus on only one in this essay—the place in the church of gay and lesbian Christians who are in committed relationships.[3]

Acknowledging the complexity of current discussions, I will use two terms, intended to be neutral and descriptive, of the two sides of the issue of gays in the church.

The first I will call the *restrictive* perspective. In this view, there should be restrictions placed on the participation of all sexually active gays in the church. These restrictions could range from total rejection to acceptance as participating non-members to restricting the possibility of gays exercising ordained leadership.

The second perspective, the *inclusive* perspective, holds that the "gayness" of a church person (including being in a committed same-sex relationship) should have no bearing on church participation. Typically, this perspective would argue (1) that moral values such as opposing sexual promiscuity, adultery, and sexual abuse that the church affirms in relation to heterosexual sexual practices should apply to gays and (2) that covenanted partnerships should be supported.

Many people oversimplistically assume that the basic issue may be broken down to a couple of truisms: "Believe in the Bible and restrict gays; include gays and deny biblical authority."

However, the reality is more complex. My position, as I will sketch it in this chapter, may very briefly be summarized as follows: A careful, respectful reading of the Bible *as a whole* supports the inclusive perspective. The Bible's overall message emphasizes God's mercy and God's movement to bring healing out of brokenness to all who trust in God. The Bible portrays God's welcome of people made vulnerable by social prejudice and exclusiveness as central to God's merciful movement toward human beings. This movement toward welcome establishes a strong benefit of the doubt toward churches welcoming gay Christians without restrictions based on their gayness. The burden of proof is on those who would have the churches adopt restrictive policies. I will argue that this burden of proof is not satisfactorily met.

When we consider how different people within the church approach the Bible in relation to sexuality issues, we may identify four general tendencies. I would characterize them as follows, thinking especially of how they approach the biblical texts that are usually cited as directly touching on homosexuality.

(1) Restrictive with a more conservative biblical hermeneutic. This view focuses on direct biblical references: "The Bible opposes homosexuality and so should we." Most, though not all, restrictive writers operate here, including Mennonite Willard Swartley and the author he relies on most heavily, Robert Gagnon.[4]

(2) Restrictive with a less conservative biblical hermeneutic. This view focuses on natural law: "The Bible is not necessarily central; the key issue is that homosexuality is unnatural." Those in the

Roman Catholic tradition tend to fit more in this category. A well-reasoned articulation of this perspective has been made by James Hanigan,[5] who certainly affirms the authority of the Bible but who ultimately bases his restrictive argument more on natural law.

(3) Inclusive with a more conservative biblical hermeneutic. This view focuses on biblical themes: "The Bible does not oppose homosexuality; since it supports inclusion of vulnerable people so should we." People in this category take the anti-gay texts seriously, but argue that they do not provide a basis for the churches being restrictive based on the best interpretation of those texts. A prominent book that reflects this approach is Letha Scanzoni's and Virginia Mollenkott's *Is the Homosexual My Neighbor?*[6]

(4) Inclusive with a less conservative hermeneutic. This view focuses on liberative texts and dismisses anti-gay texts as inapplicable: "The Bible is opposed to homosexuality (when it mentions it) but we need not be because of the priority we place on liberation." Most inclusive writers probably fit best in this category including, most prominently, Walter Wink.[7]

We notice here that people on the restrictive side can have either a more or less conservative biblical hermeneutics. This is also true of people on the inclusive side. It is crucial to note that the dividing line is not actually the issue of biblical authority. The dividing line is to be found elsewhere. At least in relation to the perspectives I will discuss in this book, the dividing line seems to lay with understandings of the *content* of the Bible.

In what follows below, I will approach the core biblical texts from a perspective closest to the third option sketched above. That is, I will approach the issue with a conservative hermeneutic. I will argue for an inclusive stance concerning gays and the church from a perspective reflecting a high view of biblical authority. I seek to demonstrate that the truism that the only way to reject the restrictive perspective is by lessening one's commitment to biblical authority is false.[8]

I do not believe that it works to reduce this issue to conservative versus liberal approaches to biblical authority. Actually, the best and most respectful straightforward reading of the Bible supports the inclusive perspective—in my opinion. One can be relatively conservative in one's view of the Bible and still come to inclusive conclusions. I will argue for the inclusive perspective because of, not in spite of, the Bible.

Our Starting Point

A crucial element of the discussion has to do with the question of our starting assumptions about where the burden of proof lies.

Do we start with the assumption that inclusive people need to prove that gays should be "in" (i.e., full participants)? Must inclusive people prove why it is okay to be inclusive because we should assume that it probably is not? In this view, we could say, gays start outside the church's circle of unrestricted participation and their supporters must find a basis for getting them in.

Or, do we start with the assumption that restrictive people need to prove that gays should be "out" (i.e., have their participation restricted)? Must restrictive people prove why it is okay to be restrictive because we should assume that it probably is not? In this view, we could say, gays start inside the church's circle of unrestricted participation and the church must find a basis for restricting their participation.[9]

Which benefit of the doubt we choose does not, of course, in itself resolve the issue. It is always possible to overcome the benefit of the doubt—but the kind of argument that must be made will follow from whether one is trying to prove that our default inclusiveness must be overridden or our default restrictiveness must be overridden.

The point we start from then becomes crucial. Hence, we must first focus our attention on our starting point. This starting point should not be arbitrary or accidental. We should examine and evaluate where we start. This is the first big piece of the puzzle of biblical hermeneutics as it relates to the church's relationship to gays.

Some reasons for putting the burden of proof on those who would be inclusive (that is, saying that the church's default position should be restrictive) may include: (1) The Christian tradition has pretty much always operated with a restrictive consensus. Restrictiveness is the historic position of the church. (2) The Christian community is called to seek for purity, to exclude unrepentant sin. Especially in our modern world where moral standards are deteriorating, the church must take a stand against sexual permissiveness. (3) A straightforward, common-sense reading of the Bible makes it clear that the Bible is against homosexuality. Believers and non-believers alike tend to assume that the Bible takes this stance.

Reasons for putting the burden of proof on the other side—to say that the church's default position should be inclusive—may include: (1) Jesus modeled inclusiveness. His treatment of people unjustly labeled as sinners in his world parallels how the church should related to vulnerable and ostracized people in our day. (2) Going back further, the Old Testament clearly teaches that the community of faith has a special responsibility to care for vulnerable and marginalized people—in that setting, the people most often mentioned were widows, orphans, and other people without access to wealth and power. (3) Paul taught that the only thing that matters in terms of one's standing before God is one's faith. Christians are those who trust in Christ, period. Not, trust in Christ plus this or that requirement.

In our work of discernment, we need carefully to examine these various points that determine our starting point. These are the convictions that will likely shape how we read and apply the biblical teaching—regardless of whether we have a stronger or weaker view of biblical authority. My perspective in this chapter operates with the assumption that the church's default position should be in favor of inclusion.

My perspective has been shaped by my pacifism. I originally accepted the restrictive perspective. In the late 1970s, my hometown held a referendum challenging the city council's gay rights legislation. That election served as a catalyst for changing my thinking. At the time, I supported the referendum (that is, I opposed the gay rights legislation). However, I became distressed at extreme hostility many of my fellow evangelical Christians showed toward gay people. My pacifist convictions led me to reflect on the significance of this hostility. I came to suspect that any moral conviction linked with such hostility needed to be questioned—not necessarily rejected but treated with suspicion.

In time, my views on gay rights changed. I came to draw on two biblical themes in particular in concluding that the church's benefit of the doubt as they examine the biblical materials should lie on the side of inclusiveness. First, the Bible, beginning with the book of Genesis, places great importance on the call to share hospitality with vulnerable people. Second, Jesus himself modeled inclusiveness toward people his faith community labeled as unworthy of full inclusion in their midst.

The central message of the Bible may be summarized in this way:[10] God created the world in love and means for all creation to be whole. In the face of human rejection of this love, brokenness comes to characterize life on earth. God grieves at creation's pain and brokenness. God's justice finds expression in God's process of making whole that which is broken.[11] God's "right-making" love (or restorative justice) works especially through communities that know and share God's love. We see this in the crucial story that comes early on in the Bible—God calling Abraham and Sarah, promising that although Sarah has been unable to bear children, God now will give the couple descendants. These descendants will bless all the families of the earth (see Genesis 12:3). God creates this particular community of the promise in order to use it as a means to bring healing to the entire world.

The rest of the Bible tells of this community of the promise—arguing throughout that God's promise remains alive. God calls the community of the promise so that all may know the healing power of God's love. Of course, many resist God's love—with terrible consequences. God's judgment falls on rebellious human beings. The story ends with hope for healing, though, even for those who resist God—Revelation's "kings of the earth" (chapters 21–22), transformed by the work of the Lamb.

Hospitality. Throughout, the Bible's call for God's people to form communities of healing finds expression in the high priority placed on the virtue of hospitality. This is the first theme that points toward a benefit of the doubt for inclusiveness. A faith community's hospitality expresses its faithfulness to God. Practically, in biblical times, human life in a largely harsh, unforgiving physical world was fragile. Desert people need each other; they rely on hospitality from others for their survival. Even more, hospitality takes on a profoundly spiritual dimension—our relationship with God is determined by our willingness to live hospitably. Faith communities that refuse hospitality cut themselves off from their life source.

Throughout the Bible, inhospitality evokes God's judgment. We see this in the story of Sodom and Gomorrah as interpreted by Ezekiel (16:49-50), in Amos's critique of Israel's injustice toward the poor, in Jesus' teaching about the sheep and goats in Matthew 25, and James's sharp words in James 2.

I want briefly to trace this theme of hospitality in the Bible, giving only a few obvious examples of what I believe may be found in detail throughout both testaments.

Two important examples actually are a little ironic in relation to the "gay issue." Both the Sodom story in Genesis 18–20 and the teaching in the holiness code of Leviticus 18–20 are concerned above all with *hospitality* as defining faithful living in relationship with God. Hospitality may be defined as "showing kindness in welcoming guests, strangers, and others in need."

The Sodom story as a hospitality story contrasts the failure of hospitality in Sodom with Abraham's hospitality as the chosen channel of God's blessing. First the angels visit Abraham prior to going to Sodom. Abraham models what Sodom should have done. He gives the angels a welcome, showing genuine hospitality. After their visit to Abraham, the next place the angels go is to Sodom. Rather than hospitality, they are threatened with rape.

This story, thus, holds up Abraham as the model of hospitality in contrast to Sodom. As a model, Abraham actually intercedes with God on behalf of Sodom—being so bold as to remind God of God's loving and just character while pleading with God to show mercy to Sodom. In contrast to Abraham's exemplary hospitality, the people of Sodom reap judgment due to their inhospitality (see Ezekiel 16:49: "This was the guilt of your sister Sodom: she and her daughters had pride, excess of food, and prosperous ease, but did not aid the poor and needy").

Leviticus 18–20 is a very different kind of literature than the stories of Genesis. These chapters are the heart of the holiness code in the Old Testament law. And at the heart of this section, in Leviticus 19, we get a clear picture of holiness according to Torah.

Leviticus 19 teaches. "You shall be holy, for I the Lord your God am holy" (19:2). Some manifestations of this holiness follow: "When you reap the harvest of your land, you shall not reap to the very edges of your field, or gather the gleanings of your harvest. You shall not strip your vineyard bare, or gather the fallen grapes of your vineyard; you shall leave them for the poor and the alien" (19:9-10). "You shall not keep for yourself the wages of a laborer until morning. You shall not revile the deaf or put a stumbling block before the blind" (19:13b-14). "When an alien resides with you in your land, you shall not oppress the alien. The alien who resides with you shall be to you as the citizen among you; you shall love the alien as yourself, for you were aliens in the land of Egypt" (19:33-34).

At its core, holiness includes hospitality toward the vulnerable people in the community—the poor, the alien, the laborer, the deaf, the blind. Elsewhere we also read of the widow, the orphan, the daughter.

Later in the Old Testament, prophets portray Israel as having lost its moorings, departing from God's will for their lives. A sure sign of Israel's crises may be seen in the *lack* of hospitality, the disregarding of the concerns of Torah for the vulnerable members of the community.

Probably most forcefully, the prophet Amos makes clear that injustice and inhospitality are sure signs that amidst Israel's apparent prosperity, something is rotten. A catastrophe is coming to the people of Israel, Amos cries, "because they sell the righteous for silver, and the needy for a pair of sandals—they who trample the head of the poor into the dust of the earth, and push the afflicted out of the way" (2:6-7). Amos goes on to assert that when the community is so inhospitable, their very worship is sinful. To tolerate such injustice and then turn to God as if it does not matter is the worst of blasphemies.

Catastrophes *are* visited upon the people. The great empires, Assyria and Babylon, bring ruin to Israel. According to the prophets, though, the deepest problem did not come from these outside enemies but from within. With its kings, its quest for prosperity, its disregard of the true meaning of holiness, the community had departed from its calling. The community was far, far away from being a blessing to the families of the earth—rather, it imitated the worst injustices of the inhospitable nations of the earth. And the community pays the price.

Nonetheless, God keeps the community going even through it failures. When Jesus comes onto the scene, the core issue of hospitality surfaces again front and center. For Jesus, the central criterion of faithfulness may be seen in the call to hospitality.

Jesus made a point of showing welcome specifically toward those considered "unclean" (that is, outside the circle of approved religiosity). And this was not simply because he had a soft spot in his heart for strays. Jesus portrayed salvation itself as directly tied to such welcome.

One time, Jesus responded to the question about eternal life with an affirmation of following the commandments—which he summarizes as loving God and loving neighbor—quoting Leviticus 19. When pushed as to whom the neighbor actually is, Jesus tells the story of the good Samaritan. This story packs an amazing punch when we realize that the kind of hospitality illustrated here (again, being linked directly with salvation) is risky, unconditional, and counter any kind of boundary line that seeks to separate faithful insiders from outsider "sinners"—remember, the Samaritans were the worst of sinners to Jerusalem-centered Jews.

One other place Jesus directly connects salvation with hospitality. Matthew 25 tells a parable of the day of judgment, the separation of those who inherit the kingdom and those who are excluded from the kingdom. What is the criterion? "I was hungry and you gave me food, I was thirsty and you gave me something to drink, I was a stranger and you welcomed me, I was naked and you gave me clothing, I was sick and you took care of me, I was in prison and you visited me" (25:35-36). When did we do these things for you? "Truly, just as you did it to one of the least of these who are members of my family, you did it to me" (25:40).

As portrayed in Matthew 25, showing hospitality leads to salvation; practicing *in*hospitality leads to condemnation. Hospitality matters.

The Bible teaches from start to finish that the authenticity of the communities that have professed their faith in Yahweh, the God of Israel, may be seen most clearly in the quality of their hospitality. By definition, this hospitality is tested most tellingly in relation to vulnerable people, the people who most need it, we could even say, the people the communities have the most difficulty welcoming. Inhospitable communities separate themselves from God—and reap the consequences.

When applied to the question of whether the restrictive or the inclusive view should be the church's starting point, the theme of hospitality points clearly toward placing the burden of proof on those holding restrictive views. What bases do we have for concluding that the norm of hospitality toward vulnerable people does not apply to gay and lesbian people?[12]

Jesus' model. Along with hospitality, the second biblical theme that supports a generally inclusive stance arises from focusing more directly on Jesus, "the pioneer and perfecter of our faith" (Hebrews 12:2). He models welcome. Almost everyone affirms that Jesus taught and practiced love. Certainly, Jesus' portrayal of love stands at the center of his message. We need to look at what Jesus actually did, however, in order to appropriate his message about love. We might discover Jesus' love may be more distinctive than we have thought.

Jesus consistently showed deep-seated and at times costly kindness and respect to particular men, women, and children. Jesus was not so much a general humanitarian. He did not make big plans for large-scale projects. Mostly, Jesus cared for specific people. He cared for Matthew the tax collector. He cared for the woman at the well. Jesus modeled for us the practice of simply accepting other actual people. He treated individuals with respect. He listened to others, was interested in them, shared food with them.

Jesus' love for particular people, however, most certainly had social consequences. He loved particular people, in all their real-life social aspects, as a political strategy. We may call this strategy the "politics of compassion."[13] Politics in this sense, may be defined, following John Howard Yoder, as "the structuring of relationships among persons in groups."[14]

Jesus and his followers formed a social organization that stood in sharp contrast to the relatively rigid social boundaries of their culture. They rejected boundaries between righteous and outcast, men and women, rich and poor, Jew and Gentile. Jesus' politics of compassion was founded on a profound understanding of God's mercy. God, as represented in Jesus' teaching (e.g., the parable of the prodigal son, Luke 15:11-32), does not discriminate but loves all people. God is our model: "Be merciful, as your Father is merciful" (Luke 6:36).

Jesus opened participation in this community to all who chose to be part of it—all they had to do was "repent" (turn toward God) and "believe the good news" (trust that God's mercy is for them). This constituted Jesus' fundamental message (Mark 1:15). In the ministry that embodied his proclamation, Jesus made unmistakably clear the openness of his community for all who wanted their lives transformed by his mercy.

One clear expression of this openness may be found in Matthew's gospel. A repeated verse in both 4:23 and 9:35 sets off a discrete section: Jesus traveled throughout Galilee, "teaching in their synagogues and proclaiming the good news of the kingdom and curing every disease and every sickness among the people." This section of Matthew shows that the "good news of the kingdom" includes both Jesus' teaching (e.g., the Sermon on the Mount, 5:1–7:29) and Jesus' healing. A partial list of the recipients of healing shows the incredible openness of this kingdom Jesus proclaimed: demoniacs, epileptics, a leper, a centurion's servant, Peter's mother-in-law, two Gentile demoniacs, tax collectors, sinners, and the daughter of a synagogue leader.

In these verses, Jesus mostly healed outsiders, people considered unclean or contaminants by the established religion. Jesus offered them mercy just as they were. He was not simply a knee-jerk iconoclast, however. He willingly brought healing to anyone who turned to him, including even a synagogue leader. Jesus' politics of compassion included all who responded.

Of these aspects of Jesus' politics of compassion, the practice of open table fellowship perhaps most powerfully speaks across times and cultures. The metaphor of table fellowship resonates deeply in the Anabaptist-Mennonite tradition, as it does in the story of Jesus. Sharing table fellowship has powerfully and concretely expressed fellowship, inclusion, and communal connection. Because of its deep symbolic significance, Jesus' practice of table fellowship reflects perhaps most profoundly his philosophy of life.

The important role table fellowship played in all the cultures of Jesus' world cannot be overestimated. Meals were not simply about people meeting their physical needs. The sharing of meals had become a ceremony symbolizing friendship, close social connections.

Joining for meals expressed one's acceptance of another as an integral part of one's community. Usually, people shared food with those of their own social class. Hence, mealtime reinforced social differences, fortifying the boundary walls between insiders and outsiders. People tended to provide hospitality toward those they expected to reciprocate—"I invite you to eat with me fully expecting that you will invite me back."

Jesus delighted in breaking bread with an enormous variety of people, regardless of their ritual cleanliness. "He directly challenged the social and religious exclusiveness associated with table fellowship," writes Scott Bartchy. "He showed radical openness."[15]

Jesus practiced a radical openness that ran contrary to the purity-oriented exclusionary practices of religious people of his time (and ours). The symbol of open table fellowship with outsiders, "sinners," excluded ones, reveals Jesus' approach with stark clarity.

Table fellowship for Jesus signified welcome into the kingdom of God. The love feast Jesus welcomed people to join had no prerequisites, no initiation rites, no insistence on purification as a prerequisite for entering. All it took was open hands—the prodigal son's return, the five thousand's acceptance of the bread and fish, the sinner woman's tears (see Luke 7:36-50).

Once it became clear that not all the religious leaders of Jesus' day would join with his radical openness, he wasted no time critiquing their boundary marker-oriented approach to faith. When the Pharisees restricted access to God's mercy to the ritually pure, excluding so many, Jesus spoke sharply in opposition. Jesus certainly offered a message of love and compassion, but this positive message carried with it a direct confrontation to those not willing to respond to it with love and compassion of their own. Show others compassion and God will show you compassion; withhold compassion and God will withhold compassion from you.

My referendum experience in the late 1970s opened my eyes to the extent that gays in our society, and also in the church, have often been treated with hostility—and worse. Some of the most vulnerable people in our society surely are sexual minorities—and as such would seem to be people who Jesus and the Old Testament law and prophets would have special concern.

Reading Christian history through pacifist eyes, I found the restrictive assumption of the importance of "this is how the church has always believed" to be unpersuasive. As I came to see it, the church as a whole has been wrong about warfare for the large majority of its history—as well as slavery. So it could also have been wrong about gays in the church. From a pacifist perspective, I assume that when the church's position (e.g., supporting war, supporting slavery, supporting restrictiveness toward gays) is hurtful to people it should be treated with suspicion.

As well, in my experience the churches have not used open and respectful processes in its treatment of inclusive congregations, dissenting individuals, or the formulation of denominational or conference statements. I do not believe we have had the kind of open discernment processes and due process that would ensure fairness and gentleness in dealing with the issues. This lack of care in our ecclesial processes also provides me a reason to be suspicious of interests that are protected by less than careful processes.

Certainly all of these points in support of starting with inclusiveness as the default position are debatable. I do not claim to have offered proof that this is where all people of good will should start! I am simply giving the bases for my perspective.

Regardless, the centrality of hospitality in the Bible and the way Jesus modeled welcome support holding inclusiveness as our starting point. However, such a starting point does not resolve the issue concerning gays in the churches. We must consider whether, in the Christian tradition, we might have decisive reasons that should cause us to overrule our starting point and conclude that the churches nevertheless should ultimately take a restrictive stance.

If we start with the inclusive assumption and seek to follow a conservative hermeneutic with the Bible, then the basic argument might go like this: What do we find if we examine the biblical teaching asking if it provides clear and persuasive bases for the restrictive position? Is there a clear basis for overturning the inclusive assumption? Do the "core texts" that explicitly mention homosexuality provide a clear basis for overriding the default inclusivist position?

Because the question of whether present-day gays by living in committed relationships are actively sinning seems to be the basic issue in dispute, the focus of our investigation should be on the issue of the alleged sinfulness of all possible expressions of same-sex sexual intimacy. We need to focus most of all on the alleged bases for asserting that even covenanted, monogamous same-sex relationships are inherently sinful.[16]

If the Bible makes it clear that gays in covenanted partnerships *are* sinning, that would be enough for someone with a conservative biblical hermeneutic to override the pro-inclusiveness benefit of the doubt. If such clarity is not forthcoming, that would do a great deal to move the inclusive position from being an assumption to being a conclusion.

In what follows, I will focus on the question of whether the Bible provides a clear basis for overriding the default position of inclusion. Does the Bible clearly condemn what many today are calling same-sex covenanted relationships?

I intend here to take a fairly unsophisticated, direct "plain sense" approach to the Bible.[17] I am interested in whether, following a reading strategy compatible with a quite conservative doctrine of Scripture, one finds clear evidence for asserting that the Bible condemns all forms of same-sex sexual intimacy as sinful.

To answer this question, we need to ascertain whether the

"condemnation" is overtly and explicitly expressed. The question of whether the Bible clearly condemns *all* forms of same-sex sexual intimacy can be answered only by considering the texts cited as directly speaking to the issue. I will focus on six passages seen to speak directly to same-sex sexuality: (1) the story of Abraham, Lot, Sodom, and Gomorrah in Genesis 18–19; (2) a similar story in Judges 19; (3) Leviticus 18–20, the holiness code for Israel's practice; (4) Romans 1:18-32, with its well-known connection between idolatry and sexuality; (5) the list of sins that often is understood to contain reference to same-sex intimacy in 1 Corinthians 6; and (6) a similar list in 1 Timothy 1.

I will approach these texts first of all in their broader context within the books of which they are part. I believe the literary units within which these scattered references to same-sex intimacy fall are the most important elements of interpreting those references. I understand the meaning of the Bible to emerge most of all from its literary units—the largest being the most important in conveying meaning: the Bible as a whole, the individual books, then sections, paragraphs, and sentences. Individual biblical words are at the bottom of the list.[18]

Biblical Texts Central to the Debate

Genesis 18:1–19:29. Genesis 18 and 19 contain two contrasting accounts of hospitality. In juxtaposing these two accounts—one being Abraham's hosting of the visitors from God, the other being the men of Sodom's attempt to gang-rape their visitors—the text focuses on the called-outness of Abraham as God's channel of salvation for all the families of the earth.[19]

If we consider the connection between chapters 18 and 19, we see that the main point of the story of Sodom is to highlight by contrast the exemplary characteristics of Abraham, not to underscore as an end in itself the point of the sinfulness of the heathen. So, the point of the Sodom story is not about homosexuality at all; it is about hospitality.

We still need to ask what precisely Sodom and Gomorrah did to be condemned. In Genesis 18:20-22, God reports to Abraham that God has heard the outcry concerning the gravity of the sins of Sodom and Gomorrah. This outcry evokes echoes of other cases where the outcry of oppressed people reaches God (for example, the outcry of Abel's blood in Genesis 4:10, and the outcry of the enslaved Israelites in Egypt in Exodus 2:23). The outcry implies social injustice, as later alluded to in the references to Sodom in Jeremiah 23:14 and Ezekiel 16:49.[20]

The story portrays the Sodomites' injustice as their brutal inhospitality. Hospitality had great significance in the desert culture of the Bible. Abraham, in the first part of Genesis 18, shows how hospitality was supposed to be practiced. The moral corruption of the Sodomite community comes through clearly in their refusal to care for Lot's visitors with generosity; they respond instead with exploitative violence.[21]

The text describes the inhospitality of the Sodomites in terms of every single man in the city (19:4) seeking to have sex with the visitors—indicating the intent to gang-rape the visitors. The sin here clearly is a *social* sin (not individual), characterizing the entire city.[22] Several of the men of Sodom were Lot's prospective sons-in-law (19:12-14), implying that while every man might have been intent on raping the visitors, not every man was homosexual. The issue clearly seems to be domination over vulnerable outsiders, not same-sex sexuality.[23]

Genesis 18–19 tells us nothing about same sex affectional orientation, same-sex loving relationships, or even about alleged ancient Near Eastern revulsion regarding a condition modern people call homosexuality.[24] This passage concerns hospitality—contrasting Abraham's welcome of strangers and intercession with God over the fate of sinful people with the brutal inhospitality of the Sodomites, paradigmatically expressed in the effort to subject Lot's visitors to gang rape as a means of humiliating and subjugating them. Its ethical exhortation centers on practicing hospitality like Abraham models—not on forbidding loving, committed, same-sex intimate partnerships.

Judges 19:1-22. Interpreting Genesis 18–19 as focusing on hospitality (and inhospitality) finds support from Judges 19:1-22, a passage that George Edwards calls the earliest commentary on Genesis 19.[25] Edwards argues that close parallels between these two passages include these points: In each case the visitors offer to stay outside and are strongly urged by their hosts not to, the cities are each utterly inhospitable with the exception in each case of a single resident alien, both hosts' houses are surrounded by a mob from the city who want to "womanize" (humiliate through gang-rape) the guest(s), the hosts both offer virgin daughters to the mob.[26]

A crucial difference between the two stories, though, supports interpreting the concern in these stories as gang rape, not same-sex sexuality. In the Judges story, the mob relents when they are given the guest's concubine to gang rape. To ravage the man's woman had a similar effect of emasculating the male guest, the concern being domination, not same-sex sex.[27]

These two passages, Genesis 18–19 and Judges 19, are the only two stories in the Old Testament that mention particular men seeking to have sex with other men, and we have no stories at all featuring women with women. In both cases, though, the desire for sexual intercourse was an expression of the desire to dominate strangers through gang-rape, not an example of general homosexuality. So these stories provide no evidence that the Bible condemns all possible same-sex sexual intimacy as sinful.[28]

Leviticus 18–20. The book of Leviticus centers on the need for Israelites to maintain clear distinctiveness from surrounding cultures.[29] The book places itself in the time of Moses, following the exodus and prior to the entry into the promised land. Leviticus challenges the Israelites to live faithfully in this land God gives them.

To survive, the faith community must follow God's law. An

inevitable consequence of faithfulness to God's law will be living as a contrast culture in relation to surrounding cultures.[30] How can Israel live as a distinct, separated people in the context of a surrounding culture that rejects their faith?

Leviticus 17–26 is called the holiness code and sketches the characteristics that should distinguish Israel as God's holy nation. Within the holiness code, chapters 18 through 20 provide the core teaching, and within that smaller section, chapter 19 plays the especially crucial role of defining holiness.

The concept of biblical holiness is best understood *relationally*. Holiness in Israel characterizes God as a relational God. Holy people are people who live in right relationship with God and with other people. The community of faith actualizes its holiness as it fosters interpersonal relationships characterized by whole-making justice.[31]

Leviticus 19 gives concrete shape to Israel's calling to be a holy nation,[32] calling the people to be holy just as God is holy (19:3). Leviticus' picture portrays holiness in relational terms. Among the commands: revere your parents; do not harvest the corners of your fields or strip your vineyards bare in order to provide "for the poor and the alien" (19:9-10); do not lie or steal (19:11); do not withhold the laborer's wages (19:13); treat the deaf and blind kindly (19:14); do not slander (19:16); respect the elderly (19:32); and be inclusive of aliens (19:33-34). We may sum up the teaching on holiness, as Jesus did, with 19:18: "You shall love your neighbor as yourself; I am the Lord."

To be a holy nation means to imitate God, to love the neighbor, to care for vulnerable ones, and to love even the alien "as yourself."[33] The core identity of Israel as a distinctive people of God centers on concern for all members of the community; this focus especially includes concern that vulnerable ones may function as community members. The legislation concerning sexual practices must be understood within this context of care for vulnerable ones that lay at the heart of the definition of holiness in Israel.

Two underlying issues motivate legislation concerning sexual practices here: (1) the need to differentiate Israel's way of life from that of the Canaanites[34] and (2) concern about procreation, continuity over successive generations.[35]

Leviticus 18 focuses on differentiating Israelite culture from surrounding cultures. The chapter begins by asserting that the Israelites "shall not do as they do in the land of Canaan" (18:3). It concludes with, "do not defile yourselves in any of these ways, for by all these practices the nations I am casting out before you have defiled themselves" (18:24).[36] The practices forbidden in Leviticus 18 and 20 are forbidden primarily because they are seen as characteristic of the peoples from whom the Israelites must differentiate themselves.

In addition to moral separation from "the nations," the Israelites also must "be fruitful and multiply" in order to continue as a distinct community. Each of the prohibitions in 18:19-23 has to do with "wasted seed." These are almost all sexual practices that cannot produce children within a socially approved family context, including sex during menstruation, adultery, male/male sexual relations, and bestiality. The one exception, the reference to child sacrifice, is certainly also a form of wasted seed, contrary to the need for children.[37]

We still must consider why specifically the list includes the command that the Israelite male "shall not lie with a male as with a woman" (Leviticus 18:22, also 20:13) and what this command might possibly refer to. This is an obscure reference. We are given no explanation as to what is in mind beyond what we can glean from the context, i.e., the concern about wasted seed and the need to be different from the Canaanites. There are no other references in the law codes of Exodus through Deuteronomy to male/male sex.

However, from the immediate context in Leviticus 18 and 20, we can with some confidence say that the problem with male/male sex here is in large part based on the problem of wasted seed. This may be part of the reason why we see only male/male sex mentioned and see nothing about female/female sex.

Since we are given no details about what the context for these forbidden practices was, we may at best speculate. The tiny bit of evidence we have does seem to point toward some sort of cultic sexual practices; note especially the reference to child sacrifice in this passage as well as the general concern about Canaanite religious practices.

We have little basis here for generalizing about the Bible's overall view of homosexuality. Leviticus 18–20 contains numerous other prohibitions that are rarely if ever understood by Christians to be determinative of the Bible's overall position. For example, in the immediate context of the above two commands, we also find prohibitions of male/female sexual intercourse during menstruation (18:19), of wearing clothes made with more than on kind of fiber (19:19), of wearing tattoos (19:28), and of planting more than one type of grain in a single field (19:19). These are rarely if ever cited by Christians in the present as proof that the Bible condemns these practices once and for all.

The main reasons for the prohibition of male/male sex in Leviticus 18:22 and 20:13 that we have any evidence for at all seem clearly context specific. Though numerous writers who argue that the Bible indeed condemns homosexuality claim that the Leviticus prohibition is based on more fundamental theological assumptions, they are unable to marshal direct evidence for this claim from Leviticus itself (or from elsewhere in the Old Testament).[38]

Certainly Leviticus 18:22 and 20:13 clearly condemn some sort of male/male sex. However, in the absence of a clear universalizable basis for such a condemnation, we do not have enough evidence to generalize from these two rather cryptic references. These two verses are not sufficient in themselves to conclude that the Bible condemns homosexuality as a broad category including both men and women.

The most we can say for sure is that these verses give us a

basis for saying that the Bible condemns male/male sex in the context of concern for wasting seed, just as it condemns masturbation and sexual intercourse during menstruation in that context, and for reflecting Canaanite religious practices. Nothing about female/female sex is inferred here. In fact, these two reasons for concern do not apply to women. So, whatever the concerns in Leviticus might be, they do not appear to be in-principle condemnation of all same-sex sexual intimacy.

The obscurity of the prohibition of male/male sex counts against using it as strong evidence that the Bible condemns all possible same-sex sexual intimacy as sinful. If it is not clear to what Leviticus is referring when it speaks of male/male sex nor why, we certainly cannot use it as strong evidence for drawing a conclusion about the biblical stance as a whole.

Finally, as numerous pro-inclusion writers point out, Christians understand Jesus' message to be their core ethical source. In seeking to understand and apply Leviticus' teaching for Christian ethics, the elements that connect most closely to Jesus (in particular, "love your neighbor") matter the most.

Each of the New Testament texts commonly discussed as speaking directly to the issue of homosexuality is found among the writings attributed to the apostle Paul.

Romans 1:18–3:31. In treating Paul's discussion of same-sex sexual intimacy in Romans 1, I will first discuss the broader argument of Romans 1–3. Second, I will discuss the place that 1:18-32 plays in that broader argument. And, third, I will discuss what significance the reference to same-sex sexual intimacy has for Paul's discussion. Why does Paul use this particular example here and what might that have to say to us?[39]

(1) The argument of 1:18–3:31. The section 1:18–3:20 as a whole centers on the problem mentioned in 1:18—human injustice (beginning in 3:21, Paul presents the solution as the revelation of the justice of God). The Greek word translated "injustice" (*adika*) is often also misleadingly translated "wickedness" or

"unrighteousness." Both of those translations reflect later Christian theological developments that presented the alienation between God and human beings in impersonal, legalistic terms.

However, Paul has in mind here a deeply personal problem. The alienation human beings have from God is *relational*, more than merely legalistic. Human beings have violated their relationship with God. This alienated divine/human relationship manifests itself in alienated human/human relationships. Human beings acting unjustly toward their fellow human beings follows from the lack of justice (wholeness) in their relationship with God.

Beginning with 1:18 and continuing through the end of chapter 3, Paul's argument proceeds as follows: Human beings outside the covenant live lives of deep-seated injustice, deserving of God's wrath (1:18-32). However, those people of the covenant who vigorously condemn the injustices of the outsiders while ignoring their own also deserve God's wrath (2:1–3:8). Adding these two statements together leads to the inevitable conclusion, *all* people fall equally short of God's justice (3:9-20). Paul's punchline, though, comes beginning in 3:21. God's mercy prevails—mercy revealed in the life, death, and resurrection of Jesus. God reveals this mercy outside religious structures that are based on works of the law (though the authentic message of Israel's scriptures witnesses to it).[40]

Paul aims his primary critique in these three chapters toward the religiously smug people of the covenant who need to be convinced that they are alienated from God. Paul portrays their false view as due to their over-confidence concerning their standing. Paul indicts Gentile sin (1:18-32) in order make his central point—the religious people too are just as much under the power of sin.

Throughout Romans 2, Paul makes it clear his deepest concern in Romans. In 2:5-6 he speaks of the hard hearts of those who in passing judgment on others, assume that God's judgment toward them would be favorable. This is a false assumption; "you, the judge, are doing the very same thing" (2:1). Paul sees this false assumption as indicating that these religious people were in as much need of repentance as those he described in 1:18-32. They are equally alienated from God and do not even know it.

Paul strongly believes that keeping the authentic law genuinely counts in God's eyes. Later in Romans, he defines the law as loving one's neighbor (13:8-10). So he states in 2:26 that Gentiles who keep the true requirements of the law will be considered part of the covenant even if they have not been circumcised.

In chapter 3, Paul concludes his critique by stringing together a litany of Old Testament passages underscoring that both types of people he has described are alienated from God and living under the power of sin. He means *both* the ungodly pagan living in blatant bondage to lust *and* the religious self-seeker living in self-deceived bondage to works of the law as the basis of their standing before God.

That Paul has an ultimately redemptive intent with his critique becomes clear beginning in 3:21. He underscores the sinfulness of both types of people to clear the ground for a new appreciation of the mercy of God. The justice (i.e., right-making or healing power) of God has been shown in an unprecedented way in Jesus.

In 1:18–3:31 Paul challenges his readers to take seriously their own sinfulness and to recognize that the blatant sins of the pagans are not the most dangerous. Rather, the sins that arise with religiosity carry much more danger. Sinful religiosity attempts to construct bases for righteousness that focus on external boundary markers—works of the law—and not on trust in God's mercy that empowers people to live lovingly and justly toward their neighbors.

(2) The role of 1:18-32 in the larger argument. In the context of Romans 1–3, the discussion of wrongdoing in 1:18-32

serves Paul's case by making two points. First, readers are set up
for what follows in Romans 2—the critique of religiosity. Second,
this critique leads to Paul's punch line: God's unconditional
mercy is revealed in Jesus apart from such religiosity.

In 1:18-32, Paul's allusions likely would have been familiar
to his readers. He assumes here that human beings are inherently creatures oriented toward worship. We all serve something
outside ourselves—if not God then idols, if not trusting in God
then trusting in things. Should we take the route of trusting in
things, we will find ourselves on a downward spiral. We will
move toward ever-increasing injustice and slavery to our lusts
that render us less than human.

Paul describes this process here by saying that God "hands
over" human beings to their injustice—as if God withdraws
God's providential care for these people and simply allows them
to reap the consequences of their idolatry.

These consequences find expression in extraordinary injustice, degrading passions and sexual obsessiveness. Idolaters lose
self-control—even to the point of women giving up "natural" self-
control for unbridled lust and men being consumed by passion
for other men (1:26-27).[41] The injustice finds a variety of expressions beyond oppressive sexuality; 1:29-31 lists twenty examples
of unjust behavior characteristic of people who choose idolatry
and ungodliness over genuine worship in the God of creation.

This passage does *not* have as its rhetorical intent negatively
analyzing pagan sexuality in order to provide regulations for
Christian sexuality. Paul does not write Romans 1 as a constructive statement on Christian sexual ethics. Rather, Paul sets his
readers up for what follows in chapter 2. When you pass judgment on such terrible sinners, "you condemn yourself, because
you the judge are doing the very same things."

Paul does not set out here to make normative, timeless pro-
nouncements that directly speak to twenty-first-century questions about the moral legitimacy of two Christians committing

themselves to each other in a covenanted, same-sex intimate partnership.

(3) Why does Paul focus on same-sex sex? Even if Paul does not center on same-sex sexuality, he does seem to see it as in some sense characteristic of the worst of pagan injustice.

However, we are limited in our quest to understand why Paul chose this particular expression of sinfulness by the lack of other passages elsewhere in the New Testament that could help us out. If Paul reflects widespread Christian assumptions about the inherently sinful nature of all possible forms of same-sex sexual relations, we simply do not have any concrete evidence for that. (The only possible direct evidence in the New Testament, the lists of vices in 1 Corinthians 6:9 and 1 Timothy 1:10, will be discussed below).

We do have some clues in the Romans 1 passage itself, though, that hint at what Paul may have had in mind in using the example he does, especially when combined with some extra-biblical historical knowledge.

The entire section, 1:18-32, focuses on injustice. The type of sexuality to which Paul refers here has to be understood as oppressive and hurtful ("unjust"). The "degrading passions" (1:26) are linked with offenses such as murder, envy, strife, and slander, among many other expressions of injustice listed in 1:29-31. The references to sexuality should be seen in the context of the broader elaboration of injustice that is associated with trusting in things rather than trusting in God.

One of the puzzles in the passage is what Paul means with his reference to women in 1:26. Too easily, interpreters assume he refers here to female/female sexual relations. However, the text itself does not clearly state this. Literally, it tells us that the women exchange "natural sexual intercourse" for "unnatural" without specifying the actual form such an exchange takes. Then we are told in 1:27 that the men, in a similar way give up "natural sexual intercourse with women" for unbridled lust for other men.

It is altogether possible that the parallel between what the women do and what the men do has to do with their passion and lust, not that the women are necessarily involved with other women. Basically, all we are told for certain about them is that they are in bondage to extreme passion. David Fredrickson argues that the underlying concern for Paul here is to hold up extreme passion or lust as the stereotypical fruit of idolatry. This would be consistent with other uses of the Greek word *kresin* (translated "intercourse" in the NRSV) in Greek writings of Paul's time and would also be consistent with Paul's thought elsewhere where he warns about the dangers of unbridled lust.[42]

It is not self-evident why Paul would offer same-sex sex per se as his paradigmatic case of the consequences of pagan idolatry. Same-sex sexual intimacy is peripheral to the Bible. It makes more sense that Paul had something else in mind that he thought would touch his readers' antipathy.

Considering Paul's historical setting provides a few intriguing clues about what Paul may have had in mind in 1:18-32. At the time Paul wrote, the sexual outrages of recent Roman emperors had scandalized practically everyone in Rome.[43] He would likely have seen these as reflecting the worst of pagan culture. His readers, living in Rome, could easily have been expected to connect Paul's general comments in Romans 1 with what they knew about Caligula and Nero.

Neill Elliot points out that among those who assassinated Emperor Caligula was an officer he had sexually humiliated. This person stabbed Caligula several times in the genitals. Could this event be echoed in Paul's words: "Men committed shameless acts with men and received in their persons the due penalty of their error" (1:27)?[44]

Following Caligula's death, Claudius's reign ushered in a brief period of relative moral gravity. However, Claudius was succeeded by another tyrant, Nero. "Paul wrote Romans during the reign of . . . Nero, whose rapes of Roman wives and sons,

incest with his mother, brothel-keeping, and sexual submission
to various men and boys prompted his tutor, the philosopher
Seneca, to conclude that Nero was 'another Caligula.'"[45]

"Surely it is reasonable to suppose, against this context,"
Elliott argues, "that by juxtaposing the senselessness of pagan
idolatry with a lurid depiction of sexual perversion Paul sought
to evoke for his readers the moral bankruptcy of the imperial
house itself." The list of vices in 1:29-31 greatly exaggerates con-
ventional Gentile morality. Not all Gentiles did these kinds of
things; in fact, few did. However, the vice list is not exaggerated if
it is "a description of the horrors of the imperial house."[46] We may
be confident that Paul did not have pagan morality as a whole in
mind in chapter 1, because in chapter 2 he makes it clear that
some people outside the covenant ("uncircumcised") are indeed
fully capable of authentically keeping the law (2:27).

Ultimately, then, in considering 1:18-32 in its broader context we discover a number of reasons why it does *not* provide
direct evidence that the Bible condemns all possible intimate
same-sex relationships as sinful. It is not written as direct ethical
teaching prescribing Christian behavior. We twist this passage
from its context if we apply it as if it directly tells Christians
what not to do.

Beyond applying these verses in ways they were not intended,
to use this passage as a basis for judging the behavior of Christians
in same-sex loving relationships turns the role they play in Paul's
overall argument on its head. Paul's concern in 1:18–3:20 is to *critique* judgmentalism, not to foster it.

Even when we look at the discussion of same-sex sex within
the 1:18-32 passage, we do not find material that applies to present-day covenanted same-sex relationships among Christians.
The example Paul gives of the consequences of pagan idolatry
focuses on injustice, people hurting other people. Paul's concern
centers on injustice, not on covenanted, loving, mutual partnerships.

Also, it is not likely that Paul has in mind female/female sex in general. The male/male sex he had in mind most likely was the kind of unbridled excess characteristic of the worst of the Roman emperors, even if he was not necessarily specifically referring to the emperors. The reference to females in 1:26 most probably refers to female participation in such sex, whether with men or women.

That is, the type of sexual activity associated with injustice and with obsessive lust seems clearly to be what Paul had in mind—not condemning all possible same-sex intimacy as sinful.

1 Corinthians 6:1-10. As with Romans 1, with 1 Corinthians 6 we have the responsibility of looking at the allusions to same-sex sexual activity in the wider context of the passage. When we do so, we will see that Paul's purpose here is *not* to give direct ethical guidance to Christians concerning homosexuality in general.

Chapter 6 begins with mention of some people in the Corinthian church taking legal action toward others in the church. In 6:7-8 Paul writes of defrauding, indicating that perhaps the conflicts had to do with economic issues. Paul's anger stems from the church not taking care of its own business internally.

Paul speaks harshly of the Corinthian Christians relying on "unbelievers" to settle their internal disputes. Earlier Paul refers to the courts of the unbelievers as unjust (6:1). Richard Hays suggests, "When the Corinthians Christians take one another to court, they are declaring primary allegiance to the pagan culture of Corinth rather than to the community of faith."[47]

Hays cites evidence that the court system in the Roman Empire systematically favored the wealthy over the poor. Quite likely the Corinthian Christians initiating the court actions were wealthy and the lawsuits were aimed at poorer members.[48] Paul writes in 6:9 that the unjust non-Christians (often translated "wrongdoers") will not inherit the kingdom of God. The Corinthian Christians imitate such unjust unbelievers when they act unjustly in similar way (6:8).

So when Paul comes to the list of characteristics of the unjust people who will not inherit the kingdom of God, he does not have sexuality per se on his mind. Rather, he chastises the Corinthian Christians for taking each other to "secular" courts, using unjust nonbelievers to buttress their own injustice. He makes an essentially rhetorical point in 6:9-10, intending to drive home his view that Christians should not trust their disputes to unjust outsiders.

The items in the list of 6:9-10 merely illustrate what the Corinthians *used to be* prior to their coming into the church. They used to be unjust, and now they have changed due to Christ (6:11). In light of this transformation, they ought to stop acting like *adikoi* (unjust people) using the courts to settle their property disputes in favor of the powerful within the church.[49]

Justice is central to Paul's point here. Because of their being made members of God's family through justification (6:11), Paul calls believers to cease acting unjustly toward one another (6:8) by going to court before the unjust (6:1).[50]

As with Romans 1, then, the central concern of 1 Corinthians 6 has to do with justice and injustice—and Paul uses the example of the injustice of pagans to challenge his Christian readers to faithfulness. He simply does *not* intend in either place to focus on constructive ethical guidelines for sexuality, and even less does he center his concern on condemning all possible same-sex intimate partnerships as sinful for Christians.[51]

Still, we do have these references in 1 Corinthians 6:9. The NRSV translates the Greek words *malakos* and *arsenokoites* as "male prostitutes" and "sodomites" respectively. The TNIV has "male prostitutes" and "practicing homosexuals." However, the meanings of these words are far from clear. It seems doubtful that they are best understood as alluding to the broad categories implied by these translations.

Paul, in 1 Corinthians 6:9-10, simply gives a list of examples of injustices characteristic of pagan judges. He does not describe how any of these different examples are problematic. Since the general context here is injustice, even if *malakos* and *arsenokoites* have sexual connotations (which is not certain at least in the case of *malakos*), most likely they connote sex of an economically unjust and exploitative type.

Malakos is a fairly common term, meaning literally "soft" with no intrinsic sexual connotations (see Matthew 11:8 = "*soft* clothing"). It is often used in a negative moral sense such as "laziness, decadence, or lack of courage." Most often, perhaps, it is used, with negative connotations, of men being effeminate.[52]

By itself, *malakos* could easily in 1 Corinthians 6:9 simply be a general term for "morally lax," linking with some of the other terms in the list such as "thieves, the greedy, and robbers." It could have sexual connotations—a man allowing himself to be used like a woman (probably for economic gain). But there is nothing to require this meaning, so the use of *malakos* here is scarcely clear evidence that Paul is condemning homosexuality in general.

Our second term, *arsenokoites*, is on the one hand even more obscure than *malakos*, while on the other hand it would seem quite likely to have more overt sexual connotations. Outside of 1 Corinthians 6:9 and the obviously derivative use in 1 Timothy 1:10, the word is never used in Paul's writings, never used in the rest of the New Testament, and never used in other surviving first century Greek writings.

Numerous scholars suggest that Paul himself may well have coined this term, combining two words from the Septuagint translation of Leviticus 20:13. According to Donald Wold, Paul "pulled together two terms used in the Leviticus text: *arseno-* ('male') and *–koitai* ('sexual intercourse'). Paul creates this compound word in order to accurately capture the meaning he sought—the active partner in the homosexual act."[53]

Certainly, Paul may have coined this word. We have no basis to say he did not—or that he did. However, to see in this word the meaning of "the active partner in the homosexual act" goes far beyond the evidence. There is no parallel use anywhere in any extant first-century Greek literature. Neither 1 Corinthians 6:9 nor 1 Timothy 1:10 hint in any other way that Paul's concern was with homosexuality. He's clearly not self-consciously articulating a thorough-going general position on Christians and homosexuality.

All we have is this single word. *Arsenokoites* likely combines words that originally meant "male" and "sex act." However, many compound words have different meanings than simply the sum of their parts. This may or may not be the case for *arsenokoites*.

Dale B. Martin surveys the few scattered uses of *arsenokoites* in the second century and concludes that it tends to be used in vice lists in the contexts of other terms generally dealing with economic injustice or exploitation. Such usage fits 1 Corinthians 6, where the list includes vices such as "thieves," "greedy," and "swindlers."[54]

Martin concludes, *arsenokoites* "seems to have referred to some kind of economic exploitation by means of sex, perhaps but not necessarily homosexual sex. Sibylline Oracle 2:70-77, likely written in the second century CE, probably provides an independent use of the word. It occurs in a section listing acts of economic injustice and exploitation. 'Do not steal seeds…. Do not *arsenokoitein*. Do not betray information. Do not murder.'"[55]

1 Timothy 1:10. The use of *arsenokoites* in 1 Timothy 1:10 follows from 1 Corinthians 6:9. Here too we find a list of vices with no further explanation. Whatever the term means in 1 Corinthians, it likely has a similar meaning in 1 Timothy. The latter usage offers no clues as to what that precise meaning might be. In both cases, the vices listed tend toward violations of justice, not violations of rules governing sexual conduct for those otherwise living just lives. If the lists refer to same-sex sexual activity at all, most likely they condemn exploitative sex used for economic purposes—as an expression of injustice.

Neither the vice list in 1 Corinthians 6 or 1 Timothy 1 provide direct, constructive ethical guidance for Christian sexual practices. Rather, they offer challenges for living justly, for turning from injustice. Most clearly, in 1 Corinthians 6, Paul argues not about sexuality, but about not trusting Christians' disputes to unjust people. First Corinthians 6 and 1 Timothy 1 do not show that the Bible condemns all possible same-sex intimate partnerships as sinful. Neither speak in a clear and direct way about homosexuality at all.

Conclusion concerning the core texts. My central question has been whether these few texts speak clearly enough to conclude that the Bible calls all same-sex intimacy sinful. In looking at each key text, I have found reasons to doubt that they support such a conclusion. The Bible does not in fact condemn all possible same-sex intimate relationships as sinful. Of course, even if my interpretations are correct, we have not resolved the issue. All I have shown is that the "direct texts" do not provide a clear basis for overriding the application of the Bible's teaching on hospitality and Jesus' ethic of welcome to including gay Christians in covenanted relationships in the churches without restrictions. I have not tried to argue that, in fact, Paul, Jesus, and Leviticus offer a clearly pro-gay stance that could override a benefit of the doubt toward being restrictive. Hence, the importance of reflecting on our starting point as we examine these texts.

We must also briefly consider two other themes that often also come up in restrictive arguments. Does the biblical view of marriage, understood as establishing marriage as normatively and exclusively being for one man and one woman for life, implicitly but clearly prohibit same-sex partnerships that parallel heterosexual marriage? Do all same-sex intimate partnerships contain inherently harmful elements that provide a clear basis for understanding them to be immoral?

The Biblical Perspective on Marriage

Many writers representing the restrictive perspective argue that part of their basis for arguing that the Bible condemns all possible intimate same-sex relationships as sinful is their understanding of the Bible's normative portrayal of male and female marriage.

In his book *Welcoming But Not Affirming*, Stanley Grenz, echoing what numerous others also say, asserts that Genesis 1 and 2 establish the importance of marriage as built into creation itself. God populates the earth ("be fruitful and multiply") through heterosexual marriage, and heterosexual marriage provides for human companionship. Departure from this norm, thus, threatens the very fabric of human community.

It is at this point that the restrictive argument understands Jesus' teaching to speak most directly to sexuality issues. Jesus directly quotes from Genesis in asserting the centrality of heterosexual marriage to God's will for human life. Jesus did not need to say more than simply that God requires sexuality to be expressed in the context of male/female marriage relationships to make clear his rejection of all possible same-sex intimate relationships.

This point about heterosexual marriage as norm lays near the heart of many restrictive writings on this topic. However, its importance may be challenged for several reasons.

(1) Using the creation account and other allusions to male/female marriage as a basis for condemning all same-sex sexual expression makes a point that the texts themselves do not make. None of the biblical allusions to marriage or male/female sexuality say that therefore same-sex sexuality is wrong. And none of the texts that allegedly reject same-sex sexual intimacy directly refer to the creation account. Admittedly several of the restrictive writers see allusions to the creation account's portrayal of marriage both in Leviticus and in Romans 1, but such allusions are quite oblique—if they exist at all.

The restrictive writers use texts that make particular points to speak authoritatively about altogether different points. We may legitimately use texts indirectly as secondary evidence for a case; however, such indirect use does not seem strong enough by itself to make a case.

(2) We may agree that the Bible presents procreative sex between males and females as normative in the context of monogamous marriage. However, logically, we are not necessarily forced to conclude from this that all other expressions of sexuality are wrong or are threats to the norm.

Our faith communities now, either explicitly or implicitly, accept as morally legitimate some forms of non-procreative sexual expression (e.g., sex between infertile married partners, sex when the partners are using birth control, masturbation) without understanding them to threaten the biblical norm. So there would seem to be no reason why faith communities would have to assume that another form of non-procreative sex (between two people of the same sex) inherently threatens the norm.

(3) Restrictive writers, in drawing upon what they see as a normative biblical view of marriage, ignore the fact that the Bible portrays marriage in quite varied ways. An obvious example is the biblical portrayal of polygamy. The Bible at least implicitly presents polygamy as a norm for marriage throughout the Old Testament—and never overtly rejects that relationship pattern in the New Testament. The Bible also notoriously seems to assume a strongly patriarchal notion of marriage, in which wives are essentially thought of as their husband's property.

Present-day Christians today tend to affirm a view of marriage (one man, one woman, equal partners for life) that does not have overt biblical precedent. This understanding of marriage appears to be a human cultural construct and not an obvious biblical option. The understanding of marriage as one man, one woman, equal partners for life has evolved over time. If this is the case, it cannot be a rejection of biblical authority or the order of creation to question whether same-gender committed relationships are inherently wrong because they violate "the one biblical view of marriage" as only between one male and one female.[56]

(4) The restrictive position seems to assume a static, timeless notion of normativity in relation to marriage—as if one ancient

book sets the once-and-for all standard. I have pointed out above that the Bible does not actually have just one view of marriage. As well, human history reflects a dynamic of many understandings of marriage evolving as human constructs. Human understandings of marriage are thoroughly culturally embedded and not based on a clear "order of creation."[57] We have no clear, absolute, once-for-all standard for marriage that provides an essential criterion for judging same-gender committed relations as inherently contrary to God's will.

Our understandings of marriage in the churches—assumed by the restrictive position and read back into the Bible as the one biblical view—surely accurately draw upon some biblical themes. However, as we consider such values as companionship, fidelity, mutuality, friendship, buildings block for community, childrearing, and procreation, we see that these attributes may also characterize same-gender committed relationships along with heterosexual marriages.

Inherent Harmfulness

Numerous restrictive writers cite evidence that same-sex sexual intimacy links directly with damaging health consequences.[58] However, these consequences do not seem to be actually to be inherent to the "same-sexness" of the relationships.

Certainly great human harm does result from the sexual behavior of many gay men—both physical problems and emotional problems clearly related in large part to the consequences of promiscuity. However, I find it difficult to see how any of these problems are related to the *same-sexness* of the partnership per se. Promiscuous heterosexuals have the same kinds of problems—and non-promiscuous same-sex partners do not.

It does seem to be a matter of empirical fact that there do exist same-sex partnerships for both men and women that are healthy and life giving. I know several such relationships among my own friends—including a couple still going strong after forty years. This empirical reality directly challenges the notion that same-sex partnerships are inherently harmful.

Some sexual behaviors among heterosexual people are harmful—coercive sex, sexually-transmitted diseases, promiscuity, unfaithfulness. Heterosexuals struggle to remain committed in covenanted relationships; divorce rates soar. However, we do not, in light of these problems, generalize about "heterosexual practice" being wrong.

Harmfulness within heterosexual intimate relationships challenges us to seek ways to foster more healthy relationships; such harmfulness does not lead us to deny the validity of heterosexual intimate relationships. We know that most human beings flourish best when they are in healthy marriages.

I see no logical reason why we cannot approach same-sex partnerships in the same way—critique the harmful practices, support the healthy ones.

Conclusion

I have tried to defend my conclusion that none of the three basic arguments commonly used to support the restrictive position are strong enough to overturn the biblical bias in favor of inclusiveness. If I am on the right track, where does this leave the churches?

Speaking to my Mennonite context, I recognize that regardless of the validity of my argument in this chapter, my denomination, Mennonite Church USA, is far from accepting it. My main hope would be simply that the perspective I have presented here could play a role in the MC USA's on-going discernment processes.

At this point, I hope for two short-term outcomes. The first is that we could reach a consensus that we need on-going, open, and safe discernment processes in which we recognize the diversity of perspectives that currently exists within our denomination. The diversity runs too deep and too wide for us to find unanimity on the inclusive/restrictive debate in the near future.

Hence, our biggest immediate challenge is to find a way to step back from fearfulness and threats to break fellowship and listen to each other.

The second short-term outcome would be movement toward a more congregational polity. Similar to the polity practiced by the former General Conference Mennonite Church, it respects that membership issues should be decided on the congregational level. On the homosexuality issue especially, given the complexity of the arguments and diversity of conclusions throughout the denomination, the most legitimate context for discernment is on the face-to-face, directly accountable level of the local congregation. As was the case with the General Conference, once a congregation is welcomed as part of the denomination, the discernment within each congregation would be respected and not put under threat of being challenged by the broader conference and denomination.

Neither of these two outcomes—a safe and open discernment processes and leaving membership issues to congregational discernment—will resolve all the issues. However, they seem to me to be prerequisites for the Mennonite Church to move beyond the chaos that surrounds us now.[59]

Additionally, I hope that most of us might agree on the importance of the church's role in supporting its members in their intimate relationships. Today's American Christian churches encounter major challenges in the face of failed heterosexual marriages and sexual misbehavior of all kinds.

I believe that all of us who believe in fidelity, monogamy, and sexual intimacy only in the context of covenanted relationships should make common cause—welcoming committed same-sex partnerships and calling all in the churches to faithfulness and high ethical standards within covenanted relationships.

Mark's Response: The Ideology of Inclusion

Ted and I agree on the importance of hospitality within the overall story and teachings of the Old and New Testaments. I have already hinted at this at several points in my longer essay. I want to elaborate briefly on this agreement as I begin my response to his essay.

Agreement Regarding Hospitality

About twenty-five years ago, as the founding director of a small Christian peace and justice organization, I was aware that refugees from various Central American countries were pouring into the United States. These refugees were often fleeing oppressive regimes, some of which were supported by the United States government. I was asked to address this subject. As I searched the Scriptures in relation to these realities, I noticed not only a few texts but a discernable pattern. Exodus 23:9 captures the heart of the matter. "You shall not oppress a resident alien; you know the heart of an alien, for you were aliens in the land of Egypt." Lest we think the teaching only pertains to prohibitions because of the words "you shall not oppress," reading further in this same chapter shows that one of the reasons for keeping the Sabbath is so that "the resident alien may be refreshed" (23:12b). The narratives and legal provisions from Exodus through Deuteronomy reiterate this theme. Because God's people were once strangers and aliens they must care for the strangers and aliens among them. This pattern, found throughout much of the first five books of the Old Testament, should reverberate through the churches that seek to live into the biblical story.

The New Testament continues and expands the Old Testament call to hospitality. One can almost hear an echo of the freed slaves in ancient Israel when 1 Peter emphasizes: "Once you were not a people, but now you are God's people" (2:10a); you are called to be "aliens and exiles" and to "be hospitable to one another without complaining" (4:9). Furthermore, just as the central theological warrant for Israel's welcome of strangers and aliens in the Old Testament was God's deliverance, so in the New Testament we repeatedly hear words like those recorded in Romans 15:7: "Welcome one another, therefore, just as Christ has welcomed you, for the glory of God."

Much of the hospitality language in the epistles of the New Testament issues a call to welcome fellow Christians. We should not minimize the challenge this presented to Jewish and Gentile brothers and sisters in Christ, who were indeed strangers to one another in the beginning. However, Christians are also to "extend hospitality to strangers" who are not from among "the saints," are not fellow Christians (see Romans 12:13; cf. Galatians 6:10; 1 Thessalonians 3:12). The writer of Hebrews likewise wants the readers to remember—echoing the story of hospitality in Genesis 18—that in showing hospitality to strangers Christians may be in for a surprise, "for by doing that some have entertained angels without knowing it" (13:2b).

As Christine Pohl says, according to the New Testament, "hospitality is not optional for Christians. . . . It is, instead, a necessary practice in the community of faith."[60] This is true not only in the teachings I have already referenced from the epistles. The Gospels portray Jesus offering a wide welcome and, as Ted says, this wideness often challenged established boundaries of his time and place.

The breadth of this challenging call to hospitality may be represented by two teachings of Jesus. The first is found in Luke 14:12-14:

> When you give a luncheon or a dinner, do not invite your friends or your brothers or your relatives or rich neighbors, in case they may invite you in return, and you would be repaid. But when you give a banquet, invite the poor, the crippled, the lame, and the blind. And you will be blessed, because they cannot repay you, for you will be repaid at the resurrection of the righteous.

Matthew 25:31-46 offers a similar challenge. It presents a picture of a final judgment when all the nations are gathered around a king. The king, like a shepherd, separates the sheep from the goats, the righteous from the unrighteous. The ones who have fed the hungry, clothed the naked, given drink to the thirsty, welcomed strangers, cared for the sick, and visited prisoners are deemed righteous. Those who have not done such things will be cast "into the eternal fire prepared for the devil and his angels." Hospitality, according to these texts, is neither selective nor optional for God's people.

Within the Gospels Jesus is portrayed as showing us what these teaching look like in practice. He welcomed a wide array of people—tax collectors, women who "had a bad name," Pharisees, and, that catch-all category, sinners. Perhaps Jesus would not have been quite so offensive if he had only *preached* good news to the poor or healed some folk (albeit, not on the Sabbath). But to welcome and eat with "sinners" challenged normal relationship patterns. The welcome Jesus calls us to extend is indeed radical. Who should not be among our guests? Does our hospitality include those who are labeled as alcoholics and drug addicts? What about pedophiles? Do we welcome homeless people, prostitutes, and strippers? And what about liberal Democrats, conservative Republicans, and idiosyncratic Libertarians or Socialists?

I would never claim that I have been very good at living out this radical call to hospitality. But I have attempted to respond to these challenges for many years. Early in my Christian life I knew a man who was a pedophile. I loved this man. In fact because he was a gifted pianist and singer—and led music in the church of which I was a part—I was often deeply moved by his ministry. In retrospect I am sure neither I nor my church dealt with him very well. But I knew I needed to be kind to this very lonely man. When later in college a friend of a friend invited me to dinner and then to join him in bed, I declined. But I knew by instinct that I must befriend this man. He and I had a bi-weekly break-

fast together for the remainder of my time at the college. Two of
my close friends were/are sex addicts. I know their stories. I love
them. Have I been the kind of friend I should be? I trust I have
been welcoming to them. As a social worker in the late '70s I got
to know many different sorts of people. I remember with fond-
ness, for instance, the apparent candor of a stripper and a prostitute in relation to their jobs and their parenting. As a child pro-
tective services social worker I was primarily charged with pro-
tecting children. And yet I was constantly dealing with parents
who were real people, with real histories and often deep wound-
edness. It was an excruciating job for me because I came to care
about most of the parents with whom I interacted. Have I been
welcoming? The call to welcome, hospitality and love of others is
indeed far-reaching and challenging.

Disagreement Regarding Hospitality

I agree with Ted that if one reads carefully and prayerfully
through the Scriptures, with Jesus at the center, we are challenged
afresh to radical and costly hospitality. However, I disagree with
Ted's decision to make hospitality into an overarching or programmatic theme within Scripture. I believe hospitality is one
moral claim among many. This may seem like a subtle difference,
but I believe it is one with large consequences. Near the beginning
of his chapter, "Toward a Theology of Welcome," Ted writes:

> My position, as I will sketch it in this chapter, may very
> briefly be summarized as follows: A careful, respectful
> reading of the Bible as a whole supports the inclusive
> perspective. The Bible's overall message emphasizes
> God's mercy and God's movement to bring healing out
> of brokenness to all who trust in God. The Bible por-
> trays God's welcome of people made vulnerable by
> social prejudice and exclusiveness as central to God's
> merciful movement toward human beings. This move-
> ment toward welcome establishes a strong benefit of the

doubt toward churches welcoming gay Christians without restrictions based on their gayness. The burden of proof is on those who would have the churches adopt restrictive policies. I will argue that this burden of proof is not satisfactorily met.[61]

The shift from seeing hospitality as a crucial imperative in the Scriptures to seeing it as an overarching theme and thereby the interpretive lens through which to see everything results in significant distortions. Let me attempt to name what I mean in several steps.

First, following God cannot be reduced to the practice of hospitality. Said differently, hospitality cannot be separated from our call to proclaim God's glory with our whole beings. Both Testaments bear this out.

Christine Pohl observes that the Old Testament accounts demonstrate that "Israel lived by God's grace, and its self-proclaimed identity as chosen-yet-alien was a continual reminder of this relationship of dependence and faithfulness, gratitude and obedience."[62] She locates hospitality within the Old Testament framework as follows:

> The complex relation between living a holy life and providing hospitality to strangers begins in early Israel. Israel understood itself as chosen by God and owing to God its singular loyalty and obedience. Israel's requirement and capacity to love aliens, to meet its social, economic, and legal obligations to them, was embedded in its relationship with God. Two interconnected concerns in Israelite law—that of protecting and including the weak, and that of maintaining loyalty to God alone—are not separable because God's holiness includes care for the weak.[63]

What Pohl rightly points out here is that Israel's relationship with God entailed "dependence and faithfulness, gratitude and obedience," or put differently, it entailed "singular loyalty and obedience" to God. This certainly included loving aliens or providing hospitality, but it also meant the people of God were called to submission, loyalty, and holiness in all areas of life.

In his careful study of moral purity in the New Testament, David de Silva observes that throughout his public ministry Jesus was redrawing the "cultural purity maps" in ways that were threatening to many. He notes: "as Jesus demonstrated, the lines separating believers from unbelievers always remain permeable for mission, for reaching out in love to bring some measure of relief or restoration, as well as for conversion and entrance into the church."[64] DeSilva further asserts that, if we are to follow the New Testament, this mission of " reaching out in love" cannot be compromised, yet "at the same time, we cannot compromise our commission to be a distinctive people 'holy to the Lord.'"[65] He goes on to say that the various New Testament authors name the lines that help us to understand what it means to be holy as our God is holy. What Jesus began is continued in the life of the churches as presented in Acts and the epistles, especially as regards the bringing together of Jews and Gentiles into one body. This reconciliation is healing for the sake of the nations. This call to be reconciled also includes a realization of our need for God's salvation that produces lives of holiness, faithfulness, and righteousness/justice (the same Greek word). This may seem like a small point, but it is not. It has substantial implications.

When hospitality or welcome becomes the overarching biblical theme it distorts or mutes the tensions within the Scriptures. These tensions must not be squelched if we are to hear the full-orbed biblical claim upon our lives. Christine Pohl names this well:

> Within much of the biblical tradition, there are tensions between living a distinctive life, holy to the Lord, and the command to welcome strangers. *Their relationship is best understood through the theological framework of covenant*—bonds of responsibility and faithfulness connecting guests, hosts, and God. *Only in this context*

can we adequately understand the simultaneous practices of inclusion and separation. Faithful believers who practice hospitality understand themselves to be in a relationship with God whose worship requires holiness, a distinct identity, and attention to the needs of others.[66]

Ted's essay lacks this tension because it misses any substantial notion that our relationship with God, our worship of God "requires holiness, a distinct identity." It fails to highlight anything additional to or beyond an "attention to the needs of others." As such, Ted reduces holiness or distinct identity to identities and behaviors that readily fit within his understanding of hospitality. For instance, in commenting on Leviticus 18 and 20, he claims "the community of faith actualizes its holiness as it fosters interpersonal relationships characterized by justice." And later: "to be a holy nation *means* to imitate God, to love the neighbor, to care for vulnerable ones, and to love even the alien 'as yourself'" (emphasis added). More specifically, he says: "the legislation concerning sexual practices must be understood within this context of care for vulnerable ones that lay at the heart of the definition of holiness in Israel." Hospitality and justice are indeed components of holiness, but used alone cannot substitute for a full understanding of holiness.

Or, moving to the New Testament, Ted says that Jesus heals many who would have been marginal to Jewish life and undoubtedly the healings were offensive to many. He is right that the variety of recipients of Christ's healing reflect "the incredible openness of this kingdom Jesus proclaimed." Likewise, Christ's table fellowship included a wide variety of people, again including those with whom most respectable Jews would not have associated, much less shared a meal. Without a doubt this is true. Then what is missing?

What is missing is any notion of repentance. In Luke 5:31-32, Jesus responds to the critics who accuse him of eating and drinking with tax collectors and sinners with the words: "Those who are well have no need of a physician, but those who are sick; I have come to call not the righteous but sinners to repentance."

Miroslav Volf comments on such passages, i.e., those that contain a combination of welcome and repentance, as follows: "[Jesus] was no prophet of 'inclusion' . . . for whom the chief virtue was acceptance and the cardinal vice intolerance. Instead, he was the bringer of 'grace,' who not only scandalously included 'anyone' in the fellowship of 'open commensality' . . . but made the 'intolerant' demand of repentance and the 'condescending' offer of forgiveness (Mark 1:15; 2:15-17)."[67]

Ted also fails to point out that everyone who follows Jesus is called to deny themselves, pick up their crosses, and follow him. Those who repent and believe are called to a specific identity. They will come to be named as "Christian." When they form communities, they will be called the "body of Christ," the "people of God," and various other terms designating that they are a distinct people gathered in the name of Jesus. They are called to be righteous, just, and holy. As mentioned earlier, this then creates tensions. For, in the midst of being called to justice/righteousness/holiness, this people are always called to be hospitable, to welcome strangers. If these welcomed strangers choose to become a part of this people of God they are called to repent and trust in the God revealed in Jesus. They are called to love God with their whole being. Following from this—as many Jews and Gentiles had to learn—they must abandon non-Christian ways and become a part of a people who are called to holiness, justice, and righteousness. These new peculiar people are then, among other things, to be hospitable to more strangers. And the cycle continues.

Ted and I agree that hospitality is an indispensable characteristic of God and therefore of the people of God. However, I do not believe that God's purposes and calling can be reduced to hospitality. It is much broader than that. (I will return to this issue in the last two sections of this essay.)

Biblical References Concerning Homosexuality

I will make only a few remarks regarding Ted's interpretations of the biblical texts related directly to homosexuality. I am basically not going to engage in dueling exegesis or hermeneutics in relation to the texts in question. Others have dealt much more fully with the details of the texts and the times in which they were written. I have read much of this literature and rest more or less content with where I stand. But for those who want a fuller treatment than we have provided, I would point you to literature Ted and I have referenced earlier. I would urge serious students to read some of the major studies offering varying perspectives before reaching a conclusion.[68]

I do want to offer a few reflections on Ted's interpretive comments on Romans 1–3. I was not surprised by his interpretation of the specifics of the text dealing with homosexuality (1:18-32). These arguments have been made before; I remain unconvinced. As far as I am concerned, Richard Hays, Thomas Schmidt, Willard Swartley, and Robert Gagnon have quite convincingly shown the weaknesses of this sort of interpretation. If someone wants to examine Ted's arguments carefully, here is what I would recommend. Since Ted is dependent mostly on essays by David Fredrickson and Neill Elliott, read their essays. Then read Robert Gagnon's substantial responses to both authors.[69] With all of their reflective comments in mind, go back to Romans 1:18-32.[70]

What surprised me about Ted's interpretation of Romans 1–3, however, is that he seems to be using these chapters to call for what Bonhoeffer referred to as cheap grace. It is one thing to say that Romans 1 does not have relevance for current debates about homosexuality. It is another to say: "Paul taught that the only thing that matters in terms of one's standing before God is one's faith. Christians are those who trust in Christ, period. Not, trust in Christ plus this or that requirement." Ted then joins this to his claim that "Paul's concern in 1:18–3:20 is to *critique* judgmentalism, not to foster it" (emphasis his). These comments and others in Ted's essay seem to drive a wedge between faith and faithfulness, between trust in God and righteousness. Ted mentions one moral concern that he claims is central to these chapters. He writes: "The entire section, 1:18-32, is concerned with injustice."[71] So despite what he seems to be implying by the ambiguous word "judgmentalism," I would imagine that God and a Christian should judge injustice as wrong.[72]

I trust you recognize what has happened here. I do not doubt that Ted's intention is, as he said, to be "inclusive with a more conservative biblical hermeneutic." But I think he has failed to fulfill this self-description in relation to "a more conservative biblical hermeneutic." It appears that those things that fall foul of his narrow definition of holiness get muted or defined out of the biblical picture. As I noted earlier, this has led him to mute Jesus' call to repentance and the creation of a peculiar people gathered in Jesus' name. The whole of the biblical message is redefined by his understanding of hospitality.

I was further surprised and disheartened with Ted's comments regarding marriage. I have believed for some time that churches that shift from the traditional view on homosexuality should at least shore up the convictions about and importance of marriage. Being fairly conversant with a wide range of literature on these subjects and having some knowledge of gay, lesbian, bisexual, and transgendered activist groups connected to denominations, I often thought my hopes unrealistic. Nonetheless, in my imagination, sometimes this would happen. And I thought Ted might be the person to aid this process. But that has not happened.

Now, I would grant that in various ways these are complicated matters. We need to admit that marriage and the family have evolved over time as understood and practiced by Christians.[73] And if we are to read the Bible honestly on these matters we are compelled to employ a thoughtful and carefully considered hermeneutic. However, such carefulness ought not lead to the rather radically relativizing comments Ted makes. For example,

"Present-day Christians today tend to affirm a view of marriage (one man, one woman, equal partners for life) that does not have overt biblical precedent. This understanding of marriage appears to be a human construct and not clearly the only biblical position." Or again: "The restrictive position seems to assume a static, timeless notion of normativity in relation to marriage—as if one ancient book sets the once-for-all standard."

What if I replaced Ted's statements with the following: "This understanding of pacifism ('love your enemies' equals not killing those to be loved) appears to be a human construct and not clearly the only biblical position. The pacifist position seems to assume a static, timeless notion of normativity in relation to violence—as if one ancient book sets the once-for-all standard." Ted and I would agree that there is not a simple message in the Bible, from Genesis to Revelation, that equals pacifism. We have to do some interpreting, interpreting that both of us, I would have thought, believe needs to respect the integrity and the authority of the Scriptures and finds its central rootedness in Jesus. This does not relativize our commitment to pacifism. It simply reminds us that an argument has to be made—and can successfully be made—that this is the biblically based Christian position that makes sense. I would suggest something similar in relation to marriage.[74]

Ted is right that polygamy exists in the Old Testament, though not as a "norm" as he claims.[75] It is interesting to realize that the New Testament says little to counter such practice, although 1 Timothy 3:2, 12 and Titus 1:6 bear consideration. I would have thought that, contrary to what Ted implied, what Jesus, echoing Genesis, says about marriage (see Matthew 19:4-6 and parallels) would serve as "overt biblical precedent." Many have thought that it does. But more to the point, why is it that Ted only offered a deconstructive approach to the traditional Christian understanding of marriage rather than shoring up that same approach in the midst of calling for a shift to affirm committed gay and lesbian relationships (marriages?)? I am certain

Ted and I will have many further invigorating conversations concerning this topic.

One of the reasons I have not offered dueling exegesis is that I confess that sometimes after I have read yet another essay or book on this topic, I want to echo the following comments from British ethicist Oliver O'Donovan. "Faced with yet another attempt to get at the meaning of *arsenokoites* by philology, I cry: Enough! You have satisfied the curiosity of a generation!"[76] Or, on another occasion O'Donovan said: "interpreters who think that they can determine the proper ethical application of the Bible solely through more sophisticated exegesis are like people who believe they can fly if only they flap their arms hard enough."[77]

Also in relation to biblical interpretation, let me quote from one of the great Christian provocateurs of all time. Fully cognizant of the fact that it cuts several ways, I offer this parable from Søren Kierkegaard:

> Imagine that it says in the New Testament that it is God's will that every human being is to have 100,000 dollars [*Rigsdalere*] (we can surely imagine it!)—do you think there would be any question about a commentary? I wonder if everyone would not say: This is easy enough to understand; no commentary is needed; let us for God's sake stay away from commentaries—therefore, out, out with all commentaries.
>
> But what stands in the New Testament (about the narrow way, about dying to the world, and so on) is no more difficult than this matter of 100,000 dollars. The difficulty lies somewhere else, in its not pleasing us—and therefore, therefore, therefore, therefore we must have commentaries and professors and commentaries. We are not "running the risk" of its becoming ambiguous—no, that is precisely what we want, and we hope that little by little with the cooperation of commentaries, it will become ambiguous. . . .
>
> We have invented scholarship in order to evade doing

God's will. This much we certainly do understand—that face to face with God and his obviously understood will to say "This I will not do"—this no one dares to do. We do not dare do it that way, so we protect ourselves by making it seem as if it were very difficult to understand and that therefore we—he must indeed be flattered by this and regard it as praiseworthy in us—study and investigate etc., that is, we protect ourselves by hiding behind big books.[78]

Having read hundreds of essays and more than a dozen books on topics related to homosexuality, I finally believe that the biblical texts are relatively clear—as they were generally believed to be within the Christian tradition until roughly thirty years ago. However, I also believe that some of the central disagreements over this issue are mostly not about the details of texts, but rather are at a more macro theological level. In Ted's case I fear he has unintentionally substituted an ideology of inclusion for the full biblical message, a message that includes a call to hospitality.

The Problem of Inclusivity

Let me define what it is I mean by "an ideology of inclusion." The problem is signaled in Ted's essay by the fact that he substitutes the word "inclusiveness" for hospitality and then renders this term into an overarching, almost all-defining concept. Elizabeth Newman, in her recent book on hospitality, points to what is problematic here. In her discussion of "inclusivity" as a distortion of true Christian hospitality, she argues that the current ideology of inclusiveness names no identity, no central good beyond itself. It is simply an affirmation of the inclusion of everyone, the celebration of diversity for its own sake. She believes that this ends up "underwriting a consumeristic and aesthetic way of life," a way of living that is essentially "noncommittal" and valorizes individualistic freedom and autonomy.[79]

Philip Turner states the implications of the current ideology

of inclusiveness more fully in the following discussion. Turner
suggests that the argument begins as follows:

> The great news of the Christian gospel is this. The life
> and death of Jesus reveal the fact that God accepts and
> affirms us. From this revelation, we can draw a further
> conclusion. God wants us to love one another, and such
> love requires of us both acceptance and affirmation of
> the other. From this point we can derive yet another.
> Accepting love requires a form of justice that is inclusive
> of all people, particularly those who in some way have
> been marginalized by oppressive social practice. The
> mission of the church is, therefore, to see that those who
> have been rejected are included.

Turner goes on to point out that however well-intended the
above description of the Christian gospel is,

> In respect to God, [the doctrine of radical inclusion] pro-
> duces a quasi-deist theology that posits a benevolent God
> who favors love and justice as inclusion, but acts neither
> to save us from our sins nor to raise us to new life after
> the pattern of Christ. In respect to "the neighbor" it pro-
> duces an ethic of tolerant affirmation that carries with it
> no call to conversion and radical holiness.

With such a perspective,

> The atoning power of Christ's death, faith, justification,
> repentance, and holiness of life, to mention but a few,
> appear at best as an antique vocabulary to be either out-
> grown or reinterpreted. So also does the notion that the
> church is a community elected and called out by God
> from the peoples of the earth for a particular purpose.
> That purpose is to bear witness to the saving event of
> Christ's life, death, and resurrection and to call people to
> believe, repent, and live in an entirely different manner.

The conclusion of this misuse of inclusivism is indeed destructive to the Christian witness because

To be true to itself [a theology of radical inclusion] can find room for only one sort of witness, namely, inclusion of the previously excluded. Indeed, the connection of the existence of the church to a saving purpose makes little sense because salvation is not an issue for a theology of radical inclusion. God has already included everybody, and now we ought to do the same.[80]

I trust that these comments from Newman and Turner make it clear that my focus on the issue of homosexuality is about much more than this one issue. It is about the future integrity of the church and its adherence to the gospel of Jesus Christ, a gospel that is to be embodied by a people who are forgiven and redeemed by God and then called and enabled to live faithfully across time to the glory of God. Most arguments for the affirmation of homoerotic relationships almost always make moves similar to what Ted has made, moves that, however well intentioned, end up muting or significantly distorting important components of our overall understanding of the Christian faith.

Conclusion

I know Ted reasonably well and respect him. I do not question his intentions. But I do not believe he has offered "a more conservative hermeneutic," as he claims to have done, In fact, he has—despite his best motives—implied a seriously reductionistic account of the Christian faith. Signals of this are present many places in his essay—the overarching role assigned to hospitality, the use of hospitality and inclusion as interchangeable terms, the muting of any concerns regarding righteousness or holiness that do not fit within the ideology of inclusiveness, and no account of the need for repentance or salvation for those who would become a part of the body of Christ.

In a nutshell one could say that Ted has substituted the current ideology of inclusiveness for a full, rich, biblical, and theological account of hospitality, an account that would then be located in the overall biblical message, which would include the above matters (both in the long quote from Philip Turner and my summary statements just given).

And then specifically in relation to matters of sexuality we need to refuse to be Gnostic or docetic—i.e., writing as if we are something other than humans, living embodied lives in communities that exist across time. Sex is a gift to be celebrated. It is also a powerful force that can be destructive as well as glorious. We must reflect on what it means to be embodied, with gendered differences and with drives and lusts. We must attend to the need for structures for behaviors, structures that organize our lives into families and communities, structures that consider the existence of relationships across time.[81]

In the presence of God we are called to live our lives in holiness, in righteousness and in justice—knowing that our loving, gracious and forgiving God calls us to welcome the strangers while also remembering that the commandment that bids us to love our neighbor, even our alien neighbor, also calls us to love the Lord our God with our whole being.

Ted's Response: Constraining the Conversation

I appreciate Mark's thoughtful response. He has challenged me to work harder at clarity—which can only be a good thing. I feel the need to restate the basic argument I make in my longer essay. I fear I may not have made my concerns apparent enough.

When I began my longer essay with discussion of the important biblical theme of hospitality, I focused on this theme in order to articulate a general framework for considering the issue of how churches might relate to gay and lesbian Christians. I did not intend to reduce Christian ethics to hospitality as *the* overriding concern of the Bible—nor, certainly, to present hospitality as an autonomous principle separate from the faith community's relationship with God. I strongly believe that our call to hospitality is given to us in the context of our call to be in covenant relationship with God—through the revelation of God's will through Torah (and reiterated by Jesus and Paul).

I will grant that I do use the terms "hospitality" and "inclusion" in ways that assumes a close connection between the two. I understand the call to hospitality to include as a key element the inclusion in the faith community of all who seek to follow God. As well, in Torah, the prophets, and Jesus special attention is paid to including vulnerable people who seek to follow God, those who the community may tend to want to exclude or at least limit its care for.

However, I tried to be careful to use "inclusion" in a sense that subordinates the call to inclusiveness to the call to live faithfully to Torah and the word of Jesus. So, when I define "inclusion" in relation to questions concerning gay and lesbian Christians in intimate relationships, I include two components: (1) that the moral values the church affirms in relation to heterosexual intimate relationships (e.g., opposing sexual promiscuity, adultery, and sexual abuse) should equally apply to same-sex intimate rela-

tionships and (2) that *covenanted* partnerships should be supported (indicating that there is a "covenant" [or marriage] expectation
for all sexual intimacy).

In the paragraph that follows my defining "inclusiveness" in
this way, I set out my basic argument. I speak of the churches
under the influence of the biblical emphasis on hospitality giving
the benefit of the doubt to the inclusive approach. That is, when I
speak of this benefit of the doubt I have the understanding of
inclusion in mind that I have just defined—in the context of the
expectation of covenant fidelity for all sexual relationships. Hence,
I am *not* implying by the use of "inclusive" "an ethic of tolerant
affirmation that carries with it no call to conversion and radical
holiness" (Mark's quote of Philip Turner).[82]

I believe that when the churches do recognize particular types
of behavior as sinful, they should in some sense (depending on the
situations—this is an important element of pastoral discernment)
restrict the participation in the churches of those guilty of such
sinful behavior. That is, I am most decidedly not advocating
"cheap grace" nor wanting to establish in the churches a practice
of inclusion without repentance or turning.[83]

So what I mean to say about hospitality is that its importance in the Bible challenges us to be very careful in how we
understand and apply the faith communities' responsibility to
draw conclusions concerning the sinfulness of community members' behaviors. This care is especially important—based on clear
biblical teaching—in relation to vulnerable people in our midst,
those the communities tend to marginalize.

I appreciate Mark's own discussion of hospitality in the first
couple of pages in his response, especially his conclusion, "the call
to welcome, hospitality, and love of others is indeed far-reaching
and challenging." This is really pretty much all I am trying to say
as well.[84] Mark does not say that this "far-reaching" call sometimes
is non-binding or that we are at times justified in being inhospitable. So I am not sure we actually disagree about hospitality.

I am *not* arguing that the importance of hospitality and inclusion proves that the churches should uncritically welcome all gays and lesbians into full participation regardless of whether they are violating the churches' standards concerning covenant fidelity as the context for sexual intimacy. I am simply saying that the churches are enjoined by the importance of the call to hospitality to be very careful and solid in our discernment before we conclude that those Christians sharing in same-sex, monogamous covenanted intimate relationships are per se living in sin and should have their participation in our communities restricted.

It is possible, within my argument, for communities to recognize the importance of hospitality and inclusion (as I define inclusion) and still take a restrictive stance concerning same-sex partners. All they would have to do is establish that the benefit of doubt toward inclusion should be overridden. However, I go on to present the case that the three basic grounds most likely to be used for such an overriding do not withstand scrutiny— the grounds of direct biblical commands, of the meaning of marriage, or of the intrinsic harmfulness of all same-sex intimate partnerships.

This is why for the case I present in my essay, close attention to the "direct texts" that allegedly establish the intrinsic sinfulness of all possible same sex intimate relationships is so important. I suggest that we need to have clear and strong bases for concluding that the call to hospitality should not lead us to welcome same-sex partners who live within the parameters of the churches' convictions concerning covenanted faithfulness.

I try then to show that such clear and strong bases are not forthcoming when we engage in careful reading of the direct texts. I am disappointed that Mark chooses not to engage my argument on this level. His dismissive tone ("I am not going to engage in dueling exegesis or hermeneutics") does not seem to recognize or respect the type of case I try to follow here.

His later comments concerning some of my points regarding

1 Corinthians 6:9 (quoting Oliver O'Donovan, "Faced with yet another attempt to get at the meaning of *arsenokoites* by philology, I cry: Enough! You have satisfied the curiosity of a generation!" and "interpreters who think they that they can determine the proper ethical application of the Bible solely through more sophisticated exegesis are like people who believe they can fly if only they flap their arms hard enough") seem not only mean-spirited but also to misrepresent what I am trying to do.

It seems to me that the people Mark depends on and cites as authorities (though he does not summarize their arguments and show how they apply—e.g., Robert Gagnon and Willard Swartley) are the ones who base *their* case on philology (as does Mark himself when he cites as a fact that *arsenokoites* refers to male homosexuals). The points I make concerning 1 Corinthians 6:9 are (1) that the meaning should be determined by its context in the larger argument of 1 Corinthians 6, not by philology, and (2) we can't base our conclusions on the clear meaning of this one word *arsenokoites* anyhow because its meaning is unclear and by the nature of the case can't help but be unclear.

Mark concludes that I have *not* offered "a more conservative hermeneutic," but instead have "implied a seriously reductionistic account of the Christian faith." He can say this only by projecting on to me his definition of "inclusion" in defiance of my own definition and by focusing on my *conclusions* that he assumes cannot be "conservative" rather than on my method. Since he does not much engage my exegetical discussion, he has not shown how my *approach* to the Bible is problematic.

Mark, and other restrictive writers, dismiss the arguments of pro-gay writers such as Walter Wink for not taking the Bible seriously enough. So I try to meet them on the level of the biblical "direct texts" only to find my approach dismissed as "reductionistic" when I try to show that the *content* of the Bible does not support Mark's views. Maybe my interpretation of the biblical texts is not the best—but Mark doesn't show *why*, and he doesn't point to any problems in my methodology.

I realize I may not have been clear enough in my affirmation of the "importance of marriage" (though in footnote 61, I state that I "believe that one man, one woman, equal partners for life is the norm for today's Christians" [and I cite my agreement with the important books by David Myers and Letha Scanzoni and by William Stacy Johnson that make a theological case for gay marriage based on a very high view of marriage] and in my definition of "inclusion" I state that this has to do with churches affirming the importance of supporting covenanted partnerships characterized by monogamy and mutuality).

However, Mark seems to miss the point of my discussion of marriage—which is to affirm the sanctity of marriage while suggesting that we have the freedom to expand our definition of marriage to include same-sex couples (but not to minimize in any way that fidelity, mutuality, lifetime commitment, and accountability before God in the faith community are part of the definition of marriage). I do not mean to *relativize* our commitment to marriage. I fail to see how affirming the commitments of those same-sex couples who want to pledge their lifetime troth to one another before God and the church relativizes marriage—especially in light of the horrendous failure rate of married heterosexual couples to remain faithful to their commitments.

I agree with Mark that biblical holiness should be a central category that shapes Christian life. However, it appears that we may understand holiness a bit differently. I understand God's holiness ultimately as God's commitment to bring healing to humanity.[85] Jesus, as God Incarnate, embodied God's holiness by entering into the broken human environment (not remaining separate from it) and bringing healing. Mark would need to show that he is not using holiness primarily as a justification for inhospitality, or *explain* why and when holiness does justify inhospitality.

As I suggested in my response to Mark's longer essay, he does not explain *why* Christ-following gays in intimate relationships are living in sin simply due to the same-sexness of their partnerships. His response to my chapter essentially takes me to task for positions I don't hold (e.g., his "ideology of inclusion" that he projects on me despite my own definition of inclusion, which does set it in the context of a call to rigorous discipleship) and fails to engage what seem to me to be the core issues at stake.

Intentionally or not, he seems to take as settled his conclusions concerning the Bible and the obvious sinfulness of gays. By not engaging the discussion on the level of justifying those conclusions, he constrains the parameters of our "conversation" and runs the risk of perpetuating the reduction of the church's debates about homosexuality to mere power struggles.

PART 3:
DISCUSSING KEY ISSUES

— Chapter 5 —

Mark's First Question
What about Macro Theological Issues?

Mark's Question:

Ted, toward the end of my initial response to your two essays I quoted Oliver O'Donovan's provocative statement: "Faced with yet another attempt to get at the meaning of *arsenokoites* by philology, I cry Enough! You have satisfied the curiosity of a generation!" I went on to quote another statement from O'Donovan as well as offer a long quote from Søren Kierkegaard. Your response indicated that you thought these comments were directed at your exegetical work. They were not. I apologize if I was not clear enough. Toward the end of that section I said what I was intending to signal by the following general statement: "some of the central disagreements over this issue are mostly not about the details of texts, but rather are at a more macro theological level."

There are a number of questions, at this "more macro" level that I could ask you. I will ask two. Here is the first one. I have said that it is unusual for people with your position both to articulate a clear affirmation of marriage and, accompanying that, a rationale for why sexual intercourse outside of marriage is wrong. Would you at least provide an outline of your position in regards to both marriage and sex outside of marriage? And as an amplification of the latter, articulate why it is you believe, if you do, that a sexual relationship between siblings is wrong (assuming in this case that they are consenting and respectful of and loving toward each other).

Ted's Answer:

Thanks for the questions, Mark. I'd like to say first, though, that I think one of the key differences between your approach and mine seems to be about whether these "macro theological" issues are central to the particular issue we are discussing. I understand that issue to be the moral acceptability among Christians of same-sex committed partnerships.

I have framed my argument in favor of acceptance in terms that do not depend upon a specific perspective on such macro issues. Thus, in relation to your specific questions, I don't see why a person could not have a "conservative" view of the wrongness of "sex outside of marriage" and still believe that same-sex marriage is okay. One could (*should*, I personally would say) have the same negative view of same-sex partners having sex outside of marriage as one has toward heterosexual partners having sex outside of marriage.

Likewise, I don't see why a person could not have a conservative view toward "a sexual relationship between siblings" and still think a sexual relationship between a married same-sex couple is acceptable.

So, on the "macro" issues of sex outside of marriage and sex between siblings, I see no logical necessity for a person who approves of gay marriage, for the sake of consistency, to be accepting toward sex outside of marriage or sex between siblings. Logically, it would seem that the opposite should be the case. The same logic that supports *marriage* for people in same-sex relationships would also support marriage as the context for all intimate sexual relationships.

The question of the moral legitimacy of same-sex marriage, on the one hand, and the issues of sex outside of marriage and sex between siblings, on the other hand, seem like totally distinct issues. I don't see how the "macro" issues of sex outside of marriage in general or sexual relationships between siblings would have anything to do with one's view concerning same-sex marriage. In the one case, the issue seems to be whether marriage is the exclusive context for sexual intimacy. In the other case, the issue seems to be who may legitimately be married. To want to expand our views of who may legitimately be married to include same-sex partners does not in any way have to imply expanding our views of the legitimate context for sexual intimacy beyond marriage.

I don't see any inconsistency between affirming the moral legitimacy of same-sex marriage and believing in the intrinsic sinfulness of sex outside of marriage or of sex between siblings. It clearly seems to be possible to hold to all of these views following from the same basic theological-ethical methodology. For example, see the two recent books advocating that the churches should affirm same-sex marriage (both of which would clearly seem to oppose sex outside of marriage and sex between siblings): David Myers and Letha Scanzoni, *What God Has Joined Together: The Christian Case for Gay Marriage* and William Stacy Johnson, *A Time to Embrace: Same-Gender Relationships in Religion, Law, and Politics.*

For the writers of these two books (and for me, as well), support for gay marriage follows from an affirmation of marriage as the only legitimate context for full sexual intimacy. Such support is part of a high view of marriage. Thus, arguments in opposition to "sexual intercourse outside of marriage" and to "sex between siblings" may well be identical for many supporters *and* opponents of same-sex marriage.

Since, as I tried to make clear in my earlier essays, I do believe sexual intercourse outside of marriage is wrong—and I certainly believe sex between siblings is wrong—I don't mind speaking to your specific questions. But it seems pretty simple; I don't expect we would disagree on much.

I will use the three points I raised in my main essay. I suggested that the main reasons people could decide that same-sex intimate partnerships are *always* wrong would be: (1) the Bible overtly forbids all such possible relationships, and/or (2) human experience clearly shows that all such relationships are harmful or likely to be harmful, and/or (3) support for any such relationships would severely undermine people's commitment to the institution of marriage.

Whereas, in my main essay, I argue that in relation to none of these three points do we have strong reasons for opposing same-sex marriage in principle, here I will suggest that in relation to all three points we *do* have bases for in principle opposing sex outside of marriage and sex between siblings.

(1) The trajectory of the biblical teaching on marriage clearly leads to the conclusion that it is the will of the God of the Bible that two people who enter into a permanent, covenanted, life-long partnership as a married couple are to share exclusive intimate sexual relationships with one another—implying that any intimate sexual relationships outside that context are sinful. So the Bible clearly speaks against sex outside of marriage. The Bible does overtly forbid such behavior.

(2) It seems clear to me from what I know of human experience that sexual relationships outside of a marriage commitment are harmful. They tend to separate the joyful expression of physical intimacy from the deepening of love that energizes people in marriage relationships to sustain their commitments to the long-term and socially necessary yet difficult work of building lasting partnerships that provide the glue for the thriving of human community. They also tend to stunt the emotional growth that sustained sharing in sexual intimacy provides in the context of permanent commitments.

(3) And sexual relationships outside of marriage, especially adultery, undermine the institution of marriage in general. Infidelity undermines a couple's trust and their ability to sustain

vulnerability with each other. Pre-marital sex, especially with a series of partners, also may well diminish the special bond that connects married couples to one another in unique ways.

Concerning siblings having sex, I have little more to say. This seems like a universal taboo that, for Christians, surely also follows from a sense that the Bible clearly opposes it. It harms those who may do it, and it undermines the institution of marriage.

I would add, too, that I am not aware of any sibling sexual relationship where both people "are consenting and respectful of and loving toward each other." I tend to believe that such a relationship is not possible. So this seems like a completely hypothetical question. Perhaps in your response to my comments you could say a bit more about why you would have raised this question.

Mark's Follow-up

Ted, thank you for your careful and thoughtful responses to my question. You are right of course that, in the main, I would agree with what you have said. In retrospect I realize that throwing in the bit about sibling incest probably seemed like a red herring. I certainly didn't intend it to be a trick question, though it may have seemed like that. I don't disagree with your response on that. I am of course aware that not only does the Bible prohibit incest (in Leviticus, it should be added) but there is an almost universal taboo against it. Nonetheless, I've decided that it can be an interesting exercise to attempt to go beyond our almost gut response to try to articulate why it is wrong (aside from being prohibited in the Scriptures). What purposes are served by saying it is always wrong for siblings to have sexual intercourse with each other. I think such reflection can help to clarify some things about the nature of sex and embodiedness. You didn't really offer that sort of reflection, but that's okay.

(Perhaps a better question would have been the following: Do you believe that cohabitation is wrong, even if a par-

ticular couple are caring, loving and respectful in their relationships with each other? How does your response relate to
the three criteria you gave for why sex outside of marriage is
wrong?)

You gave three reasons why sex outside of marriage is
wrong. They are good reasons. But I do have some questions. First, if the Bible is definitive for affirming marriage
then why is the "male and female" part optional? This is not
about debating the meaning of a Greek word that might
mean homosexual, rather there is no question but that both
in Genesis and in Jesus' affirmation of this account, marriage
is between a man and a woman.

Second, the three factors you named for prohibiting sex
outside of marriage are (briefly stated): the Bible; all such relationships are harmful; and undermining the institution of
marriage. Given what you've said numerous places, what I
wonder about is how you weigh each of these points in relation to the others? What seems to me to be the case is that
you have decided that the biblical affirmation of marriage
between a man and a woman can be overridden because gay
and lesbian "marriages" are not harmful and do not undermine the institution of marriage. How do you discern that
our current understanding of whether something is harmful
can override a biblical teaching?

You see, a part of what puzzles me is that in your longest
essay what seems to be driving your argument has nothing to
do with marriage as such. Rather, a passion to be inclusive and
just—understood in a certain way—seems to drive your argument. In your response to my longer essay you said that a part
of the debate is: what is "the issue"? Then you said that the
issue for you was not about accepting or not accepting gay or
lesbian relationships, but rather it is about emotional violence
to gays and lesbians. What you seemed to suggest—here and
elsewhere—is that sex and how we deal with it institutionally

or communally is relatively unimportant even when the issue at hand is sex and marriage. Rather you seemed to say that even then, *the* issue is violence or inclusion or justice. This was one of the reasons I said there were important "macro" issues involved. I still tend to think there are.

Ted's Final Comment

Your comments here, Mark, point to several important issues.

I would agree with you that cohabitation is wrong. I think two of the three criteria I discussed directly apply—the biblical norm of marriage and the undermining of the institution of marriage. The third criterion (overt harm) does seem perhaps less obvious in your scenario. Pastorally, I would want to know why the couple did not marry. In principle, though, I would assume that there likely would be some harm insofar as the unwillingness to marry officially may relate to an unwillingness to commit fully to the partnership or stem from an unwillingness to be accountable to a faith community for the sustenance of the partnership.

Your question about why, "if the Bible is definitive for affirming marriage," is "the 'male and female' part optional" is important. This one probably does touch on what I suspect might actually be the heart of our differences.

The allusions to male and female in Genesis and Jesus clearly describe the typical intimate relationship. They are not overtly presented as an exclusive prescription. The central points being made in these two texts have to do with issues other than denying the potential validity of same sex marriage. I don't see marriage as *exclusively* male and female as a positive, overt "biblical teaching." It is at most an inference.

It is not necessarily inappropriate to draw normative conclusions from a descriptive reference. However, the reasons for doing so should follow from other considerations as well. The descriptive allusions do not stand on their own. What other reasons would there be to forbid same-sex partnerships? I don't really see any.

The general trajectory within the Bible and in contemporary Christian practice seems to be to move from restrictive specific commands (say, in the Old Testament) toward more flexible practices (relevant examples would be the acceptance of women in church leadership, willingness to charge interest on loans, and unrestricted inclusion of divorced and remarried people in churches). Your argument seems, in contrast, to move from implicit biblical allusions to more restrictive specific commands that are never stated in the Bible.

I see the three factors I suggested (Bible, harm, undermining marriage) as being roughly on the same level, each informing the other in our discernment processes. I am suspicious of any use of the Bible that does not link our use of biblical prohibitions with actual practical bases for the prohibition. When we don't have such a link, we risk violating the Bible's own guidance (Jesus' concern about seeing people being made for the commands instead of commands being made for people).

Part of my concern with your type of argument is that it seems to me that you are distorting the overall message of the Bible (1) by minimizing the Bible's concern with hospitality/care for vulnerable people and (2) by treating a descriptive allusion of the typical arrangement of marriage as a normative command for one exclusively valid model. So, I actually think my argument is more faithful to the overall message of the Bible than yours.

—— Chapter 6 ——

Ted's First Question
What is Wrong with This Picture?

Ted's Question

You clearly do not see much merit in my interpretations of the key "direct" biblical texts (Leviticus 18–20; Romans 1; 1 Corinthians 6). I would like you to explain to me where my analyses go wrong.[1]

Let's focus on 1 Corinthians 6. I will summarize the line of reasoning that is at the core of my argument:

(1) I assume that Paul has a reason for giving his vice list in 6:9-10, so I ask to what use is he probably putting this list. The immediate context (6:1-8) gives us one possible answer: his objection to people taking fellow church members to secular courts. The unbelieving judges are unjust (6:1, "unrighteous" in NRSV).[2] To illustrate that these nonbelievers are unjust (6:9, "wrongdoers" in NRSV), Paul gives this list of vices. Some of you in the church used to be unjust like this (6:11, underscoring that Paul is using this list to illustrate the unbelieving judges, not to describe those presently in the church), but now that you are made just (6:11, "justified" in NRSV), don't turn back to the injustice of the non-believers when you have disputes with each other.[3]

(2) With this context, we turn to the list of vices itself. We may assume they are meant to illustrate the injustice of the unbelieving judges. It's a broad indictment that includes

sexual sins; all of the terms may be understood under the rubric of injustice if this term is understood in a broad sense of social behavior that causes harm and in general undermines the well-being of the community.[4]

(3) The meanings of terms applied to homosexuality are obscure. *Malakos* is used in several ways in the Bible and other contemporary literature. Thinking of it in relation to the concern for injustice could lead to seeing it to mean "morally soft" in a general sense, a use consistent with how the term is used elsewhere. *Arsenokoites* is extremely rare; we have little to go on concerning its meaning. It seems believable that Paul would have in mind male/male sex that was of an economically exploitative type.

(4) So contrary to the standard account, Paul is not making a broad general statement addressed to people in the churches telling them that under no circumstances would intimate same-sex relationships be acceptable. Rather, he seems to make a more contextual statement warning church members not to entrust their disputes to unjust, immoral non-Christian judges who are like those who engage in the kinds of behavior alluded to in the vice list.

What do you think is wrong with this picture?

Mark's Answer

Ted, thanks for posing this question. I have given brief responses to points in your interpretation in footnotes attached to your question. However, mostly I want to offer my own interpretation. Then you (and the reader) can compare it with your interpretation (both above and in your earlier essay). Let me make one thing clear as I begin. The reason my earlier comments on this passage were geared toward homosexuality was because that is the subject of our book; thus we are mostly focused on that for the purposes of this book. In case it is not obvious, I do not see homosexuality as the central subject in this passage.

On 1 Corinthians 6:1-11:

(1) Anytime we read a letter we need to ask about a number of contexts. To keep this simple I will name only a few elements drawn from the letter itself. First, Paul begins by reminding the Corinthians that they are being "sanctified in Christ Jesus" (1:2). In writing this letter Paul's hope is centrally that the Corinthian Christians will hear a reminder that they have "received not the spirit of the world, but the Spirit that is from God, so that we may understand the gifts bestowed on us by God" (2:12). For what we need is "the mind of Christ" (2:16b). Paul is convinced, however that, in relation to the Corinthians, he "could not speak to [them] as spiritual people, but rather as people of the flesh, as infants in Christ" (3:1). Thus he needs to speak critically. There are a number of specific issues Paul will address in this letter, criticizing their wrongdoing as well as calling them to embody the righteousness and justice to which they are called as the body of Christ.

2. Many commentaries, including the recent ones by Richard Hays and Anthony Thiselton, note that the larger context for understanding 6:1-11 is really chapters 5–7. It is interesting to notice that chapter 5 opens with concerns about sexual immorality, and verse 12 in chapter 6 returns to this theme. Thus verses 1-8 in chapter 6 are a digression within the context of the prominent theme in chapters 5–7. It is also interesting to notice that, though chapter 7 is primarily about sex and marriage, it also has a substantial digression, offering reflections on living Christianly in our various roles in life (7:17-24: circumcised/uncircumcised and slaves).

Anyone who knows Paul's letters very well, it seems to me, ought not to be surprised by what seem like digressions within passages. They are not uncommon. I would suggest that the main theme (in chapter 7 that is sex and marriage) *and* the subtopic/s ("let each of you lead the life that the Lord has assigned") should both be taken seriously. Then adequately to understand how one relates to the other requires a careful reading of the whole passage within the context of the chapter, sometimes within a larger context, as well as attending to specific wording to attempt to discern the interconnections and the meanings of each.

3. Let me next comment on the paragraph immediately preceding chapter 6 (5:9-13). This is especially relevant for two reasons. First, it addresses the issue of inclusion or hospitality. In verse 9 Paul says: "I wrote to you in my letter not to mix indiscriminately with [sexually] immoral people."[5] Paul then adds two other important things. On the one hand he expands the list of wrongdoers with whom we should not associate indiscriminately: the sexually immoral; greedy; idolaters; verbally abusive; drunkards or people who exploit others. On the other hand he makes it clear that this does not mean we should not associate, in a general way, with those outside the church who do such things; otherwise we would have to abandon association with the world. Paul seems here to be attempting to retain the peculiarly righteous/just identity of the church while also insisting that Christians, with their peculiar sanctified identity, are to engage, welcome and love those who are outside their community.[6]

The other relevant reason to discuss these verses (5:9-13) is because they provide a clue as to why he discusses lawsuits in 6:1-8. In 5:12-13 Paul ends this subsection of the letter, offering reflections on distinctions between being inside and outside the community and on the need for judgment or discernment. Perhaps as Paul named this subject it made him think of another, related subject. In any event, these reflections appear to serve as a segue into the next subsection, which will deal with another issue in the Corinthian church community related to insiders, outsiders, and making judgments.

4. Considering what has already been said, of course 6:1-8 is a subsection with its own subject. As I said above, given that the prominent subject from chapters 5–7 is sex then the immediate subject here is something of a digression. However, I have already suggested the connecting theme that led him to segue into this subject. Besides, Paul will loop back to his larger themes, as I will

discuss in a moment. The primary theme throughout 6:1-6, it seems to me, is that Christians should be able to use discernment/judgment among themselves rather than taking their conflicts before non-Christian courts. In fact, in 6:7-8 Paul calls Christians to be willing to be wronged rather than engage in wrongdoing—another reason not to go before "pagan" courts with their grievances. As Richard Hays puts it:

> Paul is upset with the Corinthians because they are failing to act as a community, failing to take responsibility for one another. Just as they have failed to discipline the incestuous man [5:1-13], so they are failing to take responsibility for settling their own disputes. . . . When the Corinthian Christians take one another to court, they are declaring primary allegiance to the pagan culture of Corinth rather than to the community of faith. . . . Let the point be registered clearly: In 1 Corinthians 6:1-11 Paul has not really changed the subject from the topic of chapter 5. In both cases the problem is "a failure of the church to be the church."[7]

5. At the end of this passage (6:1-8) about the Christian community and the pagan courts Paul again creates another segue, this time to one of his more general themes. In 6:8 Paul says that these Corinthian Christians are doing wrong (*adikeite*). Then at the beginning of the next subsection (6:9-11) Paul says: "Do you not know that wrongdoers (*adikoi*) will not inherit the kingdom of God?"

On the one hand this is intended as an admonition to those who are doing wrong in the specific ways he has named in 6:1-8— quite possibly connected to economics (then, as now, the rich have more power in the courts) but also simply for taking each other before a pagan court when they shouldn't.

On the other hand, Paul's connecting "wrongdoing" to a more general list of sinful behaviors loops back to the list given in 5:9-13.[8] Then there is the list itself: those who are sexually immoral; idolaters; adulterers; *malakoi*; *arsenokoitai*; thieves; the greedy; drunkards; the verbally abusive; the exploitative. (6:9-10) (I will discuss the meaning of the two untranslated terms later). Again, he underscores: "none of these will inherit the kingdom of God." He concludes: "And this is what some of you used to be. But you were washed, you were sanctified, you were justified, in the name of the Lord Jesus Christ and in the Spirit of our God" (v. 11). This circles back to the beginning of the letter, where Paul had addressed the Corinthian Christians as "those who are sanctified in Christ Jesus."

6. What I was puzzled by in your interpretation is how you can see all of these terms as falling simply under your category of (social) justice. Some certainly would be so categorized. And in fact I believe it is imperative that here, as in 5:9-13, matters like sex should not be emphasized in such a way that concerns about greed and economic exploitation are trivialized. But I also believe the reverse is true. Sexual immorality, adultery, idolatry, and the two terms related to homosexuality, cannot simply be subsumed (and thus trivialized for what they are fully) under the contemporary understanding of justice.[9] No, all of these point to a Christian community called to live a sanctified life, a life of righteousness and justice daily and in every dimension of life (as opposed to wrong-doing). As Richard Hays puts it: "The concern of the passage as a whole is threefold: to call the Corinthians to act as a [Christian] community, to condemn litigation as an instrument of injustice, and to assert the transformed identity of the baptized."[10]

7. Now let me turn to the two terms for practicing homosexuals (*malakoi*; *arsenokoitai*). I have read numerous discussions, taking various positions, regarding the meanings of these terms. Adequately to discuss this would be to replay all those details. I cannot do that here but I will offer a brief summary.

Let me begin with *malakoi*. The NRSV translates this word as "male prostitute." Anthony Thiselton prefers "perverts," adding in brackets that the reference is probably to those who participate in pederastic practices (i.e., sex between a man and a boy).[11] Given that the word refers to "soft" or "effeminate" behavior and in some contexts refers to sexual behavior, and given that it is located next to another word referring to homosexual practice, it is likely that it refers to someone who is a passive partner in male same-sex behavior (although maybe with more specific connotations, as suggested by Thiselton).

But let me make fuller comments on *arsenokoitai*, about which we can be clearer. It is hardly adequate to say, as you do: "We have little to go on concerning its meaning. It seems believable that Paul would have in mind male/male sex that was of an economically exploitative type." There is nothing about the word, or the textual context, that would indicate it has something to do with economic exploitation. It is a much more adequate reflection of most contemporary scholarship to say, with Richard Hays, that "although the word *arsenokoitēs* appears nowhere in Greek literature prior to Paul's use of it, it is evidently a rendering into Greek of the standard rabbinic term for 'one who lies with a male [as with a woman]' (Leviticus 18:22; 20:13)." And, as Hays also says, it reflects "standard Jewish condemnation of homosexual conduct."[12] How so?

Simply put, the word, *arsenoikoitai*, has to mean something. And it has to mean something that Paul, a Jewish follower of Jesus, believes should be included on this list of "wrongdoers." Given that, as far as we know, it was standard practice at the time of Paul for Jewish leaders to condemn homosexual practice; given that this word was very likely created either by a Hellenistic Jew or by Paul, a rabbi and a serious student of the Septuagint (the Greek translation of the Old Testament); and given that the Septuagint uses the words *arsenos* and *knoitēn* as the words to refer to the prohibition: "you shall not lie with a male as with a woman." (Leviticus 18:22; 20:13)[13], it is not difficult to see how Paul came up with the compound word, *arsenokoitēs*. It is hardly a word about whose origin we "have little to go on."[14]

What seems incredible to me is that John Boswell, in his very influential 1980 book, *Christianity, Social Tolerance and Homosexuality*, never considers the significance of these Septuagint words for the meaning of this compound in the New Testament. Perhaps it is because of the following misinformed belief: "It would simply not have occurred to most early Christians to invoke the authority of the old law to justify the morality of the new: the Levitical regulations had no hold on Christians and are manifestly irrelevant in explaining Christian hostility to gay sexuality."[15] And what seems very unfortunate to me is that Boswell, with this sort of shoddy argument, has had and continues to have a huge influence on very many people.[16]

Before I finish this section on the debate about these terms, let me say a couple of things. First, I am well aware that the vast majority of the readers of this book are not going to read the essays I have referenced for a fuller discussion of these two words. Rather, what often seems to be accomplished by what Boswell and you have said is that doubts are raised. More than a few readers will be (or have already been) convinced, simply because questions have been raised by scholars, that there must be legitimate questions; we don't really know what Leviticus, Romans, 1 Corinthians, 1 Timothy or Genesis say about the issue before us. Thus, who are we to take a stand, much less continue to "pontificate" on this issue? That is what I fear too often happens.

Anyone who regularly reads scholarly literature knows that virtually everything under the sun—certainly anything about which people have strong opinions—is contested. Questions are raised. But that doesn't mean the questions are legitimate. That doesn't mean the alternatives posed are right. I think it should count that the church has mostly been of one mind about this issue until roughly thirty years ago. (It should be said that this includes the pre-Constantinian early Church Fathers.) I am well aware that sometimes this clear conviction led to the horrible treatment of gays and lesbians. And in no uncertain terms such treatment should be denounced. It also happened in certain periods of time that those who violated marriage vows were horribly treated. Again, such behavior should be denounced. But in both cases the question of whether or not the belief in the wrongness of homosexual behavior or the rightness of marriage commitments are neither affirmed nor brought into question by the linkage of such beliefs to wrongful violence as a way of reinforcing the dominant culture's norms.

In my main essay I offered some discussion of the most immediately relevant passages of Scripture. And I do believe it is important that we look carefully at such passages (though I believe that work has been done carefully and more thoroughly by others than you and I could do it). But I think one of the reasons I have shied away from offering this sort of detailed discussion of all of the passages is because, in some ways, I think it is a diversion. I tend to think we would get farther if we simply stipulated that the Bible says homosexual practice is wrong. Then let's spend our time arguing about whether or not we still agree with that and why. That is what was done in a recent essay by the prolific and respected New Testament scholar, Luke Timothy Johnson. He says that the Bible teaches that homosexual practice is wrong. Then he attempts to say why it is we can no longer believe this.[17] I think he is unsuccessful in his arguments. But at least he has opened up the right conversation, even if I disagree with his position.

Ted's Follow-up

I appreciate your thoughtful discussion of 1 Corinthians 6 and its place in our conversation. I found it illuminating to read your more extended interpretation of this passage and how it informs your theology. However, I didn't get what I was especially looking for—a clear, concise explanation of where precisely, in your view, the logic breaks down in my interpretation.

In extrapolating, though, I have noticed several problems

you identify. These lead you to reject seemingly without qual-
ification the interpretation I give. I will focus on four in my
response.

(1) You state that Paul ends one subsection on lawsuits
(6:1-8) and then turns to a discussion of "one of his more
general themes" in a new subsection (6:9-11). If it is true
these are separate units of thought, then I likely am incorrect
in suggesting that they illustrate the behavior of the non-
Christians to whom Paul is telling the Corinthian believers
not to take their lawsuits.

However, I believe, in seeking to read the text looking
for its plain sense (the common sense reading), one can
validly make an argument for following the King James,
NRSV, and TNIV, in seeing 6:1-11 as a single unit. And if
we look at it as a unit, we then legitimately ask how the vice
list makes sense in relation to the rest of the unit of which it
is part. Then we notice that the same word that introduces
the vice list in verse 9 (*adikoi*, which literally means "unjust"
or "unrighteous") is used at the beginning of the unit of the
judges who run the secular courts (verse 1).

Since Paul's concern in 6:1-8 is to warn the Corinthian
Christians not to utilize these courts, it seems sensible to
understand 6:9-11 as providing evidence for why they should
not be relying on unjust people to decide their disputes. So
when Paul states in verse 11, "this is what some of you used
to be," he is referring *both* to verse 1 and verse 9, because
those two verses are referring to the same *adikoi*. Part of my
reason for using "unjust" in both cases in my exposition is to
make clear that we are dealing with the same term in both
verses—something the NRSV obscures by translating the
first *adikoi* as "unrighteous" and the second as "wrongdoers."

I agree with you that the "what some of you used to be"
in verse 11 refers to "those presently in the church." These
present believers had in the past lived in ways alluded to in

the vice list. Then they were "washed," "sanctified," and "justified"—that is, transformed and freed to follow God's will. So they must not turn back to the unjust ways of those "will not inherit the kingdom of God" (verse 9). But why is Paul saying this here? I suggest that in the context of this unit of thought (6:1-11), Paul concludes his argument about not going to court by reminding the believers that since they are freed from these vices they should not submit their disputes to those still under bondage to "injustice" (or "wrongdoing" or "unrighteousness"). That is to say, the vice lists illustrates the way of life followed by non-Christians from which Christians have been freed.

Let me repeat how this fits with my overall argument. I am seeking to follow a straightforward reading strategy, trying to discern the plain meaning of the text. I am also asking for clear biblical evidence that we have direct and obvious commands that would forbid same-sex covenanted partnerships among Christians. If the allusion to male/male sex in 1 Corinthians 6:9 is meant by Paul to illustrate the behavior of non-Christian judges and what some Christians *used to do* before they were justified, then it would not seem to count as a direct and obvious command speaking to Christian behavior.

(2) You suggest I inappropriately fit sexual immorality under the rubric of a "contemporary understanding of social justice." I am not sure what you mean by that phrase, but I think you seem to mean something quite different from what I mean by justice/injustice and what I think Paul means by *dikaisune/adikia*. In my question, I define injustice briefly as "a broad sense of social behavior that causes harm and in general undermines the well-being of the community." Justice, likewise, could be defined here "as social behavior that fosters the well-being of the community."

I don't see in this definition a sense that I am saying, as

you claim, that I believe that "any behavior to be wrong must be shown to show immediate and obvious harm (*immediate* and *obvious* are important here)." And I also don't see how this understanding of justice/injustice requires me to redefine each of the vices, as you assert.

What I am actually trying to do is understand how Paul himself uses these *dik-* terms. I understand Paul to be following in the tradition of the prophets and Jesus in centering his concern on relationships. These vices are problematic because of how they bring alienation to relationships. Paul's concern about sexual misconduct seems obviously to be a social issue for him because of the damage it does to people's relationships (which, of course, makes it an issue in their relationship with God). As with Jesus' great command that links love of God and love of neighbor, Paul's theological ethics do not separate religious and social nor personal and social.

Using "justice" as the root English word (cf. also "injustice," "unjust," "justification," et al.) seems best for translating all the *dik-* words. It conveys the sense that Paul has the same general set of concerns in mind whenever he uses such a word (a sense lost when we use such disparate English terms as "righteousness," "wickedness," "wrongdoing," "injustice," "justice," et al.). Plus, if we are careful to define justice in the biblical sense as I have tried to do (and not in the "contemporary" sense you project onto me), using it consistently might help protect us from religious/political and personal/social dualisms that are foreign to biblical thought.

(3) You suggest that I fail to recognize the clarity of meaning Paul had in mind in his use of malakos and *arsenokoitai* in his vice list in 6:9-11—that they refer to "active" and "passive" partners in male/male sex.

In your own comments, though, I actually see a sense that these words have uncertain meanings even as you are definite in what you say they do mean. You say, "the word [*malakos*] refers to 'soft' or 'effeminate' behavior and in some contexts refers to sexual behavior." So, you admit, in some contexts it does not refer to sexual behavior. And, as we see in Matthew 11:8 ("soft robes"), sometimes it simply means "soft" and does not refer to behavior at all.

Perhaps the meaning of *malakos* should be determined by the word that follows it (*arsenokoitai*) as you say, but why not the word before it ("adulterers")? There clearly is nothing intrinsic to the word itself that requires us to see it as referring to homosexuality. Your idea that *malakos* refers to "someone who is a passive partner is male same-sex behavior" is no more than speculation.[18]

With *arsenokoitai*, you acknowledge that "this word was very likely created either by a Hellenistic Jew or by Paul." My point would not be to deny that it is possible that Paul made up this word with the Septuagint rendering of Leviticus 18:22 in mind, only that we simply cannot know this because Paul never says and there are no other accounts of why this word was coined.

You are correct, of course, that this word "has to mean something." But that is scarcely evidence that its meaning is what you claim it *certainly* is. Nor do we in fact have much evidence to support your flat statement that "it was standard practice at the time of Paul for Jewish leaders to condemn homosexual practice." We have only scattered references to antipathy toward specific male behavior, inadequate support for generalizations about "standard practice" for an entire culture—and inadequate support for a comprehensive rejection of all possible same-sex intimate relationships.

(4) You suggest that I am being especially obtuse is resisting the clear stance of the Bible that "homosexual practice is wrong."

You conclude with a few comments that cast doubt on the legitimacy of my entire discussion. "What often seems to be accomplished by what . . . you [have] said is that doubts are raised [that would lead people to assume] there must be legitimate questions [concerning the scholarly consensus that the Bible unequivocally opposes all possible same-sex intimate partnerships.] But that doesn't mean [your] questions are legitimate. . . . I tend to think we would get farther if we simply stipulated that the Bible says homosexual practice is wrong. Then let's spend our time arguing about whether or not we still agree with that and why."

Perhaps you are correct in implying that I am completely off base when I try to develop arguments in favor of accepting the moral legitimacy of same-sex covenanted intimate partnership on biblical grounds. But I do not believe you have shown me *why* through a thorough response to the arguments I have articulated.

I sense that your assumptions about the clarity of the Bible's message concerning what you call "homosexual practice" are so powerful that you can't even imagine how anyone could successfully challenge that clarity. Hence, you don't seem to see a need to answer directly the arguments that do try to challenge that clarity.

However, as a person who still does doubt the certainty you and many others have about the Bible's teaching, I am not likely to accept your simply stipulating "that the Bible says homosexual practice is wrong" without much more of an explanation than what you have offered about why my counter-arguments are wrong.

Mark's Final Comment

Ted, again, thank you for your full and thoughtful responses and critiques. I really do believe that this exercise has some usefulness, I hope for others as well as ourselves. I will first respond by dealing with some of your critique of the details of my interpretation of 1 Corinthians 6:1-11. I will then offer some final reflections on some macro issues very much related to this passage and others.

First some comments on 6:1-11 as a unit. To begin with I don't think you have responded to my claim that really the overall unit of thought runs from chapter 5 through to the end of chapter 7. But then of course we can subdivide that further; most Bibles do. Most commentators I am aware of (and certainly the two I referenced) seem to follow more or less the route I took. That is to say, as I suggested with the use of the word "segue," in some ways of course there is a connection in chapter 6 between verses 1-8 and 9-11 (thus they are in that way functioning as a unit). "Wrongdoers" is the word that connects them. Then in verses 9 and 10 Paul names a variety of specific wrongdoers, i.e., unrighteous and unjust people. This list was intended to remind the Corinthians that they were not to be wrongdoers—because they were "washed," "sanctified" and "justified." So, just as verses 9-11 connect to the previous subunit of 1-8, they also point back to the end of chapter 5 and significantly connect all of this to themes announced at the beginning of the letter and named in various ways throughout the letter (written to those who are being saved, being sanctified).

However, I have questions about what you have attempted to do, through calling these verses a single unit. You seem to be attempting to homogenize the various terms in verses 9 and 10 so that they all mean what you mean by "justice." Most translators realize that's not what should be done. Thus they translate the general term as something like "wrongdoers," thereby allowing all of the specific terms (e.g., the sexually immoral, the idolaters, the greedy) to retain their particular and full meaning. Whether any particular term is then to be categorized under the label "unjust" or "unrighteous" requires discernment on the part of the translator to know which English word to employ where, to catch the specific moral and theological nuance.[19]

Next let me make a few more comments on my discussion of

the Greek terms for someone who practices same-sex sexual relations. You raise questions about the claim that "it was standard practice at the time of Paul for Jewish leaders to condemn homosexual practice."[20] You are quoting my quote from Richard Hays, a well-respected New Testament scholar at Duke Divinity School, a pacifist, and someone who has written several academic essays on the subject of homosexuality. Of course in looking at the ancient world we never have as much evidence as we might like. Partly because of that and partly because of other factors, any issue about which people disagree is debated. There is rarely a uniform opinion across the board. But I would invite those who are truly interested in the details to read several scholars on this question then discern for themselves the accuracy of what Hays says was the "standard practice."[21]

In a footnote you raise the question about how these two terms in this passage in 1 Corinthians relate to female homosexual practice. The simple answer is: they don't. I may have referred generically to homosexual practice, thinking that every reader could see by the specific terms involved that, of course, the references are to males. I apologize if I was not clear enough here. The issues addressed by specific letters of the New Testament were occasioned by the life of the congregations in question. We can only guess that the question of lesbianism, as with many other issues, either was not raised or for whatever reason was not addressed. But of course the matter of lesbian relations is addressed indirectly by Genesis and Jesus affirming marriage as between a man and a woman and directly by Paul in Romans 1.

Toward the end of your reflections you assert that my assumptions are so powerful that I can't really hear challenges put to these suppositions. I understand how it might sound like I begin with "assumptions." But I would suggest that there is a significant difference between *assumptions* and *conclusions*. Over a period of more than twenty-five years, having read, e.g., all of the literature I referenced on the two Greek words for men engaged in some form of same-sex behavior (and much else on that topic), I think I am warranted in having come to some conclusions. Because I continue to wrestle, I am genuinely open to new arguments that might name something important I have missed—or simply don't get. But there is nothing about your detailed discussions that is new in this sort of way. Most of it I have read numerous times. I am not beginning with assumptions; I am beginning this particular conversation with conclusions based upon extensive reading, conversations, and reflection.

Now let me once again attempt to name a set of macro issues that, seem to me, to skew your discussion of this set of concerns. They are intertwined issues, thus I will not attempt to discuss them separately. Moreover these are difficult to discuss because they are really related to so many other issues, which will have to be discussed elsewhere.

The first is justice. Let me make it clear: I am in favor of justice. What Christian who truly cared about being biblical wouldn't be concerned about justice? I have given much of my adult life to working on issues of peace and justice (six years professionally for a peace and justice organization I founded). Moreover, I continue to believe that caring for the poor and the marginalized within our Christian communities and the larger society is one of the vital issues of our day. Even so, I want to raise questions.

Does it not seem odd that each passage you deal with here in detail finally has the same message: pursue justice! Whether Leviticus 17–26, Romans 1 (or 1–3) or 1 Corinthians 6:1-11—they are a call to care for the marginalized or in other ways pursue justice. I would urge readers to read each of these passages, with a couple of commentaries to assist them: is this really the dominant (or only) message of these passages? Or is it true that there is an intermingling of a call to holiness, righteousness, justice, and worshipping the true God—with a number of specifics that simply must be named in their particularity, refusing to mute the complexity of what it means to be faithful to God as embodied people who are to live our lives within communities with a peculiar identity, communities that exist across time?

One issue here is that justice, though a vital Christian word, is also a slippery term. And yet a slippery term that is loaded with contemporary meaning for those who tend to agree with you or even care about peace and justice. Did the reader notice that you (and I) do not need to define justice. We all know what it means. But do we? Scott Bader-Saye is helpful here, when he says: "Absent any agreement about the substance of justice, the term comes to function like a cipher."[22] And function it does, in powerful ways.

But you see, biblically understood, justice is interchangeable with the word righteousness for a reason. Read through any careful Bible dictionary article on righteousness/justice and you will note the rich complexity.[23] One of the central points that most such articles will make is that the word for justice/righteousness fundamentally refers to our right relationship with God. This is huge, with profound implications! The fundamental meaning of this term is that we (the people of God) are to be faithful to God, to be holy, to be righteous.[24] Thus the first thing to note about justice is that whatever justice/righteousness refers to in terms of behavior it is defined by God. Righteousness begins with our right relationship with God. God then, in the context of our relationship with him, makes us into the people we are to be (sanctifies us, joins us to the covenantal people of God). Thus we are made righteous/just/holy. Then our knowledge of and relationship to God defines our identity as well as all of our relationships. Our relationships are to reflect our peculiar identity in the God and Father of our Lord Jesus Christ. And since they are "relationships" then of course our behavior toward others should reflect our just/righteous identities—and give witness to the God who has made us who we are.

If you (and the reader) have followed me to this point, do you see what you have done? You have made two important

interpretive moves. First, you have depended on the current connotations of the word *justice*. In doing so, you have implicitly
muffled or even silenced other meanings that the Scriptures give
to these words, meanings that appropriately enrich and complexify our moral and theological language, integrating it fully into
the whole of our life of faith and trust in God.

Related to this is that you have placed a distorting grid over
the whole of the Scriptural story. Hospitality (=inclusiveness)
and contemporary understandings of justice are used as all-
inclusive of the biblical message. That is what can lead you to
see justice as *the* message of Leviticus 17–26, Romans 1–3 and
1 Corinthians 6:1-11. It's why you see no tension between hospitality and holiness. One can test whether or not a particular
theme is broad and complex enough to be seen as a way to view
the whole of the rich and full biblical story.[25] But care needs to
be taken. Such an overarching scheme can easily be distorting.
I'm sure it is not your intention to distort, but I nonetheless
think it is the result of your approach.

Finally, this is one of my last (solo) comments in this book.
Let me end this by naming a few things I don't want to be
missed. First, I do not believe homosexuality is the most important issue facing Christians today.[26] Second, I care deeply that we
as Christians embrace the call to pursue justice, compassion, and
welcoming the stranger, especially those who are difficult for us.
Third, if we are to continue to call for sexual fidelity within the
church we must care for those who truly desire to be so committed but fail from time to time. Fourth, if we are to continue to
call for sexual fidelity within the church we must attend to the
relational needs of those who are single. Fifth, I believe we as a
church must love those among us who feel marginalized or even
sinned against by our moral positions. Sixth, though we must
speak the truth we must never forget that we must speak it in
love. Seventh, we must never forget our own fallibility; humility
is a virtue. This means, among other things, that we cannot sim-

ply silence voices who say we are wrong. Such voices must be allowed to speak into the process of discerning what the Spirit of God is saying to us today.[27]

---- Chapter 7 ----

Ted's Second Question
Why Is Same-Sex Intimacy Intrinsically Sinful?

Ted's Question

In your thinking, what precisely is it that makes same-sex sexual intimacy intrinsically sinful? That is, if you factor out elements that are also sinful for heterosexuals (e.g., adultery, promiscuity, coercion, physical harm), what is left that is sinful per se about the couple being gay?

Let me describe a scenario (which is largely based on a couple I know, though I do not know some of the intimate details of their particular relationship). Two women, both Christians, become friends and then fall in love with each other. They decide to become a couple and begin working with a minister on premarital counseling. Then they have a public union ceremony. Only then do they become fully sexually intimate. They live as a married couple, sharing life together, actively participating in a church, and remaining committed to monogamy. Their friends are enriched by the love they share with each other. Maybe at some point they even decide to have a child together, either through adoption or through one of them being "artificially" impregnated. What would you say is sinful about this relationship?

219

Mark's Answer

In some ways I have already answered this question at various points in my long essay. But since you did not see what I said as responding to this specific question, perhaps the reader doesn't either. So let me offer some direct comments.

The answer is simple in some ways. However, to unfold the details involves more than I can offer here. But let me attempt to begin an answer with two basic biblical and theological ways to frame it. The first would be to focus on our call to be holy—to live holy or sanctified lives. Holiness is, after all, the lens through which Leviticus and 1 Corinthians, and perhaps 1 Timothy, view behaviors and thus the lenses through which the opposite behaviors are considered unrighteous, unjust or unclean. I have already offered some reflections along these lines in my earlier comments on Leviticus (in my long essay). However, it would warrant further discussion.[1]

The other approach, the one I am elaborating on here, is to frame my comments around *shalom*. As Cornelius Plantinga Jr., says:

> The webbing together of God, humans, and all creation in justice, fulfillment, and delight is what the Hebrew prophets call *shalom*. . . . In the Bible, shalom means *universal flourishing, wholeness, and delight*—a rich state of affairs in which natural needs are satisfied and natural gifts fruitfully employed, a state of affairs that inspires joyful wonder as its Creator and Savior opens doors and welcomes the creatures in whom he delights. Shalom, in other words, is the way things ought to be.[2]

Shalom refers to all of life. However, in this case I simply mean to point to one way in which God intends to encourage human "flourishing, wholeness, and delight." Rooted in the creation passages in Genesis 1 and 2, and Jesus' affirmation of them, Christians have traditionally believed that marriage is one of the social institutions that is intended to facilitate flourishing, wholeness, and delight. In order for it to do that the specifics of marriage must be attended to: a male and female leaving their homes, publicly making a life-long promise to care for and love each other, giving birth to children, raising children within a nurturing environment, with the realization that everything is to be done for the glory and in the service of God.

Of course all of us know that none of this works out perfectly. We live in a fallen world. There are various ways in which the shalom of a family may be challenged—poverty, mental illness, infertility, the abuse of alcohol, domestic violence, adultery, or the birth of a child with disabilities, to name a few. All or any of these realities serve to "vandalize" the shalom of a family, and at least in some ways the larger society.[3] It also needs to be said that these forms of damage to wholeness and well-being are not alike. Each must be taken seriously. And each must be responded to appropriately and according to the ways in which it damages the wholeness of a family and society. This is complicated. Let us just say that all of these realities need to be named as vandalizers of shalom. Following that acknowledgment, and equipped with a rich understanding of sin, wisdom and discernment are required on the part of family members and others to know how to respond to the varying realities in ways that reaffirm our commitment to the gospel and, as much as possible, restore wholeness.[4]

What I would suggest is that, until recently, it was assumed that homosexual practice was also one of the violators of the flourishing and wholeness that God desires for us. After all, it was believed, all of the components of marriage need to be present for marriage to serve shalom in the ways intended. We cannot simply pick and choose. "Male and female God created them" is one of these necessary components for understanding what marriage is. This is not only what the Bible teaches. Christian and Jewish wisdom have continued to affirm this across the centuries almost uniformly from the time of Leviticus until just a few decades ago.

One of the reasons I have read widely on this subject over the years is I have entertained the thought that maybe the biblically rooted wisdom of the past on this subject is wrong. Maybe we truly do have new insights into homosexuality, bisexuality, and transgendered identities that should lead us to embrace new ways of living that truly do encourage flourishing and wholeness, not just for a particular set of two individuals but for families and society. This is what I've listened for as I've read and as I've had conversations. I have not been convinced. Moreover, as I've read and listened I continue to have profound theological problems with much of what I hear. Let me name simply a couple of these.

I really do believe that many today, including Christians, have a woefully inadequate understanding of sin. Especially in relation to sex, "sin" is often only connected to behaviors that obviously produce immediate or at least short-term harm. When you add this to the dominant individualism, too often underwritten by a therapeutic culture sometimes linked to cheap grace, then all that matters is an affirmation of individuals in their own behavior or, at best, a couple in theirs (if their behavior is not "harmful" to each other). That is what leads more than a few to have "justice-love" as their only substantive moral criterion for thinking about sexual ethics.[5]

Another persistent problem I see is Gnosticism or docetism—a denial of our basic human embodiedness. If we are to avoid this denial we must affirm the need for social structures and institutions that order our embodied, communal existence across generations and therefore across time. To avoid this denial we must attend to the particularities of being male and female.[6] To avoid this denial in relation to sex means that we have to respect the fact that sex was never meant to be "safe." As Kari Jenson Gold puts it, "Surely the words are ludicrously contradictory! Sex can be many things: dark, mysterious, passionate, wild, gentle, even reassuring, but it is not safe. If it is, it's not likely to be very sexy."[7] Marriage and the family are the primary ways we institutionalize our acknowledgment of the complex realities of our sexual, embodied, and communal existence across generations.

Let me pose a different scenario from the one you pose in your question, Ted, but similar in important ways. Like yours, mine is drawn from a couple I know, with a few details altered. A man and a woman are Christians actively participating in their church. They have lived together for over forty years but have never gotten formally married. In their state there is no such thing as common law marriage, so they are not legally married. Their relationship is exclusive in the same way a faithfully married couple's is. They have a mutual relationship in which they treat each other with care and respect. What would you say is sinful about this relationship? (One could easily pose a scenario related to the many who live together for some period of time before they are married. Stipulating that they are truly loving toward each other, the same question: what would you say is sinful about this relationship?)

For those who believe a biblically informed faith teaches that we should be married, the answer is obvious. They should be married. And following from this, one could argue that affirming their non-marital relationship undermines true marriage. But I've met many people (including Christians) over the years to whom this answer is not obvious. One could argue that someone who does not believe this needs to become a Christian or at least to be more seriously Christian so that the Scriptures would be authoritative. That may indeed be right. One can also attempt to give other practical reasons why marriage is important and even mandatory for Christians who don't want to be living in sin.

However, once you've begun to say this and act upon the implications, two things happen. First you offend those who think that there is nothing wrong with a couple simply living together, as long as they are truly loving toward each other. In fact, you may be accused of being a sinner yourself for not being loving, affirming, inclusive, etc. Second, to make an argument to the contrary you have to name ways in which the institution of marriage, with its particularities, is important as a way of regulating sexual relationships, structuring the commitments of couples and caring for children. Then we are back where I began.

That is to say we are back to shalom. From my perspective shalom—flourishing, wholeness, and delight—is rooted in who God is and who God desires us to be, as biblically understood. Thus in relation to marriage and the family we seek to understand what this means through serious, reflective and theologically informed biblical study.

After much study I have come to reaffirm the traditional view that the affirmation of marriage and family—and God's desire to use them for our flourishing and well-being—requires that I say that it is destructive of this well-being formally to affirm homosexual practice through institutionalizing it in a newly defined "marriage" and reconfigured "families." For those who are unconvinced by the Bible, more and more studies are being done to show specifically how formally affirming gay and lesbian relationships is destructive to our social existence, a vandalism of shalom.[8]

Having decided this does not make life easy. Not if we believe in God, the God made flesh in Jesus Christ, rather than an ideology. We still must love couples who are cohabitating without being married. We must love gays and lesbians who believe the stance of the church is wrong. We also must continue to affirm the identity of the church called to live faithfully, knowing our failings. And we must affirm the biblical understanding of marriage and the family, acknowledging our failings here too.

Ted's Follow-up

Mark, I appreciate your thoughts in response to my question about what is sinful per se about the fact that my friends are both women. However, I did not find in your comments a clear and direct answer. You did say several things that are worthy of further reflection, though.

You mention as one way to respond to my question the centrality of our call as Christians to live holy, or sanctified, lives. Of course, I agree. But my question remains. What specifically is "unholy" about my friends' relationship? In every observable sense they *are* holy in how they live. Their relationship is characterized by grace, beauty, and mutual up-building; they have worship of God and commitment to Jesus as central in their lives; they do many works of service and compassion. So, *why* is simply the fact that they are both women enough to condemn their relationship?

You emphasize more the theme of "flourishing" (shalom) and the problem of sin as a "vandalizing of shalom." You state that marriage is a crucial, God-established means of facilitating human flourishing. I agree, and so do David Myers, Letha Scanzoni, and William Stacy Johnson in their important books supporting same-sex marriage. I also basically agree with your description of the key elements that constitute the marriage ideal. So I don't see that the partners being of the same sex intrinsically vandalizes the flourishing marriage intends to facilitate. I see, in fact, in a number of same-sex couples I know, genuine flourishing, including in a few cases the nurturing of children.

However, I don't think this statement you make is fully warranted: "It was believed that *all* of the components of marriage need to be present for marriage to serve shalom in the ways intended" (emphasis added). An obvious exception is the presence of children. Certainly today, we would agree that heterosexual couples that remain childless still may serve shalom. Many Christians would also agree that people who are divorced and remarried may still serve shalom even if they were not in their first marriages able to sustain the life-long promise. So we do have precedents for a bit more flexibility in how we think of marriage in the context of shalom.

We need to ask what the broader purposes are that marriage serves. Why is it so important? The central purposes may include, among others, providing a context for the deepest expressions of love, joy, and intimacy with another human being; the nurture of children; providing stability and the basic building blocks for human community; and discipline for fidelity and resistance to the terrible problems caused by adultery and promiscuity.

Are any of these broader purposes not possible to be met in same-sex marriages? I don't see why not. You ask if there are "new ways of living that truly do encourage flourishing and wholeness" in reference to same-sex partnerships. Leaving aside the question of how "new" such partnerships actually are, I would just say that the answer must certainly be yes—proven by the actual existence of such partnerships. I referred a real couple in my original question. Roberta Showalter Kreider's book, *Together in Love*, contains numerous stories of others.

You write of the "need for social structures and institutions that order our embodied, communal existence across generations, and therefore across time. . . . Marriage and the family are the primary ways we institutionalize our acknowledgment of the complex realities of our sexual, embodied and communal existence across generations." As I have written above, I basically agree with this understanding of the importance of marriage. However, I suggest that this view of marriage actually should lead us to *affirm* same-sex marriage. There is no reason why the value of the continuity provided by marriage would not apply to same-sex couples too.

I am not sure what you mean when you write of the "particularities of being male and female." I am uncomfortable with being too essentialist concerning gender identity, though. If we reject the view that sees homosexuality as simply a matter of genetic determinism, we should also recognize the same about heterosexuality. Various human beings have a spectrum of sexual identities. We do not all fit into neat little slots of either maleness or femaleness, clearly distinct from each other. Regardless of how we understand gender, though, my main point here would be to say we need also to think about exceptions, those who are unable to flourish in opposite-sex partnerships.

I do not find your scenario of the cohabitating couple particularly illuminating. I agree that, all things considered, they are wrong not to be married. However, the crucial difference between your scenario and the one I offered in raising my original question is that for some reason your couple does not affirm marriage as the appropriate context for their sexual relationship whereas my friends emphatically do.

Your use of the term "homosexual practice" (note the singular) in your conclusion (and throughout this book) implies a problematic double standard. You seem to say that for our moral discernment there is only one meaningful category of sexual behavior for same-sex couples, whereas we all recognize numerous distinct categories of sexual behavior for heterosexual couples—some morally appropriate and others not.

I will grant that there are sexual practices that involve same-sex couples that "vandalize shalom" (just as do some opposite-sex practices). However, I fail to see how this supports the conclusion that all same-sex relationships should be opposed—just as the existence of heterosexual practices that vandalize shalom does not lead us to conclude all opposite-sex relationships should be opposed.

I think we should follow the same strategy in relation to same-sex behavior as we do with opposite-sex behavior. We differentiate between shalom-enhancing and shalom-vandalizing practices, seeking to empower people to engage in the former and to discourage people from engaging in the latter.

If there are some understandings of same-sex marriage and families that are destructive of human well-being—as there well may be, parallel to problematic understandings of opposite-sex marriage and families—we should seek to make the case for understandings that enhance well-being, just as we do with opposite-sex relationships.

Mark's Final Comments

If any of this discussion has been hard (and it has been) this is perhaps the hardest for me. That is partly because I am convinced once again, through this discussion, that there are what I have referred to as "macro" issues that are shaping our disagreement more than the details of how we read a handful of texts. And these macro issues are difficult to name in a way that sheds light on our subject. It requires on the one hand adequately naming a large, complicated subject, and on the other sufficiently specifying how that subject relates to the matter at hand. Let me try, one last time, to name what I think needs to be named.

To remind the reader, your initial question was: "In your thinking, what precisely is it that makes same-sex sexual intimacy intrinsically sinful? That is, if you factor out elements that are also sinful for heterosexuals (e.g., adultery, promiscuity, coercion, physical harm), what is left that is sinful per se about the couple being gay?"

Let me also remind the reader what you have not made explicit. You did not say: "If you eliminate the fact that for almost two thousand years Christianity has understood the biblical texts on marriage and homosexual practice to prohibit all homosexual relationships, then what makes these relationships inherently sinful?" You are not convinced that the biblical texts mean what I (and two thousand years of church history) say they mean.[9] Thus you have eliminated that as a justification for why homosexual practice is wrong. And thus through this maneuver you have shifted the burden of proof. Having made that unstated move, you then pose the challenge: try to show me and others who more or less agree with me why it is that God would say loving, committed same-sex relationships are wrong. What is it that makes them wrong? You then reply to my more than five-page response by saying: "I did not find in your comments a clear and direct answer."

What I did not provide, I hope, is a simplistic response to your question. And I did not name some of the specifics I had named in earlier essays. If one re-reads my reflections on the various passages of Scripture that relate directly to gays and lesbians—including the way in which I connect Romans 1 to my discussion of facts in the last main section of my long essay—one can get a fuller picture of my thinking about sin. But in my response to your question, I certainly was attempting to answer the question.

On the one hand, I take the same approach as you do. That is, this is fundamentally about the Scriptures (including our Lord) defining what marriage is; our violation of that is sin (then believing you are wrong in saying that the one component—being male and female—is optional).[10]

It is when someone is not swayed by the biblical and traditional understanding of marriage and the related prohibition against homosexual relationships that a person has to try to answer the "why" question that you asked. *Why* is this behavior sinful? The approach I elected to take was to focus on shalom and its violation because it seemed appropriate. Perhaps I was not as clear as I should have been in what I said. I am certainly aware that I did not go into detail about the specifics related to homosexual practice that would suggest a "violation of shalom" (and would suggest its relevance even in relation to those who want to be "married" as gays or lesbians).

The challenge is that only if one is willing to look at the relatively substantial evidence that gay and lesbian sexual relationships do violate shalom does one know what I am really referring to. I allude to these matters in the last section of my long essay. I did not want to repeat all of that. But even there I did not go into gory detail. If I may be so bold, I would suggest that a Christian who is going against two thousand years of Christian tradition should feel compelled at least to read some of the basic writings regarding these matters, being open to be challenged by data that seek to confirm the traditional Christian wisdom regarding these matters.[11]

One of the things I am aware of as I speak of shalom, of social structures and even more of the detailed data, is that it is very tempting to over-personalize this issue. I don't know whether this is a peculiarly American temptation. But it has seemed to me it may be. My wife and I were living in London, England, on September 11, 2001. When we returned to the United States, I was struck by the way detailed news reports were often given about the events of September 11, 2001. More often than not the focus was on hurting individuals—victims of the tragedy, family members who continue to suffer.

Now of course we must know the very human and personal face of tragedies. It is an important and relevant component of the whole picture. However, it seems to me the over-emphasis on this can also be distorting. The personalizing of "9/11" emotionalizes the event and thus resonates with our present belief system at an emotional level.[12] Again, this is a part of the whole. But only a part. The emotions can easily be tied to freedom, democracy, and the American way—to a renewed national identity, patriotism, and nationalism. However, adequately to evaluate 9/11 is to ask difficult questions regarding foreign policies, Islam, what causes terrorists to be terrorists, these particular targets in this particular country, etc. To answer such questions adequately is complex. It cannot happen simply through the provision of moving individual stories of an American tragedy.

Likewise, I want everyone—everyone!—to think about gay and lesbian issues with real gay and lesbian people in mind. I want Christians to personalize this set of issues. But, having said that, personalizing is insufficient by itself. It is not enough to know some lovely gay and lesbian individuals or couples. It is not enough to know the pain they feel from being excluded from marriage. We must ask tough questions related to the issues I named toward the end of my main essay. This is not nearly as easy or as pleasant as simply having warm relationships and offering an affirmation of people. No, it is the hard, necessary work that acknowledges the complexities of sex, gender, and child rearing—and the need for certain social structures, rather than others, to shape our identities.

Let me offer a few related comments about cohabitation. Since cohabitation before marriage is becoming more and more common, many of us know people who have cohabitated. Partly because I grew up in a non-Christian environment, I have known many cohabitating couples since I was a child. And of course as individuals and as couples these people vary. Some are wonderful and treat each other respectfully and lovingly, and others do not. However, if one is to give a rationale for why such cohabitation is wrong (beyond simply saying it is unbiblical or not marriage) then one will have to make an argument that is formally similar to mine, though of course differing in some of the particulars. But how does one really demonstrate (to those not inclined to be convinced) that cohabitating, without the benefit of marriage, is inherently destructive?

What gives the church the right to tell a cohabitating couple who, in a particular instance are caring of and faithful to each other, that what they are doing is inherently sinful? How can we say that their relationship is vandalizing shalom? I could tick off perhaps a list of five or six authors who have attempted to show through extensive study why cohabitation is really destructive, not necessarily of the two individuals involved, but societally. However, serious, quality studies, as far as I can remember, didn't really start to emerge until sometime in the 1990s, even though arguments for cohabitating began to become "mainstream" in the 1960s. After all, these are complicated matters; collecting data and evaluating them over an adequate amount of time is challenging.

In an earlier discussion you addressed cohabitation briefly. I agreed with what you said. I wonder if you would go further? Would you agree with what I've said in the last paragraph? I get mixed signals from you. Note what else you said in your initial question: "That is, if you factor out elements that are also sinful for heterosexuals (e.g. adultery, promiscuity, coercion, physical harm), what is left that is sinful per se about the couple being gay?" Let me acknowledge that you are signaling that your list is only a set of examples ("e.g."). But my guess is the items listed are not arbitrarily chosen. It should be noted that nothing on this list pertains to a loving, respectful, committed couple who are cohabitating. What this list suggests is that your functional definition of sin is what I had named earlier: that which causes fairly immediate and obvious harm to the individuals or couple in question. Thus you said about my earlier response: "I did not find in your comments a clear and direct answer." What you did not find was a set of reflections regarding how the particular lesbian couple harmed each other. But one of my points is that this is about more than an individual or a couple—it is about the shalom that God desires for us as a community.[13]

I hope it is obvious to the attentive reader that there are what I have referred to as "macro issues" involved here. I have discerned at least four troublesome macro questions related to what you have written throughout this book: (1) Is hospitality/inclusiveness a legitimate term for interpreting the biblical story as a whole? Or is it in fact distorting of a rich and full biblical theology if it is placed in that role? (2) Is it legitimate to say that "justice" as you use it can assume the redefining role you have given to it? Or do we need additional words—such as holiness, sanctification, righteousness, and faithfulness—that might add vital theological and ethical nuances to our discussion and thereby appropriately complexify our understanding of what it means for us to live moral lives? (3) Is sin a more complex and multi-layered word than the way in which you have seemed to employ it in our discussions?

(4) Does a subject like sex require a certain sort of treatment because of the way in which it is integrated into our very being? Is this why sexual immorality is such a prominent topic in the New Testament? And is it the case that much of our writing that ignores these realities is Gnostic or docetic—mostly ignoring our embodiedness, our particularities as males and females and therefore our need for morals tied to social structures regulating behaviors across time?[14]

I agonize every time I write on or speak publicly on this issue. That is for at least two reasons. First, I believe that large issues, like the ones I've named in the last paragraph, are as important as the particulars of specific texts. These are difficult to name and difficult to discuss. But they are vitally related to our ongoing faithfulness as the people of God. And, second, I know that more than a few believe that in continuing to call the church to hold to the traditional view on this issue I am calling on the church to continue to hurt people, to sin! I feel the sting of the accusation. I continue to listen. Because I know that I am fallible and because I believe a living God is Lord, I am aware that I may be wrong. We need continued discernment. But until I am convinced that the Spirit of God is clearly speaking on this issue—in apparent contradiction of biblical texts—then I will continue to issue the call. To be convincing an argument needs to reflect a full, rich biblically rooted theology and ethic rather than mostly reflect the current moral and sexual zeitgeist.[15]

I have tried to be honest in this book. I have tried to be as clear as I could be about the place where I find myself in relation to this set of issues. Because I believe I am called to be a teacher within the church, I ask that the church seriously consider what I have offered here. I have also decided, in relation to the present contentious discussions within the church, to offer my considered position in the context of a discussion/debate with a respected colleague and friend who differs. I appreciate your candor, frankness, thoughtfulness and vulnerability. I have learned from you. I hope our discussion will serve the ongoing discernment within the church regarding these matters that matter.

Chapter 8

Mark's Second Question
How Do You Understand Core Theological Themes?

Mark's Question

Here is another question on a macro level. I realize that I have made some relatively critical comments about your understanding of hospitality and, by implication, how your understanding of hospitality connects with your understanding of other moral and theological issues. You said some things about these matters in your response essay. But could you begin to name the elements of what you see as a full biblical and theological understanding of the following: justice/righteousness, faith/trust/faithfulness, holiness, sanctification (as these relate to salvation, redemption, repentance, the Christian community)? I say "name the elements" intentionally because I know these are all huge issues. But I wanted to give you an opportunity to clarify what you mean in ways that might challenge my readings of what you've said.

Ted's Answer

Again, I note that we apparently disagree as to the importance of these "macro" issues in relation to the subject at hand. I would need to know more about your specific views on "justice/righteousness, faith/trust/faithfulness, holiness, sanctification (as these relate to salvation, redemption, repentance, the Christian community)" to be certain, but I suspect that whatever differences we might have concerning these themes would provide no intrinsic reasons to disagree on issues concerning the place of gays in the churches.

That is, I am pretty convinced that one could have a "strict" or "conservative" or "traditional" view of the importance of purity and the need to be clear in opposing sin, et al., and still support same-sex marriage.

I have argued throughout my essays that I believe supporters of same-sex marriage in the churches do not have to base their position on a lessening of the rigor of Christian ethical standards. In fact, it is *because* of my desire to be ethically rigorous, faithful to God's revealed will through Torah, Jesus' message, and the rest of the Bible, that I believe in inclusiveness. What makes same-sex marriage morally acceptable is that the Bible establishes a benefit of the doubt in favor of hospitality toward vulnerable people (such as present-day gays and lesbians), affirms the value of monogamous life-long marriage partnerships, and provides no clear reasons to disqualify same-sex couples from the blessings and responsibilities of the marriage covenant.

So the sin issue in relation to the argument I develop is not whether we should be strict in opposing sin. My position easily allows for a very strict stance. Taking an inclusive stance concerning gay marriage while still holding to high ethical standards concerning sex outside of marriage seems totally consistent to me. The sin issue in my argument is whether we define gay marriage as intrinsically sinful. In my long essay, I have presented an argument for why we should not. This is not in any sense an argument to weaken the churches' opposition to sinful behavior.

I personally have what I would call a strongly relational view of important biblical themes such as justice, faith, holiness, and sanctification (and, for that matter, of sin and injustice as well).

However, I don't see this relational view as necessary for a person to accept my argument concerning the churches taking an inclusive as opposed to restrictive stance (and please remember that I do not accept your portrayal of my use of the motif of inclusiveness). A person could have a more command-oriented and strict purity view in relation to these themes and still accept my general argument. This is so because I argue that same-sex marriage does not, simply by the fact that it is same-sex, violate any of the Bible's commands or lessen the Bible's high standards for moral purity.

I can't image how you could define justice/righteousness, et al., in ways that would undercut the argument I have actually made (in distinction from the argument you at times seem to project on me). To answer your question nonetheless…. Because I think about themes of "justice/righteousness, faith/trust/faithfulness, holiness, sanctification" relationally, I believe that the God of the Bible is profoundly interested in whole relationships.

In the biblical story, God's response to human rejection was grief and a resolve to restore these broken relationships through persevering love. Justice has to do with restoring to wholeness that which has been broken. Holiness is the involvement of God in cleansing rebellious human beings of our corruption, if we will let God do this. I understand the Greek word *pistis* as having a rich meaning that includes trust and faithfulness. To have "faith" in the biblical sense is to trust in God as the object of worship, to turn from idolatry and sin, and to live faithfully in response to the commands of God that are given as part of God merciful healing initiative. A faithful, holy, and just person believes in God, repents of one's sin, turns from idols, accepts God's forgiveness with gratitude, and responds to God's generosity and justice by living with generosity and justice in relationship to other people.

In my book, *God's Healing Strategy*, I present God's "strategy" of blessing all the families of the earth through the witness of Abraham's descendants as a central rubric in the Bible. "Healing," of course, implies that something is wrong that needs transformation. That is, I read the Bible as containing a message of sharp critique of the human condition, a call to repentance/turning to God, and a call to transformative/restorative justice that manifests God's holiness as a disposition to heal that which has been damaged—in the human heart and in human societies.

Gay people are no different than non-gay people—we all need to trust, to respond with faithfulness, to imitate Jesus' way of the cross. "Living under the power of sin" is a tragedy for everyone who does so—and we all need to be cleansed of our sin and freed from idolatry by our trust in God's mercy expressed in Jesus' life, death, and resurrection—gays, as gays, no more or less than anyone else.

I believe the issue to be this: for gays, would their marrying a person of the same sex itself be a cause for alienation with God? I would say no, not because I don't think genuine sin (wickedness, idolatry, injustice) leads to alienation with God. All people who live in sin will alienate themselves from God and make themselves subject to God's wrath. A gay person who worships the nation-state, who oppresses other people, who is greedy, who lives in bondage to sexual promiscuity, will be alienated from God—in the same way a straight person would be. However, this alienation will have nothing to do with that person being gay or being married to a person of the same sex.

The importance of hospitality with regard to my argument concerning same-sex intimate relationships does not arise as a means to weaken the church's standards concerning sin and sexual impurity. I do *not* accept a counter-posing of hospitality (and inclusiveness) vs. holiness (and high standards of ethical behavior).

Rather, the place of hospitality in this constellation of biblical themes is that it goes hand-in-glove with justice/holiness/faithfulness. We see a clear expression of this in Leviticus 19, where at the heart of the holiness code holiness itself is presented in terms of offering caring attention to vulnerable people in the community (widows, orphans, resident aliens).

I understand gay and lesbian people in our society to be a present-day example of vulnerable people—all too often treated disrespectfully, even violently. The call to hospitality is a call to reach out with care to these vulnerable ones. Such care does not imply a lessening of our core moral imperatives concerning values such as sexual purity. However, I am suggesting, we should take care to make sure we have clear and strong bases for, amidst our care, drawing a line that would restrict the involvement of these vulnerable people in our faith communities.

As an expression of our commitment to living in harmony with our justice-seeking, holy God, we seek to imitate Jesus' style of welcome. Jesus differentiated between "sinners" such as, on the one hand, the woman caught in adultery who was both forgiven and challenged by Jesus to change her ways and, on the other hand, poor or ill people who were declared unclean due to the cultural biases of the religious institutions and offered unconditional welcome by Jesus. These latter cases of welcome by Jesus did not signal a weakening in his commitment to holiness; in fact, they were expressions of such a commitment.

If it turns out that we do not have clear, strong biblical and theological bases for taking a restrictive stance toward same-sex couples (which is what I have tried to show is the case), we are upholding the biblical call to holiness and righteousness when we offer welcome to these couples—and hold all accountable to our shared calling to ethical rigor and faithfulness.

Mark's Follow up

Thank you, Ted, for your thoughtful responses to my questions about very large issues. I will only make a few comments here and continue my conversation in response to your comments on my reflections on 1 Corinthians 6:1-11, since you raise some of the same questions there. I don't want to be any more repetitive than necessary. But I do want to offer some response here in order to prod you to say more.

You have said several times that you have a "relational" view of the terms I've asked about. All of these terms are relational, of course. But they are not only about our relationships with each other. Biblically understood these terms are all fundamentally rooted in who God is and therefore our relationships with God. Thus the richness and complexity of the terms, taken together, name both who God is and who God makes us to be as the people of God. Of course that necessarily includes our relationship with each other within our community and those outside the Christian community. Then, it seems to me, the trick is to realize not only that these two—our relationship with God and with each other—must be held together but also that one cannot simply be collapsed into the other. Moreover, we need to realize the perennial temptation to do precisely that.

I just re-read several long dictionary articles on righteousness.[1] Emerging from these essays I was reminded of why Bible translators elect not to do what you suggest in another of our discussions in this book, namely always to translate the Greek New Testament words that have *dik* as a root with a form of the word just (i.e. just/justice/unjust/injustice/justification; rather than these words plus righteous/righteousness/unrighteous/wrong-doing/wrongdoers, etc.). What most translators realize is that there are various theological and ethical nuances that would be lost both in the world of the New Testament as well as our English-speaking world if we only used the "justice" related words to translate the various Greek words derived from the *dik* root (related to but also going beyond what I named in the previous paragraph).

Another related topic is your statement: "I do not accept a counter-posing of hospitality (and inclusiveness) vs. holiness (and high standards of ethical behavior)." Of course these are not generally oppositional terms. And we are always called to live into both. However, do you never see these in tension? Most obviously, biblically, I would point to the books of Leviticus and Deuteronomy as naming the tensions between the two. Elsewhere in our discussions here I have referred to 1 Corinthians 5:1-13; that passage suggests the tension (especially in the context of the whole of 1 Corinthians). But really anytime we realize that our Lord calls us as a community to holiness and then includes within that call the call to be welcoming, there is the possibility of tension between the two.

Earlier I mentioned my friend who is sexually addicted. This man has also been married five times and is presently married. If this man were a part of your congregation how would you simultaneously call this man to live a holy life while welcoming him? Would your call to holiness always seem like "welcome" to him? Or would your warm embrace, your "welcome" always be a call to true holiness? If one attempts to think through the particulars, complexities and tensions arise. I think in real life, if we truly care about both holiness and hospitality, we have a significant challenge on our hands.

I hope the reader will recognize that what I have been saying is parallel, in significant ways, to what I said in the first section of my longer essay on the double-love command. The issues are related of course. I do not question your motives. And let me say again that I am well aware that these are genuinely complicated issues. Maybe I have misunderstood you. But I fear that you have done what I name in the second section of my longer essay. Which is another way of saying that I continue to believe that there are macro issues involved here, issues that matter in how we interpret specific texts and how we see those texts related to the whole (as well as defining that "whole").

Ted's Final Comments

Mark, thanks for the "prod … to say more"!

When I say that my understanding of justice, righteousness, faith, holiness, et al., is relational, I do not say that this is about "only our relationships with each other." I present the relational dynamic holistically. For example, this is what I wrote above: "A faithful, holy, and just person believes in God, repents of one's sin, turns from idols, accepts God's forgiveness with gratitude, and responds to God's generosity and justice by living with generosity and justice in relationship to other people."

It seems to me that you distort my argument by implying that, with regard to our relationship with God and with each other, I "collapse one into the other." I wonder if maybe only a person who is inclined to *separate* these two types of relationships in order to relativize our calling to practice justice, generosity, and hospitality would perceive my comments as collapsing these two relationships into one.

My main reason for wanting to be consistent in using forms of the word "just" in translating New Testament *dik* words is, as I said, to make it clear that all of these *dik* words are closely related. When we do this, we need to be clear that we are using "justice," et al., in their biblical sense, not the modern, Western sense. Our goal should be to let the biblical meaning of the various terms come through as clearly as possible, which doesn't happen, I fear, when we use disparate terms in our translations.

That the two dictionaries you consulted privilege righteousness over justice surely reflects their own theological and ethical biases. I tend to suspect these biases reflect the long tendency of wealthy, comfortable, and nationalistic Christians to rest comfortably with biblical interpretations that powerfully mute the prophetic and messianic call to transformative justice (cf. Micah 6:8 and Matthew 5:6) and underwrite a sense that biblical faith is mostly concerned with "pie in the sky bye and bye."

We are finite human beings with our own anxieties and

blind spots, and our faith communities can't help but be imperfect, manifesting all too many of these anxieties and blinds spots (often even exacerbating them). Therefore, in practice certainly we will typically have a hard time holding holiness and hospitality together. However, we too easily succumb to the tendency to underwrite these human weaknesses with our theology.

Theologically, I believe it is essential to affirm the biblical picture that God's hospitality is a manifestation of God's holiness. If we take Jesus as our normative revelation of God, we must recognize that it was *because* Jesus was holy (as the Father is holy) that he forgave sins as a means of empowering people to become more godly. It was because Jesus was holy that he unconditionally forgave the "woman in the city, who was a sinner" who washed his feet (Luke 7:36-50).

I will close by suggesting that we will (at this point) simply have to agree to disagree that there is a necessary link between your macro issues and my argument for inclusivity. I will repeat one last time that those who believe that same-sex covenanted intimate partnerships are *not* inherently sinful do not need a weaker view of sin in order to maintain their inclusive stance.

While I grant that you and I do apparently disagree on some of your macro issues, I am convinced that a person could agree with each general point you make about holiness, righteousness, and sin and still be inclusive. I know quite a few who do and who are.

PART 4:
CLOSING MATERIALS

Chapter 9

Naming the Common Ground

We have found through the course of this conversation significant points of agreement even as we have continued to disagree in crucial ways. In this concluding chapter we want to name some of these points of agreement so that these aren't lost in the midst of our naming the disagreements.

In some ways, Ted considers himself to be on the "right wing" of the inclusive side because of his commitment to working with the Bible and his affirmation of very high standards for sexual behavior and the affirming of committed, monogamous relationships. Mark likewise sees himself to be on the "left wing" of the traditional side given his commitment to genuine conversation regarding differences, his concern that the churches not act too quickly to silence dissidents on these issues, and his deep concern for gay and lesbian people as people. Both of us, however, would also tend to challenge the "right wing" and "left wing" images. Each sees himself as simply trying to be faithful to the biblical witness.

We would like to conclude by naming six points of agreement.

(1) **Centrality of the Bible.** We both seek to ground our ethical understandings in the Bible. We both understand ourselves as Christian theologians who, in our methodology give the Bible clear priority over creeds, traditions, experience, and reason when drawing on all these sources for Christian theological and ethical discernment. We both understand ourselves to be doing theological ethics after our teacher, John Howard Yoder.

And we both read the message of the Bible as being best, and most succinctly, summarized in Jesus' call on his followers to love God and to love neighbor as a summary of the law and prophets. We do differ in how we read and apply certain parts of the Bible, but this difference sits within the commonality of affirming the centrality of the Bible and of following very similar reading strategies (at least in theory) in how we approach the Bible.

We agree that the Old Testament Law (Torah), including the holiness code in Leviticus, contains extremely important guidance that Christians should seek to follow, given that Jesus obviously understood his message to be upholding Torah. We agree in seeing Jesus as the heart of the Bible, the source of our most normative guidance for life and faith. We agree in valuing Paul as our most important Christian theologian and interpreter of Jesus. Where we disagree, it seems, is *how* we interpret these three central sources—not in seeing them as central, nor even in how we prioritize them.

(2) **The importance of care and respect for vulnerable people.** We agree that Torah issues an unavoidable call for the people of God to care for the vulnerable people in its midst (widows, orphans, non-Israelites); that the prophets spoke sharp words of rebuke toward the community when vulnerable people were treated violently; and that Jesus' ministry embodied and articulated a special concern for vulnerable people—including those who are mistreated and people who were labeled "sinners" by the community.

We both strongly oppose homophobic violence and scapegoating. We also agree that throughout Christian history, including in the present, there have been those who identify themselves as Christians who have treated gay and lesbian people harshly. Such behavior must be named for what it is: sin. Moreover, given that we are always to care for those who are vulnerable among us, we must do so with gays and lesbians who are among the vulnerable. We do differ, it seems, in how much weight we put on this concern for vulnerable people in relation to other ethical concerns—but we do agree that it is important.

(3) **Affirmation of marriage as the only morally valid context for sexual intercourse.** We agree that sexual expression is a powerful, morally significant part of our lives. Our sexual practices are not to be treated casually. We agree that the Bible is ultimately clear that God's will for human beings is that the deepest expressions of sexual intimacy require profound commitment between partners (i.e., marriage). We agree that marriage is formally and publicly committed and covenanted, accountable to the community, and is blessed by God.

We agree that churches have the calling to support intimate relationships—to hold us all accountable to the commitments we make to fidelity, mutuality, honesty, and nurture in our marriages; and to provide encouragement, hopefulness, and positive role models that may help all of us to experience the joys and opportunities for spiritual and emotional growth that committed relationships provide.

We agree that, for most human beings, we thrive best when we can experience healthy marriages—sharing our lives with intimate others, including support for child-rearing. The churches, again, should nurture and support our efforts to live faithfully in our families.

Obviously we differ in whether or not we believe marriages should be limited only to heterosexual people. But we do essentially agree on what we understand marriage to entail for those joined together and that sexual intercourse outside of marriage is not morally acceptable.

(4) **Social constructivism.** We both believe that the dynamics that shape our sexual identities and practices are very complex and, still to a large extent, beyond our ability fully to understand. Along with recognizing these complexities, we both reject a kind of genetic or biological determinism that would assert that our sexual identities are set in concrete by our genes and that that determines our behavior.

That is to say, we are both in some sense "social constructivists" (affirming that to some extent our identities and therefore our behaviors are the product of our social environments). Then there are, within the agreement, somewhat different understandings of the significance of social constructivism.

For Ted, one consequence of the social constructivist perspective is to affirm that we each ultimately are responsible for our behaviors; that we have choices; and that certain choices may indeed be understood as sinful. None of us are required by genetics or biology in general to sin.

For Mark, our biological makeup resides within basically three social environments. First, there is the body. Second, there is the immediate social environment—the family, most fundamentally. Third, there are the various larger social environments (church, school, various subcultures, society as a whole). All of these interact with our biological makeup in complex ways to determine what characteristics within that makeup will be expressed. Two important things follow from this understanding. First, our social environments are partly responsible for who we become. Second, the whole concept of "choice" is thus problemetized. Which is not to say that choice is a meaningless concept, only that it acquires a fuller and more complex meaning.

Thus you can see the disagreement within the broad agreement. But we don't disagree in understanding sexual identity to be complex and, at least for many people, somewhat plastic and, even more, in understanding human behavior to be a matter that we all can and must take responsibility for.

(5) **Oppose a double standard in the churches with regard to the sexual sins of heterosexuals and gays.** We agree that the churches should not single out gays. Infidelity and impermanence in marriage are major problems for *heterosexual* Christians. We both believe that it is inappropriate to minimize those heterosexual problems in focusing more on same-sex issues as the locus for concerns regarding sexual misbehavior.

(6) **Welcome gay, lesbian, bi-sexual and transgendered people into our lives and into our churches.** Both of us believe

our lives and our churches should be expressions of hospitality. For both of us this certainly includes gays, lesbians, bisexual and transgendered people. We are both aware that our "welcome" will not be seen as welcoming by some. For Mark that is because he thinks sexual intercourse is intended only for a man and a woman who are married. And for Ted this is because he believes sexual intercourse is intended only for those who are married (gay, lesbian or straight).

Chapter 10

Ted's Annotated Bibliography

Over the past twenty years or so, I have steadily read theological literature relevant to the discussion among Christians concerning homosexuality in our churches and society. What follows is a list, with some comments, of twenty of the books that I have found most helpful—and that I would recommend to others.

Balch, David L., ed. *Homosexuality, Science, and the "Plain Sense" of Scripture*. Grand Rapids, MI: Eerdmans, 2000. An important collection of essays reflecting many of the scholarly debates among Christian theologians from various places on the spectrum.

Crompton, Louis. *Homosexuality and Civilization*. Cambridge, MA: Harvard University Press, 2003. A helpful and thorough historical survey of the treatment of gay people in Western culture. The writer is himself a gay man.

Edwards, George R. *Gay/Lesbian Liberation: A Biblical Perspective*. New York: The Pilgrim Press, 1984. Though the scholarship is now a bit dated, this is an important scholarly biblical and theological argument in favor of inclusion from a Presbyterian New Testament professor deeply informed by pacifist and liberation theology.

Gagnon, Robert A. J. *The Bible and Homosexual Practice: Texts and Hermeneutics*. Nashville: Abingdon Press, 2001. A massive and influential detailed examination of biblical themes. Could be read as lacking objectivity and focusing more on details than broad themes. Grants no validity to opposing views.

Grenz, Stanley J. *Welcoming but Not Affirming: An Evangelical Response to Homosexuality*. Westminster/John Knox Press, 1998. Perhaps the most irenic, carefully thought out, and clearly argued presentation of the restrictive perspective concerning homosexuality.

Hanigan, James P. *Homosexuality: The Test Case for Christian Social Ethics*. New York: Paulist Press, 1988. An important but unfortunately largely overlooked presentation of a Roman Catholic, natural law-oriented case for taking a restrictive stance concerning homosexuality. A careful, irenic presentation with a compassionate tone.

Hays, Richard B. *The Moral Vision of the New Testament: A Contemporary Introduction to New Testament Ethics*. San Francisco: HarpersSanFrancisco, 1996. Includes a closely argued chapter on homosexuality making a case for the restrictive position. The rest of the book provides a broad theological and ethical context for making this case based on New Testament writings.

Holben, L. R. *What Christians Think about Homosexuality: Six Representative Viewpoints*. North Richland Hills, TX: Bibal Press, 1999. A quite helpful resource that summarizes with sophistication and in some depth a spectrum of views held by Christian scholars. Besides being an excellent introduction to various of the arguments, this book also helps show how diverse the spectrum of views on these issues is.

Johnson, William Stacy. *A Time to Embrace: Same-Gender Relationships in Religion, Law, and Politics*. Grand Rapids, MI: Eerdmans, 2006. A most important presentation of the case for Christians affirming same-sex marriage by a Presbyterian theologian, minister, and lawyer. Combines sophisticated theological analysis with careful treatment of legal issues and reflections concerning the place of this discussion in our wider North American society. Johnson's view on marriage closely parallels what I've argued for in this book.

Kraus, C. Norman, ed. *To Continue the Dialogue: Biblical Interpretation and Homosexuality.* Telford, PA: Cascadia Publishing House, 2001. A pioneering collection of fifteen essays representing a spectrum of perspectives (though tending toward the inclusive side), followed by a variety of short responses. One of the first published attempts by Mennonite scholars to reflect on these issues.

Kreider, Roberta Showalter, ed. *Together in Love: Faith Stories of Gay, Lesbian, Bisexual, and Transgender Couples.* Kulpsville, PA: Strategic Press, 2002. An illuminating collection of several dozen stories of committed relationships among Christian sexual minorities. The second of a series of three books complied by Showalter to give voice to people often not heard in church discussions. The first book was *From Wounded Hearts: Faith Stories of Lesbian, Gay, Bisexual and Transgender People and Those Who Love Them*, second edition (Kulpsville, PA: Strategic Press, 2003 [1st edition, 1998]) and the third, *The Cost of Truth: Faith Stories of Mennonite and Brethren Leaders and Those Who Might Have Been* (Kulpsville, PA: Strategic Press, 2004).

Myers, David G. and Letha Scanzoni. *What God Has Joined Together: The Christian Case for Gay Marriage.* San Francisco: HarperSanFrancisco, 2005. An argument in favor of same-sex marriage by two thinkers often identified as evangelical Christians. As Myers is a sociologist and Scanzoni a professional writer, the book is not extremely sophisticated theologically. But it does present a clear argument strongly oriented toward the practical benefits of marriage.

Nissinen, Martti. *Homoeroticism in the Biblical World: A Historical Perspective.* Minneapolis: Fortress Press, 1998. A scholarly treatment of many of the biblical passages. The author strives for objectivity, ultimately arguing for an inclusive reading.

Rogers, Jack. *Jesus, the Bible, and Homosexuality: Explode the Myths, Heal the Church*. Louisville: Westminster John Knox, 2006. A passionate argument in favor of inclusion from a retired theology professor and church leader. Rogers, a Presbyterian who taught for many years at evangelical Fuller Theological Seminary, writes engagingly from his own experience about how his views have evolved.

Scanzoni, Letha Dawson and Virginia Mollenkott. *Is the Homosexual My Neighbor? A Positive Christian Response*. Revised edition. San Francisco: HarperSanFrancisco, 1994. When first published in 1978 it created a sensation as two prominent evangelical writers made the case for an inclusive stance. The revised edition remains important for building its case on a relatively high view of biblical authority.

Seow, Choon-Leong, ed. *Homosexuality and Christian Community*. Louisville: Westminster John Knox Press, 1996. Another collection of scholarly writings that include a spectrum of perspectives. This one is notable because all contributors were members of the Princeton Theological Seminary faculty at the time of publication. Therefore it reflects debates among mainstream Protestant theologians.

Siker, Jeffrey, ed. *Homosexuality in the Church: Both Sides of the Debate*. Louisville: Westminster John Knox Press, 1994. A helpful collection of scholarly essays representing a variety of perspectives. Particularly useful in collecting both Roman Catholic and Protestant viewpoints.

Swartley, Willard M. *Homosexuality: Biblical Interpretation and Moral Discernment*. Scottdale, PA: Herald Press, 2003. A major work from an important Mennonite New Testament scholar. Argues with an irenic tone for the restrictive stance. Disappointingly thin on biblical interpretation and reflection on hermeneutics considering the author's background.

White, Mel. *Religion Gone Bad: The Hidden Dangers of the Christian Right*. New York: Jeremy Tarcher/Penguin, 2006.

A sharp critique of the ways the Christian Right in the United States has sought to exploit the homosexuality issue for political advantage.

Wink, Walter, ed. *Homosexuality and Christian Faith: Questions of Conscience for the Churches.* Minneapolis: Fortress Press, 1999. A collection of short, mostly popular-level essays by prominent Christian thinkers arguing in favor of the inclusive stance. Wink's essay has been widely circulated as a classic statement of the view that while the Bible is negative about same-sex relationships, present-day Christians should not be because of Jesus' call to love and compassion.

Chapter 11

Mark's Annotated Bibliography

Like Ted I have been reading literature on this subject for more than twenty years. Let me say three things about my selections. First, I have chosen articles as well as books. Some of the most helpful things I have read have been articles. And besides, many would like to have some brief pieces that are helpful. Second, as I hope has been made clear in my contribution to the book, I believe that biblically informed theology is central for our approach to this subject (as well as others). However, I have mentioned a number of non-theological writings. This is because of my conviction that many Christians seem naïve about the complex realities of sex and the ways in which these realities relate to our readings of biblical texts and our reflections on sexual morality. Thus I believe we have to name the sexual worlds in which we live. And finally, I want to mention that I have made references to a number of other works in my annotations. These can be found in my fuller but unannotated bibliography on my faculty website at Eastern Mennonite Seminary (as well as scattered throughout my footnotes or on a website such as Amazon).

Ash, Christopher. *Marriage: Sex in the Service of God.* Vancouver: Regent College Publishing, 2005. Overall I believe this to be one of the best books I have read on a theology of marriage. In some ways the subtitle names what is crucial and peculiar about this book. Additionally, it is full of deep engagement with biblical texts and theological writings in a way that reflects profound Christian wisdom and insight. (Which is not to say I would agree with everything in the book. For example, I would suggest that chapter fourteen should be read in conjunction with the book by Carrie Miles, listed below.) Compare to Rodney Clapp, *Families at the Crossroads: Beyond Traditional and Modern Options*.

Barger, Lilian Calles. *Eve's Revenge: Women and a Spirituality of the Body*. Grand Rapids, MI: Brazos Press, 2003. A very helpful book, naming issues related to the intersection of women, embodiedness, and spiritual life in a way that enriches and informs needed conversations. For comparison see Stephanie Paulsell, *Honoring the Body: Meditations on a Christian Practice*.

Blankenhorn, David. *The Future of Marriage*. New York: Encounter Books, 2007. Blankenhorn is one of the foremost authorities on the family in the United States. In this well-written and carefully researched book, he attempts to show how redefining marriage and the family (by formally affirming gay and lesbian relationships as marriage) is destructive of society, especially children. (Also see the parallel book of essays *The Meaning of Marriage*, edited by Robert P. George and Jean Bethke Elshtain and on recent shifts in Canada: *Divorcing Marriage*, edited by Daniel Cere and Douglas Farrow.)

Bradshaw, Timothy. "Baptism and Inclusivity in the Church." In *Baptism, the New Testament and the Church*, ed. Stanley E. Porter and Anthony R. Cross, 184-204. Sheffield: Sheffield Academic Press, 1997. Long before I began this book with Ted, I was convinced that the modern notion of inclusiveness, fully embraced, is destructive of the faithfulness and integrity of the church. This essay, which links baptism to covenantal faithfulness, and the essay by Philip Turner (chapter ten in *The Fate of Communion*), which I quote from extensively in my response to Ted's main essay, are two of the best I have read on the subject.

Bradshaw, Timothy, ed. *The Way Forward? Christian Voices on Homosexuality and the Church*. London: Hodder & Stoughton, 1997. (Second edition, London: SCM Press, 2003; Grand Rapids, MI: Wm. B. Eerdmans, 2003). Along with the book edited by David Balch that Ted listed, I believe this is the best among the many collections of essays on the subject. I would especially highlight the essay by John Colwell (on Romans 1) and the essay by Anthony Thiselton (on hermeneutics). But the confession of faith that all the essayists use as a reference point is helpful. And to show some of the diversity of views in Britain, most of the essays are useful (not least the essays by Rowan Williams, Oliver O'Donovan, Elizabeth Stuart and Michael Vasey).

Carey, John J. "Body and Soul: Presbyterians on Sexuality." *Christian Century* 108 (May 8, 1991): 516-20. This brief essay is a summary of a book-length document produced by a committee appointed by the Presbyterian Church (USA). The summary was written by the chair of the committee; the document was never ratified by the official body of the church. The central moral principle enunciated by the document is "justice-love" joined to a critique of patriarchy, homophobia, and heterosexism. I have included this essay because I believe it is a clear summary of a very common view held by many well-meaning people within the church. For evidence that this approach is still very much alive see the 2003 collection of essays *Body & Soul: Rethinking Sexuality as Justice-Love*, edited by Marvin Ellison and Sylvia Thorson-Smith. (See Camille Paglia's trenchant criticisms of the document, listed below.)

Gagnon, Robert A. J. *The Bible and Homosexual Practice: Texts and Hermeneutics*. Nashville: Abingdon Press, 2001. This is, without question, the most thorough book written on the subject; the varied and numerous endorsing blurbs also suggest it is backed by good biblical scholarship. Moreover, Gagnon has become the foremost Christian scholar in the

United States on this subject, as far as I know. If you visit
his faculty website you will see that he has written book-
length critiques of the book edited by David Balch as well
as the books by David Myers and Letha Scanzoni and by
Jack Rogers. He has also written lengthy critiques of Walter
Wink, not to mention many briefer articles and critiques.
See: www.robgagnon.net.

Greenberg, David F. *The Construction of Homosexuality*. Chicago:
University of Chicago Press, 1988. Used by writers with various positions on this issue, this expansive, historically oriented sociological study covers multiple cultures across time
to show that simplistic understandings of similarities and
differences regarding homosexuality in varying cultures are
just that—simplistic. For comparison see the 2003 book by
Louis Crompton, *Homosexuality & Civilization*.

Hays, Richard B. "Homosexuality." In *The Moral Vision of the New
Testament*, 379-406. San Francisco: HarperSanFrancisco,
1996. This is a careful essay by a well-respected New
Testament scholar. He has also written a popular-style article
for *Sojourners* magazine (July 1991; reprinted various places)
and a scholarly article on Romans 1 (*Journal of Religious Ethics*,
Spring 1986). It should also be mentioned that Hays, a
Methodist, is a pacifist.

Jones, Stanton L. and Mark A. Yarhouse. *Homosexuality: The Use
of Scientific Research in the Church's Moral Debate*. Downers
Grove, IL: InterVarsity Press, 2000. Jones is a psychologist
who has written other academic pieces on various dimensions of sexuality. This book is well-written, thoroughly
researched, and nuanced in its conclusions. A briefer version
of their findings is published in the David Balch edited volume (listed in Ted's bibliography). An update was published
in 2005, written by Jones and Alex Kwee (*Journal of
Psychology & Christianity*, Winter 2005). Also see Stanton L.
Jones and Mark A. Yarhouse, *Ex-Gays?: A Longitudinal Study*

of Religiously Mediated Change in Sexual Orientation and Janelle Hallman, *The Heart of Female Same-Sex Attraction: A Comprehensive Resource.* Compare their work to: Edward Stein, *The Mismeasure of Desire: The Science, Theory, and Ethics of Sexual Orientation*, Matt Ridley, *The Agile Gene* and Richard Lewontin, *The Triple Helix: Gene, Organism and Environment.*

Miles, Carrie A. *The Redemption of Love: Rescuing Marriage and Sexuality from the Economics of a Fallen World.* Grand Rapids, MI: Brazos Books, 2006. This is one of the small handful of very good books on a theology of marriage of which I am aware. This one very specifically offers a theology of marriage and sexuality quite consciously within the context of the challenges of our contemporary culture. I would also mention the idiosyncratic but thought-provoking book by Francis Watson, *Agape, Eros, Gender: Towards a Pauline Sexual Ethic.*

Moberly, Walter. "The Use of Scripture in Contemporary Debate About Homosexuality." *Theology* [British journal] 103 (July-August 2000): 251-58. This is a superb essay for succinctly presenting the issues in as neutral a fashion as I could imagine. Would be perfect for group study.

Paglia, Camille. "The Joy of Presbyterian Sex." *The New Republic* (December 2, 1991): 24-27. (Reprinted in her *Sex, Art, and American Culture.* New York: Vintage Books, 1992.) Paglia is a provocateur, so be aware of that. But this self-described ex-Catholic pagan of "wavering sexual orientation," through her critique of the 1991 Presbyterian document on human sexuality, implicitly offers an extraordinary and insightful set of critical reflections on the too often naïve approach of much liberal writing on sexuality, writing that ignores the power of *eros* and the rich moral and theological heritage of the Christian faith. (See John Carey, above. Also see some of Paglia's other essays on homosexuality in her first two books of essays.) Very different but also provocative and insightful are the British Christian ethicist, Michael Banner's two chapters on sex in his, *Christian Ethics and Contemporary Moral Problems*.

Regnerus, Mark D. *Forbidden Fruit: Sex & Religion in the Lives of American Teenagers*. Oxford: Oxford University Press, 2007. Based on extensive surveys and selected interviews, this book is attempting to show how, in real life, religion and sex intersect in the lives of American teenagers. To fill out the picture on contemporary American sexuality I would also see: Kevin White, *Sexual Liberation or Sexual License? The American Revolt Against Victorianism*; Roger Streitmatter, *Sex Sells!: The Media's Journey from Repression to Obsession*; and Miriam Grossman, *Unprotected: A Campus Psychiatrist Reveals How Political Correctness in Her Profession Endangers Every Student*. I would additionally still consult the 1994 book *Sex in America: A Definitive Survey* and the critique of it in Richard Lewontin's book of essays, *It Ain't Necessarily So*.

Roberts, Christopher Chenault. *Creation & Covenant: The Significance of Sexual Difference in the Moral Theology of Marriage*. London: T & T Clark, 2007. Originally a doctoral thesis, this book provides a careful and thoughtful historical survey of theological reflection on the subject, beginning with early church fathers. It is a model of the research we need on this sort of subject.

Rogers, Eugene F., Jr. *Sexuality and the Christian Body*. Oxford: Blackwell, 1999. Rogers attempts to make an argument for homosexual marriage in more or less traditional terms. More than a few believe he has failed in his argument. But his book is, in its own terms, careful and substantive. The book is well worth wrestling with. I would do so in light of the following critiques: a forum on the book in *Modern Theology*, July 2000; article-length reviews by Douglas Farrow (*International Journal of Systematic Theology*, November 2003) and Gilbert Meilaender (*First Things*, April 2000);

and the critique in Christopher Roberts' book (see above, pages 198-219).

Rudy, Kathy. *Sex and the Church: Gender, Homosexuality, and the Transformation of Christian Ethics.* Boston: Beacon Press, 1997. This book is intriguing—and disturbing. It is intriguing because it makes a theological argument that, to some of us, may sound compelling (building partly on Stanley Hauerwas and Rodney Clapp). It is disturbing because it uses this theology to argue for casual sex among friends ("communal" sex according to Rudy, called "polyamory" in some circles)—learning from what she sees as a prototypical gay male lifestyle that sex is a way to welcome strangers into and affirm friends within our community. An argument for "polyamory" is hardly unique to Rudy within the religious gay and lesbian community. Especially read in light of Marjorie Garbor's *Vice Versa: Bisexuality and the Eroticism of Everyday Life*, it would seem a worthwhile exercise to ask: what is wrong with Rudy's theological argument?

Schmidt, Thomas E. *Straight & Narrow? Compassion & Clarity in the Homosexuality Debate.* Downers Grove, IL: InterVarsity Press, 1995. Most of this book is a careful biblical and theological study by a Presbyterian New Testament scholar. Schmidt's style is quite irenic. Nonetheless, his book infuriated many because of two chapters in which he summarizes a considerable amount of literature on facts about gays and lesbians. It was especially his chapter "The Price of Love," about negative health consequences, that really angered some. Having discussed his research with him, I know that through 1994 Schmidt had done considerable research in medical and social science journals for this book.

Smit, Laura A. *Loves Me, Loves Me Not: The Ethics of Unrequited Love.* Grand Rapids, MI: Baker Academic, 2005. Because singleness has been given far too little attention, this book is vital for kick-starting our discussion of the complicated realities of being a Christian who wants to be sexually faithful and yet finds herself or himself to be single—perhaps for a very long time. Also similarly illuminating is Caroline J. Simon, *The Disciplined Heart: Love, Destiny & Imagination.*

Sprigg, Peter and Timothy Dailey, eds. *Getting It Straight: What Research Shows about Homosexuality.* Washington: Family Research Council, 2004. Some of my readers may dismiss this sort of book out of hand. I would suggest that, if read with open mindedness and discernment, this book points to some of the medical and social science literature that challenges certain simplistic understandings.

Stout, Jeffrey. "How Charity Transcends the Culture Wars: Eugene Rogers and Others on Same-Sex Marriage." *Journal of Religious Ethics* 31 (Summer 2003): 169-80. This is a wonderfully lucid essay arguing for the affirming position. Though based somewhat on a theological book, the argument is about society at large. I would compare this to the earlier lucid statement, also rooted in theological cues but geared toward society at large, "The Homosexual Movement: A Response by the Ramsey Colloquium." *First Things* (March 1994): 15-20. Read together the essays provide helpful grist for the mill.

Taylor, Daniel. "Deconstructing the Gospel of Tolerance." *Christianity Today* (January 11, 1999): 43-52. As with the issue of inclusiveness, I have come to believe that sloppy notions of tolerance are a threat to the identity of the church. This sensitive and smart essay helps to name why such a concern is legitimate. Taylor has expanded this essay into a small book, *Is God Tolerant?*

Van Leeuwen, Mary Stewart. *My Brother's Keeper: What the Social Sciences Do (and Don't) Tell Us About Masculinity.* Downers Grove, IL: InterVarsity Press, 2002. A wonderfully challenging book that raises important questions. I would read it in conjunction with the two sociological studies: W. Bradford

Wilcox, *Soft Patriarchs, New Men: How Christianity Shapes Fathers and Husbands* and Steven E. Rhoads, *Taking Sex Differences Seriously*. I would perhaps add the intriguing and quite insightful book by the lesbian journalist who feigned being a man in order to enter the world of males: Norah Vincent, *Self-Made Man*. This latter work, especially, should not be confused with a Christian book; some of its course language and descriptions are not for the squeamish.

Woodhead, Linda. "Sex in a Wider Context." In *Sex These Days*, ed. Jon Davies and Gerard Loughlin, 98-120. Sheffield: Sheffield Academic Press, 1997. Among many books and articles I have read on sex this is probably my favorite single theological essay, if I had to pick only one. Though it is very different, I would also mention the very insightful essay on sex by Philip Yancey in his *Rumors of Another World*, published as the booklet, *Designer Sex*.

Notes

Introduction

1. Mark became a pacifist in 1971, within a year of becoming a Christian and as a Baptist. Already among these Baptists he was beginning, as an eighteen year old, to "embrace the radical gospel message of following the way of Jesus." Thus, among other things, he became a conscientious objector approximately five years before reading Yoder. But Yoder helped him to understand how pacifism was related to the whole of the Christian faith. See his account of this in: Nation, "The First Word Christians Have to Say About Violence Is 'Church': On Bonhoeffer, Baptists, and Becoming a Peace Church," in Nation, *Faithfulness*, 83-115.

2. Mark had been involved in peace and justice work for most of the four years he was in Louisville, Kentucky, before going to seminary. He went to AMBS specifically to train to do professional peace and justice work, which he then did for six years immediately following graduation.

Chapter 1

1. An earlier version of this essay was published as "Six Perspectives on the Homosexuality Controversy" in Kraus, *To Continue the Dialogue*. Used with permission.

2. This essay is written in a similar spirit as a recent book: Holben, *What Christians Think About Homosexuality*. However, whereas I have elected to focus in some depth on a few representative writers, Holben offers a more synthetic approach drawing upon many different writers.

3. The numbers in parentheses refer to page numbers in the books being discussed.

4. See also Wold, *Out of Order*.

Chapter 2

1. This is a slightly revised version of an essay originally published with the same title in Kraus, ed. *To Continue the Dialogue*, 223-44. Used with permission. A version, virtually identical to the present one, was published as: Nation, "The Fruit of the Spirit or Works of the Flesh?"

2. Hallie, *Lest Innocent Blood Be Shed*.

3. Brueggemann, *Interpretation and Obedience*, 26, n18.

4. An issue I have struggled with in this essay is the use of language. It is perhaps impossible to use neutral language. I have usually chosen to use the term *homoerotic relations* as the matter being debated. It is the sexual behavior of gays and lesbians that, for most people, is *the* issue. *Homoerotic*, a term used by various writers in this debate, seems to be as neutral as any word I can think of to refer easily to the issue at hand. A caution: though I have adopted this language, it is still imperative that we remember that the relationships between people who identify themselves as homosexual cannot and should not be reduced to the erotic or sexual component of their relationships. This is but a reminder that this "issue" is connected to a variety of complicated matters not adequately reducible to simple terminology.

5. See Kreider, ed., *From Wounded Hearts*. For a fuller narrative of one life see White, *Stranger at the Gate*.

6. Yancey, "Why I Don't Go to a Megachurch," 80.

7. Lakoff, *Moral Politics*.

8. See Judith N. Shklar, "The Liberalism of Fear," in Rosenblum, ed., *Liberalism*, 21-38. On some of the reasons for the fear on this sort of contentious issue see, Hunter, *Culture Wars*; Hunter, *Before the Shooting Begins*; Herman, *Antigay Agenda*; and as a challenge to some of these, see Smith, *Christian America?*

9. See, e.g., David Blankenhorn, *The Future of Marriage*; Douglas Farrow, *Nation of Bastards*; Christopher Wolf, ed., *Homosexuality and American Public Life*.

10. To get an overview of the subject see Stanton L. Jones and Mark A. Yarhouse, "The Use, Misuse, and Abuse of Science in the Ecclesiastical Homosexuality Debates," in Balch, ed., *Homosexuality, Science, and the 'Plain Sense' of Scripture*, 73-120 and their recent book, Jones and Yarhouse, *Homosexuality*. For some sense of the broader debate see: Burr, *A Separate Creation*; Terry, *An American Obsession*; Rosario, *Science*; Lewontin, *Triple Helix*; and Ridley, *Agile Gene*.

11. In using "essentialist" and "social constructivist" language, I realize I am using language from the social sciences. Though such language is useful and instructive, it is also important to remember that theological language regarding, for instance, creation, sin, and corruptibility, are more determinative for Christians.

12. In case I have not been clear, let me say that I think it is a complicated mixture, thus the truth, I believe, of my previous paragraph.

13. The literature is vast, but see Greenberg, *Construction of Homosexuality*; and Garber, *Vice Versa*.

14. Among other things, the way in which "choice" often figures into these conversations is overly simplified in important ways. For some very insightful theological reflections that are relevant to these matters, see Banner, "Prolegomena to a Dogmatic Sexual Ethic," in his *Christian Ethics*, 269-309 and especially on choice, 295ff.

15. Among the many debatable points is the naming of immediately relevant texts. Most would agree that Romans 1:26-27 and Leviticus 18:22 and Leviticus 20:13 are among them. Others would include the lists in 1 Corinthians 6:9-10 and 1 Timothy 1:10. Many would concede that there should at least be discussions of Genesis 19:1-8; Judges 19:16-30; 2 Peter 2:6-7; and Jude 7. Even if one includes all of these, it is a small number of texts. Nonetheless, it is worth noting that until roughly the last thirty years these texts have set the moral norm within both Judaism and Christianity. Moreover, the prohibition against homoerotic behavior seems to be presumed within the many more general teachings about sexuality within the Scriptures.

16. For one of the most thorough, recent studies, and as a guide to other literature, see Klawans, *Impurity and Sin*. Also see Robert Gagnon, *The Bible and Homosexual Practice*, 111-46.

17. The person who has shaped much of the debate within the last twenty years is John Boswell. See his *Christianity, Social Tolerance, and Homosexuality*. Some of the other writings worth taking seriously that attempt to wrestle with the relevant texts and that come to conclusions that would make those who affirm the Church's traditional stance uncomfortable are Brooten, *Love Between Women*; Countryman, *Dirt, Greed & Sex*; Nissinen, *Homoeroticism in the Biblical World*; Scroggs, *New Testament and Homosexuality*; and Vasey, *Strangers and Friends*.

18. See, e. g., Gagnon, *Bible and Homosexual Practice*; Hays, "Homosexuality," in *Moral Vision*, 379-406; Hays, "Relations Natural

and Unnatural"; Schmidt, *Straight & Narrow?*; Smith, "Ancient Bisexuality"; and D. Wright, "Homosexuals or Prostitutes." Gagnon's book is by far the most careful and thorough book that has been published on the subject. (See additional resources on his faculty website.)

Finally, mention should be made of three excellent essays on hermeneutics. Anthony Thiselton, who probably knows as much about hermeneutics as anyone in the world, has written, "Can Hermeneutics Ease the Deadlock?" in Bradshaw, ed., *Way Forward?*, 145-96. Also see Kathryn Greene-McCreight, "The Logic of the Interpretation of Scripture and the Church's Debate Over Sexual Ethics," in Balch, ed., 242-60, and Brueggemann, "Biblical Authority."

19. As mentioned above, this is Boswell's 1980 book, *Christianity, Social Tolerance, and Homosexuality*. More recently he published *The Marriage of Likeness: Same-Sex Unions in Pre-Modern Europe*. For critical responses, in addition to some of the references to Boswell's biblical interpretations mentioned in an earlier footnote, see Williams, "Homosexuality and Christianity," and Shaw, "A Groom of One's Own?"

20. Rather than list more writings here, let me simply mention the bibliographies in two important, recent books (which themselves have very different views and approaches): Grenz, *Welcoming but not Affirming*, 187-201 and Brooten, *Love Between Women*, 363-72.

21. For one instance of a recent book that helps rescue Paul from this claim see Watson, *Agape, Eros, Gender*. Also see Collins, *Sexual Ethics and the New Testament*.

22. Paul Veyne, "The Roman Empire," in Veyne, ed., *History of Private Life*, 202. See also Rousselle, *Porneia*, and Peter Brown, *Body and Society*.

23. See, e.g., Behr, *Asceticism and Anthropology* and Miles, *Fullness of Life*. For an overview of much of the history, with substantial bibliographic guidance, see Wiesner-Hanks, *Christianity and Sexuality*.

24. Linda Woodhead, "Life in the Spirit: Contemporary and Christian Understandings of the Human Person," in Platten, et al., eds., *New Soundings*, 118.

25. One subject that should be revisited in this regard is the Mennonite understanding of church. Paul Hiebert has described what he refers to as three basic approaches to understanding church: the

bounded set, the fuzzy set, and the centered set. To oversimplify, the Mennonite Church has often taken a bounded set approach, one that focuses considerably on boundary issues that define people in or out. The centered-set approach, in contrast, focuses mostly on the center, what it is that centrally defines the church. See Hiebert, "The Category *Christian* in the Mission Task," in his *Anthropological Reflections*, 107-36. This clearly has relevance for the debates about homosexuality, as is shown in King, *Trackless Wastes & Stars to Steer By*, 115-36.

26. As Martti Nissinen, who is affirming of homoerotic behavior, says: "To the extent that Rabbinic and Hellenistic Jewish literature sheds light on the norms of Jewish society in Jesus' time, it can be assumed that public expressions of homosexuality were regarded as anomalous, idolatrous, and indecent," (Nissinen, *Homoeroticism in the Biblical World*, 118). See also Scroggs, *New Testament and Homosexuality*, 66-84 and Gagnon, *Bible and Homosexual Practice*, 185-209.

27. Volf, *Exclusion and Embrace*, 72-73. See also Gagnon, *Bible and Homosexual Practice*, 210-28.

28. For a theological argument for homosexual marriage, see McCarthy, "Homosexuality." See also Wallace, *For Fidelity* and the critique of Wallace: Budziszewski, "Just Friends." For full, recent arguments see David Blankenhorn, *The Future of Marriage* and Douglas Farrow, *Nation of Bastards*.

29. As least as a way to see what some of the issues are, consult Estlund and Nussbaum, eds., *Sex, Preference, and Family* and Wolfe, ed., *Homosexuality and American Public Life*, especially part 3.

30. For some sense of the diversity within the theological world, see Nelson and Longfellow, eds., *Sexuality and the Sacred* and Stuart and Thatcher, eds., *Christian Perspectives*.

31. As examples, see Comstock, *Gay Theology Without Apology*; Rudy, *Sex and the Church*; Stuart, *Just Good Friends*; and Comstock and Henking, eds., *Que(e)rying Religion*.

32. *Keeping Body and Soul Together*. A summary was published by the chair of the committee: Carey, "Body and Soul." It should be noted that this document was never ratified by the general assembly. Nevertheless, that this approach is still considered an important option for the church by some, see Ellison and Thorson-Smith, eds., *Body and Soul*.

33. Walter Brueggemann, "Duty as Delight and Desire: Preaching Obedience That Is Not Legalism," in *The Covenanted Self*, 35.

34. See the excerpt of the Presbyterian document published as "Sexuality and Justice-Love," 519.

35. Gold, "Getting Real," 6.

36. For other, more measured, critiques of the Presbyterian document, see Watts, "An Empty Sexual Ethic," and Michael Banner, "Five Churches in Search of Sexual Ethics," in his *Christian Ethics*, 252-68.

37. Paglia, "Joy of Presbyterian Sex," 24-25; reprinted in Paglia, *Sex, Art, and American Culture*. Also see Paglia, "Rebel Love: Homosexuality," in her *Vamps & Tramps*, 67-92.

I have serious disagreements with Camille Paglia's own views on sexuality and think some of her over-charged rhetoric unnecessary. However, her response to the Presbyterian document is an important one in at least three regards. First, she refuses to let us forget the complex emotional, relational, and physical dimensions of sexuality. Second, if, with the document she criticizes, a church is going to offer an affirmation of sexual (and homosexual) behaviors without simultaneously offering moral guidance regarding right and wrong behaviors (other than those connected to oppression and injustice), then we need to be honest, as Paglia is, as to the range of behaviors in the larger culture (most of which, incidentally, she affirms). Third, despite her own, self-proclaimed, pagan views, she wants the church to be honestly Christian, in its own views.

38. Paglia, "Joy of Presbyterian Sex," 24, 27. For her general knowledge on the subject of sexuality see Paglia, *Sexual Personae*.

39. Wendell Berry insightfully shows how well many contemporary approaches to sexuality fit with the general, consumerist zeitgeist: Berry, *Sex, Economy, Freed & Community*, 117-73.

40. Greene-McCreight, "The Logic of the Interpretation of Scripture and the Church's Debate Over Sexual Ethics," in Balch, ed., *Homosexuality, Science, and the 'Plain Sense' of Scripture*, 245. On the other hand, read within the context of her whole essay, her words hardly represent a cavalier approach.

41. Quoted in Meilander, "What Sex Is," 44.

42. Rogers, *Sexuality and the Christian Body*, 28-66. It should perhaps be noted that this is only one component of Rogers' argument. For an interesting use of Rogers' book see Stout, "How Charity Transcends the Culture Wars."

43. For other proponents of this argument, see Jeffrey S. Siker,

"Homosexual Christians, the Bible, and Gentile Inclusion: Confessions of a Repenting Heterosexist," in Siker, ed., *Homosexuality in the Church*, 178-94 and Fowl, *Engaging Scripture*, 119-27. See also arguments against this approach in Hays, "Homosexuality," in *Moral Vision of the New Testament*, 395-97, 399-400; Greene-McCreight, "The Logic of the Interpretation of Scripture," 253-60; Gagnon, *Bible and Homosexual Practice*, 460-66; and Goddard, *God, Gentiles and Gay Christians*.

44. Rogers, *Sexuality and the Christian Body*, 52.

45. Rogers' book represents the most serious attempt I have seen to make a theological argument on traditional grounds for the affirmation of homoerotic relationships. This is not to say he is successful. For a review that suggests he is not successful see Meilander, "What Sex Is." Also see the reviews of his book in *Modern Theology* (July 2000); by Farrow, "Beyond Nature," and in Roberts, *Creation & Covenant*, 198-219.

46. Greene-McCreight, "The Logic of the Interpretation of Scripture," 246-47. This is similar, formally, to what Luke Timothy Johnson suggests. See Johnson, *Scripture & Discernment*, 144-48. One could say that what Greene-McCreight is saying is vital for the ongoing integrity of the church.

47. There are many resources I would consult to wrestle with these issues. Along with writings listed in other footnotes, they would include Abraham, "United Methodists," *First Things* 84 (June/July 1998) 28-33; Banner, "Prolegomena to a Dogmatic Sexual Ethic"; Rodney Clapp, "Tacit Holiness: The Importance of Bodies and Habits in Doing Church," in *Border Crossings*, 63-74; Marva Dawn, *Sexual Character*; Jenson, *Systematic Theology*, 53-111; Meilander, "The First of Institutions"; Oliver O'Donovan, "Homosexuality in the Church: Can There Be a Fruitful Theological Debate?" in Bradshaw, ed., *The Way Forward?*, 20-36; Rolheiser, *Seeking Spirituality*; McCarthy, *Sex and Love in the Home*; "St. Andrew's Day Statement," in Bradshaw, ed., *The Way Forward?*, 5-11; Scott and Warren, eds., *Perspectives on Marriage*; Rowan Williams, "The Body's Grace," in Hefling, ed., *Our Selves, Our Souls & Bodies*, 58-68; Linda Woodhead, "Sex in a Wider Context," in Davies and Loughlin, eds., *Sex These Days*, 98-120; and Butler, "Sex or Gender?"

48. We could do worse than heed Luke Timothy Johnson's admonitions: "The church should not, cannot, define itself in response to political pressure or popularity polls. But it is called to discern the

work of God in human lives and adapt its self-understanding in response to that work of God. Inclusivity must follow from evidence of *holiness*; are there narratives of homosexual holiness to which we must begin to listen?" (Johnson, *Scripture & Discernment*, 148.)

49. On the fruit of the spirit see Kenneson, *Life On the Vine*.

50. I must thank the many friends who read and commented on an earlier draft of this essay: Jeremy Brooks, Alan and Eleanor Kreider, Phil Kenneson, Wayne and Leabell Miller, Martin Shupack, J. R. Burkholder, Margo Houts, Ted Grimsrud, Jeremy Thomson, Tim Foley, Willard Swartley, Nik Ansell, Gordon Preece, Brian Haymes, John D. Roth, Alastair McKay, Stanley Hauerwas, Fran Porter, Michael A. King, C. Norman Kraus and Mary Thiessen Nation. I hope I haven't forgotten anyone. Of course, they have varying opinions about this essay. They are certainly not to be held responsible for my approach to this issue. However, all of them have improved the essay through their comments. Thanks.

Chapter 3

1. Nation, "Fruit of the Spirit or Works of the Flesh? Come Let Us Reason Together," in Kraus, ed., *To Continue the Dialogue*, 223-44, now included, slightly revised, in this book.

2. Naming my own theological approach would be complicated. Suffice it to say, I am deeply influenced by John Howard Yoder and Stanley Hauerwas, with substantial methodological indebtedness to Karl Barth.

3. Unless otherwise noted, Scripture references are from the *New Revised Standard Version*.

4. Peterson, *Christ Plays in Ten Thousand Places*, 39, 40, 44, 41.

5. For those who are Mennonite it is also worth noting that, according to Arnold Snyder, "the theme of 'fearing the Lord' runs consistently through Anabaptist testimonies and writings, and points to a fundamental teaching" (Snyder, *Following in the Footsteps of Christ*, 30).

6. Brueggemann, "The Cunning Little Secret of Certitude: On the First Great Commandment," in *The Covenanted Self*, 65. Also see Miller, *The God You Have*; and R. W. L. Moberly, "Toward an Interpretation of the Shema," in Seitz and Greene-McCreight, eds., *Theological Exegesis*, 124-44.

7. Also see Micah 6:8. For reflections on Micah 6:8 see:

Brueggemann, *To Act Justly, Love Tenderly, Walk Humbly*. For some critical reflections on temptations related to this text for many of us who care deeply about peace and justice see Eller, *Towering Babble*, esp. 31-39.

8. Bonhoeffer, *Discipleship*, 45, emphasis in the original.

9. Bruner, *Matthew*, 413, emphasis his. (It is unfortunate that this wonderful commentary is so little known.)

10. Bruner, *Matthew*, 413, emphasis his.

11. Bruner, *Matthew*, 417, emphasis his.

12. Bruner, *Matthew*, 414, emphasis his

13. Bruner, *Matthew*, 418, emphasis his.

14. Yancey, "Exploring a Parallel Universe," 128.

15. Yancey, "Exploring," 128. It needs to be added, for those who might not know, that Yancey, a famous evangelical, knows more evangelicals by far than most of us.

16. Yancey, "Exploring," 128, emphasis his.

17. This is an allusion to the story of the good Samaritan (from the King James Version), which in Luke's Gospel is a parable Jesus gives to respond to the question, "Who is my neighbor?" (Luke 10:29-37).

18. On tolerance see Taylor, "Deconstructing the Gospel of Tolerance," Budziszewski, "Illusion," Griffiths, "Proselytizing," and Alasdair MacIntyre, "Toleration and the Goods in Conflict," in Mendus, ed., *The Politics of Toleration*, 133-55.

19. On inclusiveness see Timothy Bradshaw, "Baptism and Inclusivity in the Church," in Porter and Cross, eds., *Baptism*, 447-66; William J. Abraham, "Inclusivism, Idolatry and the Survival of the (Fittest) Faithful," in Husbands and Treier, eds., *Community*, 131-45; and Radner and Turner, *The Fate of Communion*, 243-51.

20. On compassion see: Gagnon, *The Bible and Homosexual Practice*, 210-27; and Gordon Watson, "The 'Compassion' of God as a Basis for Christian Ethical Wisdom," in Rae and Redding, eds., *More Than a Single Issue*, 232-51.

21. On justice see E. Achtemeier, "Righteousness in the OT," P. Achtemeier, "Righteousness in the NT,"; and Bader-Saye, "Violence, Reconciliation, and the Justice of God"; Bruckner, "Justice in Scripture"; Bell, "Jesus, the Jews, and the Politics of God's Justice"; and Grieb, "So That in Him We Might Become the Righteousness of God."

22. On freedom see Bader-Saye, "The Freedom of Faithfulness," and Webster, "Evangelical Freedom," in *Confessing God*, 215-26.

23. On grace see Nation, "Salvation" and Gorman, *Cruciformity*; DeSilva, *Honor, Patronage, Kinship & Purity*, 121-56.

24. On non-judgmentalism see the essays listed on tolerance and also consult Frederick Dale Bruner's commentary on Matthew 7:1-5.

25. On diversity revisit the essays listed on inclusiveness and toler- ance. But also see Bercier, "Diverse Diversities," Seligman, "Tolerance," and Wood, *Diversity*.

26. To begin to name some elements of this current cultural cli- mate see Berry, *Sex*, 117-74; Michael, et al. *Sex in America*; Streitmatter, *Sex Sells*; Morse, *Smart Sex*; and Regnerus, *Forbidden Fruit*.

27. Brueggemann, "Duty as Delight and Desire: Preaching Obedience That Is Not Legalism," *The Covenanted Self*, 35, 42.

28. "TNIV" refers to: *The Bible: Today's New International Version*.

29. Though I don't want my following comment to soften what I just said, it is also important to add that it is possible to make an argu- ment for why the prohibitions named in Colossians 3:5 all contribute to love of neighbors, though not in ways that are always obvious in our individualistic, promiscuous culture.

30. Karl Barth, *God in Action*, quoted in Carter, *Rethinking Christ and Culture*, 11.

31. D. Stephen Long, "Ecclesial Disobedience or Ecclesial Subordination to Liberal Institutions?" in Dunnam and Malony, 51. See a similar essay by Presbyterian missiologist, Darrell L. Guder, "The Context of the Church's Discussion of Human Sexuality," in Rae and Redding, eds., *More Than a Single Issue*, 105-21.

32. Hays, *Moral Vision*, 196, emphasis his.

33. Hays, *Moral Vision*, 197.

34. Hays, *Moral Vision*, 198.

35. Osborn, *Ethical Patterns*, 15-49. Osborn, a Patristics scholar, is naming a pattern he sees in the New Testament and one that recurs in four early church fathers according to his descriptions.

36. Bruner, *Matthew*, 418.

37. Wright, *The Pastoral Letters*, 9.

38. We might also reflect critically on Matthew 23:23: "Woe to you, scribes and Pharisees, hypocrites! For you tithe mint, dill, and cumin, and have neglected the weightier matters of the law: justice and mercy and faith. It is these you ought to have practiced without neglecting the others." We don't want to become so preoccupied with

this issue that we forget other vital issues. But (a) I would suggest that homosexuality is more important than tithing mint and (b) the last part of the verse reminds us that less than the most central issues still have import and need to be attended to—especially when some specifically argue that what has for more than two millennia been perceived to be wrong is now said to be right.

39. For instance, I spent more than ten years of my adult life often focused on issues directly related to matters of peace and justice.

40. On differences on the number of vices (from 36 to 110) and number of vice lists in the New Testament see O'Toole, *Who Is a Christian?* 110-18; Meeks, 68; and Collins, *Sexual Ethics*, 73-99.

41. The whole context in 1 Timothy ought to challenge our temptation to make this teaching all too comfortably only about motive (1 Timothy 6:6-10). Of course this is even more true if we place this passage in the context of the whole New Testament. There seems to be a pattern here: Mammon; idolatry; love of money.

42. For non-Mennonite readers: this is a reference to some Mennonite practices.

43. Used with permission. Names withheld to guard anonymity of persons involved.

44. See Pohl, *Making Room*, esp. on this see 127-49 and Newman, *Untamed Hospitality*. Also see Murray, *Explaining Church Discipline*.

45. One of the passages that has been challenging here is 1 Corinthians 5:9-13. This passage begins : "I wrote you in my letter not to associate with sexually immoral persons." Anthony Thiselton translates this as: "I wrote to you in my letter not to mix indiscriminately with immoral people." This makes more sense in the context of Paul's writings as a whole. (For Thiselton's justification of this translation and comments on the passage see: Thiselton, *First Epistle to the Corinthians*, 408-18.)

46. I have also come to see that some of the writings that are focused on the issues for the larger society might help us to deal with some of the Gnostic temptations within too many Christian discussions. See, e.g., Wolf, ed., *Homosexuality*; Wolf, ed., *Same Sex Matters*; George and Elshtain, eds., *The Meaning of Marriage* and Blankenhorn, *The Future of Marriage*. Two other very different essays that are helpful in their own ways are: The Ramsey Colloquium, "The Homosexual Movement," and Stout, "How Charity Transcends the Culture Wars."

47. On this huge subject I would, in general, point to writings

by John Howard Yoder and Stanley Hauerwas. Let me specifically mention: Yoder, *Christian Witness*; Kenneson, *Beyond Sectarianism*; and Carter, *Rethinking Christ and Culture*.

48. For theological clues about this see Linda Woodhead, "Sex in a Wider Context," in Davies and Loughlin, eds., *Sex These Days*, 98-120. Also see the references in note 46.

49. Let me name several references here at least to identify my approach with others: Brueggemann, "Biblical Authority in the Postcritical Period," in *The Book That Breathes*, 3-19, 183-84; Davis and Hays, *Art of Scripture Reading*, 1-5; Wright, *Last Word*; and Peterson, *Eat This Book*.

50. Kathryn Greene-McCreight, "The Logic of the Interpretation of Scripture in the Church's Debate over Sexual Ethics," in Balch, ed. *Homosexuality*, 245.

51. Greene-McCreight, "The Logic of the Interpretation," 246-47.

52. Boswell, *Christianity*, and Scroggs, *New Testament*. I know I also read Victor Paul Furnish, "Homosexuality," in *Moral Teaching*, 52-83.

53. Scanzoni and Mollenkott, *Is the Homosexual My Neighbor?* From my quick read it appears that the recent book by Letha Dawson Scanzoni and David G. Myers and the one by Jack Rogers are similarly popular in style and appear not to be well-informed by very broad reading.

54. Scroggs, *New Testament*, quoted in Anthony Thiselton, "Can Hermeneutics Ease the Deadlock? In Bradshaw, ed., *The Way Forward?* 158.

55. Walter Wink is a representative current example of this approach. See Walter Wink, "Homosexuality and the Bible," in *Homosexuality and Christian Faith*, ed. Wink, 33-49.

56. Hays, "Relations"; Hays, "Awaiting the Redemption."

57. Hays, "Homosexuality," in *Moral Vision*, 379-406.

58. Schmidt, *Straight & Narrow?*

59. Thiselton, "Can Hermeneutics Ease the Deadlock?"; Thiselton, "Vice Lists, Catechesis, and the Homosexuality Debate (6:9-10)," in *First Epistle to the Corinthians*, 440-53.

60. Jones and Yarhouse, *Homosexuality*; Jones and Kwee, "Scientific Research."

61. Swartley, *Homosexuality*.

62. Gagnon, *Bible and Homosexual Practice*. If one wants to be thorough one has to engage Gagnon's work, which is the most careful and thorough of any work of which I am aware. Not only that, he is continually writing detailed responses to significant contemporary revisionist writings. For example, he has written a book-length response to the recent book by Scanzoni and Meyers and a response to Jack Rogers. To see a listing of his other writings, many of which are posted, visit his website: www.robgagnon.net/

63. I have compiled a fifteen-page bibliography on the subject of homosexuality and the Christian faith. I have read much of what is listed there. Let me reiterate that Robert Gagnon gives the most detailed attention to biblical texts. After him I would look at Richard Hays, Thomas Schmidt, Anthony Thiselton, James B. De Young and David F. Wright. This list does not mention the relevant commentaries. (See our annotated reading lists at the end of this book for some guidance to the literature.)

64. Other texts that one would want to look at if we were trying to be thorough would be Genesis 9:20-27; Genesis 19:4-11; Judges 19:22-25 and Jude 7. (Also, of course the texts in Genesis 1 and 2 dealing with creation. I will allude to those at various places in my discussion.) For detailed commentary on these texts see the relevant sections of Gagnon, *The Bible and Homosexual Practice*.

65. I have sometimes noted that some Christians dismiss teachings that attach death as a penalty; they offer an emotional response of being offended at the notion. Before we are too quick to do this, we should be reminded that our Lord quoted such a teaching, regarding "speaking evil of father or mother," apparently quoting from Leviticus 20:9 (see Mark 7:10-13). He appeared to believe that in doing this he could both affirm the thrust of the teaching without, apparently, affirming the death penalty attached to it. Paul makes a similar move at the end of Romans 1 (v. 32).

66. See Gagnon, *The Bible and Homosexual Practice*, 117-20.

67. See, e.g., Ephraim Radner, *Leviticus*, on chapters eighteen and twenty.

68. Her seminal work here is Douglas, *Purity and Danger*.

69. Klawans, *Impurity and Sin in Ancient Judaism*.

70. Walter Brueggemann acknowledges this without, I believe, fully taking the implications of this awareness into account. See Brueggemann, *Theology of the Old Testament*, 186-96.

71. On this see: Markus Bockmuehl, "'Keeping It Holy': Old Testament Commandment and New Testament Faith," in *I Am the Lord Your God*, ed. Braaten and Seitz, 95-124 and David A. deSilva, *Honor, Patronage, Kinship & Purity*, 241-315.

72. For the sake of simplicity I have chosen not to engage two additional issues because I believe they do not affect my arguments substantively. First, I am not dealing with the meaning of the word *malakoi* in these texts, a word usually seen to refer to a passive/effeminate homosexual. Second, I am not in this essay entering into the debates about Paul's authorship of certain epistles.

73. The most careful discussion of this is D. Wright, "Homosexuals or Prostitutes?" But also for a discussion of this passage in the context of 1 Corinthians, see Thiselton, *First Epistle to the Corinthians*.

74. For a commentary on Romans that will make clear the basic contours of the first eight chapters see N. T. Wright, "Letter to the Romans."

75. I am conscious as I read the quotes from 1 Corinthians, 1 Timothy, and Romans 1 that Paul's moral language sounds harsh to many of us. Three things about this: First, such rhetoric is not very common in our more genteel worlds, but it seems simply to have been a part of Paul's world. Second, reading good biblical commentaries often helps contextualize the language. Third, with the help of commentaries, we as contemporary Christians should desire to know what these texts mean for what we believe and how we live.

76. For a fine study of the history of theological reflections on this see: Roberts, *Creation & Covenant*.

77. For an interpretation of Paul that comports well with what I have said see M. Gorman, *Cruciformity* and M. Gorman, *Apostle of the Crucified Lord*.

78. I have elected not to do heavy documentation of the various revisionists who have made these criticisms. I have read these sources. For a selection of them see Ted's annotated reading list at the end of the book. I also have a fifteen-page bibliography posted on my faculty website.

79. Linda Woodhead, "Sex in a Wider Context," in Davies and Loughlin, eds., *Sex These Days*, 98 (quoting from the *Oxford English Dictionary*).

80. This is not to say words have no power. They certainly do. And I specifically wonder if the words "homosexuality" and "sexuality," both

coming into existence in the nineteenth-century, reflect and help promote a greater divorcing of sex from relationships. That is to say, sex as used in the Scriptures is a relational term. "Sexuality" and "homosexuality" are often either abstractions or relate only to one's individual identity.

81. I would remind the reader of the literature I have referred to throughout the footnotes, especially my overview of what I consider some of the more important literature that I referred to close to the beginning of this section of my essay.

82. T. Wright, *The Pastoral Letters*, 10, 9, emphasis his.

83. This is a famous line from Lewis Carroll's *Through the Looking-Glass*.

84. Bayer, *Homosexuality and American Psychiatry*; also see the book by psychiatrist Satinover, *Homosexuality and the Politics of Truth*. By my comments I am not suggesting this process was unique to this issue; I doubt that it was. I am simply challenging the assumption that the shift that was made was done through careful deliberation, based upon significant empirical data, that then swayed the majority of the voters because of the weight of the evidence.

85. I say more or less "traditional" signaling both that I am aware there is not one traditional view and that mine in some measure differs from some positions that would use that label. By traditional I am simply meaning that I am intending my summary to reflect a deep rootage in the Scriptures and the traditions of the church.

86. This summary is deeply indebted to the wonderful essay by Linda Woodhead, "Sex in a Wider Context." In the first part of the essay she carefully, if succinctly, critiques a number of revisionist views of sex, then offers her own account of sex within marriage, based largely on Ephesians 5. I would also mention: Watson, *Agape, Eros, Gender*; Meilaender, "Sexuality"; Banner, *Christian Ethics and Contemporary Moral Problems*, 252-68, 269-309; and Clapp, *Families at the Crossroads*. I have also appreciated the very helpful book by Christopher Chenault Roberts, *Creation & Covenant*.

87. Though we should not speak as if no one who is gay or lesbian "chooses." I have been told, for instance, that the level of temporary "choosing" of lesbian relationships has increased on many college campuses.

88. What appears to be the most sophisticated study of "orientation" is Stein, *Mismeasure of Desire*. Whether or not one wants to follow

Stein in detail he demonstrates the complexity of the concept of orientation. Also see Schmidt, *Straight & Narrow?* 131-59; Jones and Yarhouse, *Homosexuality*; and Jones and Kwee, "Scientific Research."

89. See Orr, "What's Not." Orr is reviewing a book that both makes the same point and attempts to summarize much of the most recent research on genetics, namely, Matt Ridley, *Nature via Nurture.* (The title for the paperback version is *The Agile Gene.*) Also see Richard Lewontin, *The Triple Helix.*

90. My own story poses at least the following thoughts to ponder: (1) having one's earliest memories be connected to same-sex relations is not *necessarily* deterministic, (2) simplistic understandings of "choice" are just that—simplistic, (3) social environments—and the morals connected to them—are not irrelevant for what choices are made.

91. See Garber, *Vice Versa: Bisexuality and the Eroticism of Everyday Life.* Perhaps the second half of her subtitle is prophetic in relation to "celebrating" bisexuality.

92. See the careful and insightful book by psychologist, J. Michael Bailey, *Man Who Would Be Queen.*

93. Van Leeuwen, *My Brother's Keeper*, 208. Also see: Rhoads, *Taking Sex Differences Seriously*; Don Browning and Elizabeth Marquardt, "What About the Children?: Liberal Cautions on Same-Sex Marriage," in George and Elshtain, eds., *The Meaning of Marriage*, 29-52; and Blankenhorn, *Future of Marriage.*

94. Of course the results of studies vary somewhat, but the generalizations I've given hold, as far as I am aware. I have elected not to include specific statistics. For those who are interested see the nuanced discussion in Gagnon, *The Bible and Homosexual Practice*, 452-60; also see Jones and Yarhouse, *Homosexuality*, 109-10 and Schmidt, *Straight & Narrow?*, 105-8. These pages are reporting from a broad range of data.

95. A few women have reacted to my statement here, believing that I mean to be implying that, therefore, women are *responsible* for domesticating men. I certainly am not saying that. I mean to be saying four things. First, study after study affirms what I am saying; I haven't heard a better explanation of the data. Second, men *and* women need to be aware of this, if it is a reality about males. Third, both males and females should conduct themselves in a way that respects this reality. Fourth, the data seem to suggest the wisdom in the role of heterosexual marriages and families within God's design.

96. See the discussion and bibliography in Schmidt, *Straight & Narrow*, 116-22, 222-31; also on this and the next topic see the book by psychiatrist, Satinover, *Homosexuality*.

97. Again see the book by psychiatrist, Satinover, *Homosexuality*; also see Jones and Yarhouse, *Homosexuality*, 101-7 and Schmidt, *Straight & Narrow*, 112-16.

98. This is at least one of the central problems within what is one of the most serious efforts to mount a "traditional" argument to justify same-sex marriages by E. Rogers, *Sexuality and the Christian Body*. But don't take my word for it see the following careful critiques: Wannenwetsch, "Old Docetism"; Farrow, "Beyond Nature"; Meilaender, "What Sex Is"; and Roberts, *Creation & Covenant*, 198-219.

99. There is a sub-group within the hearing impaired community who do precisely that.

100. This challenge is hardly unique to this issue. With a heightened awareness of the influences of social conditions and biology, many of us struggle with how to come to grips with these complex realities. Again Cornelius Plantinga, in his book, *Not the Way It's Supposed to Be*, at least is a way to begin thinking about these issues in a way to avoid simplistic answers.

101. John Colwell, "Christ, Creation and Human Sexuality," Bradshaw, ed., *The Way Forward*, 92, 93, adapted. In trying better to understand this I have reached for analogies to homosexuality. Christopher Wolfe shows some of the ways in which the analogy with alcoholism is helpful in Wolfe, "Homosexuality in American Public Life," in Wolfe, ed., *Same Sex Matters*, 3-25, 257-61, esp. 5-11. If only taken as partial analogies it seems to me that reflections on bi-polar conditions, sexual addictions, and adults with Down syndrome all might also have some promise.

102. Moberly, "The Use of Scripture," 253. This is without question the best brief essay I have read.

103. Moberly, "Use of Scripture," 251.

104. It seems that every time I am prepared to be finished with this essay I am made aware of something else I should read on the subject. I am also aware that I simply have to say: "This is all I can do at this point" and be aware that there is always more to read, more to know. Though that is true, I do want to name two 2006 books that are probably worth consulting, that I was unable to take adequate

account of as I finish this. These are: Radner and Turner, *The Fate of Communion* and Johnson, *A Time to Embrace*.

105. For example, Mark's only reference to the 2005 book by Myers and Scanzoni, *What God Has Joined Together*, is simply to dismiss it as appearing "not to be well-informed by very broad reading" (footnote 21). He does not engage their argument in favor of monogamous, covenanted same-sex partnerships in order to show why the same-sexness of such relationships would render them immoral.

106. Mark does briefly interact with "alternative views." However, this interaction is little more than simply listing various points and dismissing them. He cites no specific writers and generally presents these points in caricatured ways. He does not deal with any sustained argumentation that has been developed over the course of longer essays or books by inclusive writers.

107. Though I didn't reference it, perhaps it was my awareness of the Welcome Letter that led me to make this positive assertion.

108. Though I do believe some urbane Mennonites are tempted to embrace what Russell Reno refers to as "Bourgeois Bohemianism." See Reno, "Sex in the Episcopal Church," in *In the Ruins of the Church*, 111-26.

109. The Brethren Mennonite Council (BMC) is an activist organization lobbying to change the Church of the Brethren and Mennonites to an affirming position regarding gay/ lesbian/ bisexual/ transgendered people. I would not try to guess as to how many others, besides writers, fit what I have said.

110. Which is not to say it never happens. I could cite various and complex examples myself.

111. I've also had lengthy personal conversations with Robert. As far as I can tell his motives are his general concern for the church and faithful discipleship.

112. In addition to other references I gave earlier see also: Thiselton, "Can Hermeneutics Ease the Deadlock?" in Bradshaw, ed., *The Way Forward*, 180-83, Gagnon, *The Bible and Homosexual Practice*, 111-46.

113. I did not go into the detail precisely because that would entail naming considerable detail. But, in addition to N. T. Wright and Gagnon, see Hays, "Relations Natural and Unnatural"; Schmidt, *Straight & Narrow*, 64-85; and Smith, "Ancient Bisexuality."

114. Hays, *First Corinthians*, 100.

115. See: Rosner, *Paul, Scripture, & Ethics*; and Thiselton, *First Epistle to the Corinthians*, 381-606.

116. See footnote 26 in that essay, I could easily have multiplied the number of references. For supportive details see Gagnon, *Bible and Homosexual Practice*, 159-83.

Chapter 4

1. Perhaps surprisingly, given the unprecedented upheaval Mennonite churches have faced over the issue of "homosexuality," the Mennonite academic community has been slow to produce careful scholarly work on these issues. Scattered pieces, more in a sociological, rhetorical, or pastoral vein, have addressed how Mennonites debate this issue (see especially, Biesecker-Mast, "Mennonite Public Discourse" and King, *Fractured Dance*). My files contain only a few fairly short *unpublished* papers by Mennonite scholars on biblical and theological aspects of the issues. Only recently has a volume of Mennonite essays beginning to address these issues been published (Kraus, ed., *To Continue the Dialogue*). Finally, in 2003 Herald Press published Willard Swartley's book, *Homosexuality*. Though I disagree with many of Swartley's points, I am grateful to him for giving us the first sustained Mennonite treatment of many of the biblical and theological issues.

2. I use scare quotes here to signal that I am conscious of the contested nature of this term itself. For most of the chapter, I will use the term "gay" as explained below.

3. For brevity's sake, I will henceforth use the term "gay" as shorthand for "self-affirming gay and lesbian Christians." Our use of words matters a great deal, and yet at this point in the discussion we have not yet comfortably settled on consensus terminology. My use of "gays" in this paper has only practical significance; I am trying to use a shorthand term that will be clear.

4. Swartley, *Homosexuality*; Gagnon, *Bible and Homosexual Practice*.

5. Hanigan, *Homosexuality*.

6. Scanzoni and Mollenkott, *Is the Homosexual My Neighbor?*

7. Walter Wink, "Homosexuality and the Bible," in Wink, ed., *Homosexuality and Christian Faith*, 33-49.

8. Most restrictive writers I know of reiterate this truism. See, for example, Robert Gagnon's assertion that taking what I call an inclusive

stance entails "a radical devaluation of the place of Scripture in the life of the church" (Robert A. J. Gagnon, "The Bible and Homosexual Practice: Key Issues," in Via and Gagnon, *Homosexuality and the Bible*, 41).

9. By "unrestricted participation" here, I am specifically referring to restrictions placed on a church person's participation in the church due only to one's being gay. The perspective I will present would accept possible restrictions due to sexual misbehavior, but these would apply equally to heterosexual and gay people.

10. See Grimsrud, *God's Healing Strategy*.

11. For more on the biblical view of justice, see Ted Grimsrud, "Peace Theology and the Justice of God in the Book of Revelation," in Swartley, ed., *Essays on Peace Theology*, 135-53; Ted Grimsrud, "Healing Justice: The Prophet Amos and a 'New' Theology of Justice," in Grimsrud and Johns, eds., *Peace and Justice*, 64-85; Grimsrud and Zehr, "Rethinking"; and Grimsrud, "Violence."

12. For an account supporting the belief that gays should, as a class, be seen as "vulnerable people," see Fone, *Homophobia*.

13. I owe this term to Marcus Borg in *Jesus*, 131-40.

14. Yoder, *Politics of Jesus*, 40.

15. Bartchy, "Table Fellowship," 796-97.

16. We certainly also need to look at other issues, probably most centrally the question of whether biblical teaching related to marriage and creation would provide such a basis, and I will discuss this issue late in this essay. However, the issue of marriage/creation is at most *indirectly* related to the issue of the inherent sinfulness of intimate gay relationships. None of the texts related to the marriage/creation issue speaks of homosexuality and none of the "core texts" on homosexuality directly refers to creation/marriage. I want to suggest that if we did not have a sense from the core texts that homosexual intimacy is wrong, we would not be concerned with the marriage/creation argument. So the most basic issue remains the core texts and whether they make the case the committed gay partnerships are intrinsically sinful.

17. Old Testament scholar Christopher Seitz argues against the tendency of many on the inclusive side to focus on sophisticated critical readings of biblical materials as a means of evading the "plain sense" of the Bible (Seitz, "Sexuality and Scripture's Plain Sense: The Christian Community and the Law of God," in Balch, ed., *Homosexuality*, 177-96.) Seitz, though, does not give us a clear explanation of what he means by

"plain sense." He appears to equate it with "the time-honored [interpretations] in church and synagogue" (189). However, I believe that our only alternatives are not either (1) higher-critical deconstructions or (2) uncritical acceptance of "time-honored" interpretations. By "plain sense" I mean a straightforward reading of biblical materials taking most seriously their literary integrity and their place in the overall canonical context. Just as Jesus and Paul challenged time-honored interpretations of their day on the basis of a plain sense reading of Torah itself, I find it most respectful of biblical authority to accept the likelihood that careful reading of the texts themselves might well cause us to reject many time-honored interpretations.

18. James Barr wrote many years ago "it is the sentence (and of course the still larger literary complex such as the complete speech or poem) which is the linguistic bearer of the usual theological statement, not the word (the lexical unit) or the morphological and syntactical connection" (*Semantics*, 263).

19. Brueggemann, *Genesis*, 163.

20. Fretheim, "Genesis," 468.

21. Fretheim, "Genesis," 473.

22. Fretheim, "Genesis," 474.

23. Edwards, *Gay/Lesbian Liberation*, 25.

24. Contrary to the position of Gagnon, *Bible and Homosexual Practice*, 75.

25. Edwards, *Gay/Lesbian*, 35.

26. Edwards, *Gay/Lesbian*, 37-38.

27. Hamlin, *Judges*, 164, and Nissinen, *Homoeroticism in the Biblical World*, 49-52.

28. Scholars who tend toward restrictive views do not as a rule ground their positions on this passage. Grenz, *Welcoming but not Affirming*, is typical in admitting that at most Genesis 19 refers to "violent homosexual rape," not "homosexual relationships between consenting adults" (40). If this is the case, the debate over the meaning of the term "to know" (Genesis 19:5)—whether it means sexual intercourse or not—is of little importance to the issue of whether the Bible condemns *all* expressions of same-sex sexual intimacy. However, both Gagnon, *Bible and Homosexual Practice*, and Wold, *Homosexuality*, do uphold the long-held association of this text with a general condemnation of all same-sex sexual intimacy.

29. Milgrom, "Leviticus," 543-44.

30. J. R. Porter, "Leviticus," in Achtemeier, ed., *HarperCollins Bible Dictionary*, 604.

31. F. Gorman, *Leviticus*, 100.

32. Baruch A. Levine, "Book of Leviticus," in Freedman, ed., *Anchor Dictionary*, 316.

33. Levine, "Book of Leviticus," 316.

34. Levine, *Leviticus*, 123.

35. Levine, *Leviticus*, 117.

36. Milgrom, "Leviticus," 544.

37. Gorman, *Leviticus*, 108.

38. See, for example, Wold, *Out of Order*, 104. Wold builds his elaborate argument for making Leviticus' prohibition a universal condemnation of *all* male/male *and* female/female sex on the use of the Hebrew term *zakar* ("male"). However, he does not cite any *direct* Old Testament discussion of same-sex sex, only inferences based on what the Old Testament says about opposite-sex relationships. Such inferences perhaps are relevant for our present-day hermeneutical task of discerning and applying biblical teaching for our sexual ethics. However, mere inferences provide little basis for making a positive case that the Bible in principle condemns homosexuality.

39. Debates over the meaning of Romans 1 dominate biblically oriented discussions of homosexuality. Richard Hays asserts, "the most crucial text for Christian ethics concerning homosexuality remains Romans 1" (*Moral Vision*, 383). Hays himself wrote a much cited essay examining Romans 1—"Relations Natural and Unnatural," as well as seven closely reasoned pages on Romans 1 in his chapter on homosexuality in *Moral Vision*. Arguing for the opposite conclusion from Hays's restrictive view of homosexuality, Victor Paul Furnish also pays close attention to Romans 1 in his chapter, "Homosexuality," in *Moral Teaching of Paul*.

What renders these discussions deeply unsatisfactory from my perspective is how writers on all sides of the issue seem to lose sight of the forest in their focus on the trees. That is, they argue as if the meaning and relevance of Romans 1 for the Bible's stance on homosexuality relies on the meaning of specific words—assuming that in some sense the main point of Romans 1:18-32 is to address the issue of homosexuality.

As I propose below, with a more contextual reading of these verses much of this narrow debate loses most of its relevance.

40. My interpretation of Romans is indebted to Dunn, *Romans 1–8.*

41. David E. Fredrickson, "Natural and Unnatural Use in Romans 1:24-27: Paul and the Philosophic Critique of Eros," in Balch, ed., *Homosexuality,* 199.

42. Fredrickson, "Natural and Unnatural," in Balch, ed., *Homosexuality,* 199-207.

43. Elliott, *Liberating Paul,* 194.

44. Elliott, *Liberating Paul,* 194.

45. Elliott, *Liberating Paul,* 194-95.

46. Elliott, *Liberating Paul,* 195.

47. Hays, *First Corinthians,* 93.

48. Hays, *First Corinthians,* 93-94.

49. Hays, *First Corinthians,* 97.

50. Hays, *First Corinthians,* 98.

51. Nonetheless, also as with Romans 1, debates concerning the application of 1 Corinthians 6 to homosexuality focus on the meaning of specific words without paying much attention to the wider context. Following the common English translations that use "homosexuals" and "sodomites," some scholars have concluded that Paul has in mind here a general condemnation of homosexuality (e.g., Gagnon, *Bible and Homosexual Practice,* 331, and Schmidt, *Straight & Narrow,* 96).

I will argue below that these are not adequate translations; my point here is that regardless of what the Greek words *malakos* and *arsenokoites* mean, if read in the context of the message of 1 Corinthians 6, they clearly are not being used to make a point about Christian sexual ethics. They are being used to make a more general point about pagan injustice and Paul's calling Christians to justice.

52. Dale B. Martin, "*Arsenokoites* and *Malakos:* Meanings and Consequences," in Brawley, ed., *Biblical Ethics and Homosexuality,* 118-19.

53. Wold, *Out of Order,* 189-90.

54. Martin, "*Arsenokoites* and *Malakos,*" 120.

55. Martin, "*Arsenokoites* and *Malakos,*" 120.

56. I'm not implying that that one man, one woman, equal partners for life is not the norm for today's Christians. I *do* believe in this ideal

for marriage. I believe in this normative ideal because it seems closely to cohere with important general biblical themes concerning commitment, fidelity, trust, mutual accountability, and the role of sexual intimacy in emotionally binding marriage partners together.

The ideal of marital fidelity and equal partnership also seems to me (from personal experience) to offer potential for fruitful living and healthy faith communities—and violations of marital ideals (infidelity, abuse, neglect) reap profoundly harmful consequences.

Nonetheless, it seems only honest to recognize that our present ideals cannot simply be read rotely as timeless, direct "biblical absolutes for marriage." They have emerged over time in the interplay of theology, practice, cultural dynamics, self-reflection, social science, and other factors.

Many on the inclusive side believe that same-sex couples are as fully capable of living with commitment, fidelity, and mutual accountability as heterosexual couples—and should be supported in doing so by their faith communities. On these themes, see Myers and Scanzoni, *What God Has Joined Together* and Johnson, *A Time to Embrace*.

57. See Ruether, *Christianity and the Making of the Modern Family*.

58. See Schmidt, *Straight & Narrow*, chapter 6, and Gagnon, *Bible and Homosexual Practice*, chapter 5, part VII.

59. In Grimsrud, "Pacifism and Knowing," I use the Mennonite church's processing of the homosexuality issue as a case study for putting into practice the pacifist epistemology I advocate.

60. Pohl, *Making Room*, 31.

61. Let me say that the phrase "to all who trust in God" might have been a significant modifier. However, he does not seem to develop this important phrase in the way the Scriptures do.

62. Pohl, *Making Room*, 27-28.

63. Pohl, *Making Room*, 136-37.

64. DeSilva, *Honor, Patronage, Kinship & Purity*, 313.

65. DeSilva, *Honor, Patronage, Kinship & Purity*, 313.

66. Pohl, *Making Room*, 136, emphasis mine.

67. Volf, *Exclusion and Embrace*, 72-73.

68. In addition to the literature we have referenced in footnotes, see our annotated bibliographies.

69. Ted provides footnotes for the essays by Fredrickson and Elliott. Gagnon provides a five page response to Elliott and a thirty-four page response to Fredrickson on his website, www.robgagnon.net.

70. Each of the other authors I mentioned above have also dealt with Romans 1. See references elsewhere in this book.

71. I was also rather surprised that Ted would suggest that *adikian* is "misleadingly translated" when it is translated as either wickedness or unrighteousness. The word is quite legitimately translated with either of those words—or injustice. I would think that Ted knows that the New Testament uses the same word for injustice or unrighteousness and the context helps determine whether the word might be more properly translated into English as injustice, unrighteousness or a related word, such as wickedness. Apparently since Ted has decided, apart from the specific context, that the meaning *must* fit with inclusivist ideology then "wickedness" or "unrighteousness" is automatically deemed an illegitimate translation.

72. For alternative interpretations of these chapters, in addition to what is offered in the relevant section of my earlier essay, I would point the reader to: N. Wright, "The Letter to the Romans," 413-86. Also, on matters related to grace and justification, see: DeSilva, "Patronage and Grace in the New Testament," in *Honor, Patronage, Kinship & Purity*, 121-56 and Gorman, *Cruciformity*, esp. 95-154.

73. See, for instance, the interesting series on "Religion, Marriage, and Family" edited by Don S. Browning and David Clairmont, which displays both variation and continuity.

74. See my brief section, "A Traditional Christian View of Heterosexual Marriage," in my longer essay.

75. See, e.g., "Marriage," *The Anchor Bible Dictionary*, Vol. 4: K-N. New York: Doubleday, 1992, s.v.

76. Oliver O'Donovan, "Homosexuality in the Church," in *The Way Forward?*, 28.

77. Quoted by Hays, *Moral Vision*, 3.

78. Quoted in Harrisville and Sundberg, *Bible in Modern Culture*, 169-70. This is not a call for anti-intellectualism; Kierkegaard himself was a brilliant man. It is simply a warning that our scholarship should be driven and defined by the gospel of Jesus Christ in profound ways.

79. Newman, *Untamed Hospitality*, 30-33, quote p. 31.

80. Philip Turner, "ECUSA's God and the Idols of Liberal Protestantism," in Radner and Turner, *Fate of Communion*, 245, 247-48, 248-49.

81. In addition to literature mentioned elsewhere, let me men-

tion: Miles, *Redemption of Love*; McMinn, *Sexuality and Holy Longing*; and Roberts, *Creation & Covenant*.

82. To support this point, I note that the terms "tolerant," "tolerance," "intolerant," and "intolerance" appear nowhere in my essay.

83. To illustrate my affirmation of the biblical call to repentance see my Bible Study lessons on most of the Old Testament prophets in the *Mennonite Weekly Review* (May 11 through August 13, 2007).

84. Mark seems to acknowledge this when he refers to me making "hospitality *an* overarching or programmatic theme within Scripture" (italics added)—though it is troubling that later he writes that for me "hospitality or welcome becomes *the* overarching biblical theme" (italics added).

85. See my book, *God's Healing Strategy*, where I posit God's "strategy" of blessing all the families of the earth through the witness of Abraham's descendants as a central rubric in the Bible. "Healing," of course, implies that something is wrong that needs transformation. That is, I read the Bible as containing a message of sharp critique of the human condition, a call to repentance/turning to God, and a call to transforming (or restorative) justice that manifests God's holiness as a disposition to heal that which has been damaged—in the human heart and in human societies. This is *not* a message of "cheap grace," "tolerance," or an "ideology of inclusiveness."

Chapter 6

1. The following footnotes attached to Ted's question are Mark's. They are Mark's brief comments on some of Ted's interpretative moves. Mark's own interpretations will follow. We encourage you to read through Ted's question first before reading Mark's footnotes—so as to get a sense of the flow of his comments.

2. Ted seems to be assuming that the adjective unjust/unrighteous (*adikon*) is naming specific, harmful behavior/s. Nothing in the text supports that claim. In fact, especially in light of the contrast with "the saints" in the same verse, the word seems, in this verse, to point to a status ascribed automatically to unbelievers by Paul (not uncommon in the Scriptures). Then this meaning is relevant for the ongoing discussion in these verses. (As I said earlier, *adikon* can mean either unjust or unrighteous. The primary referent is always, biblically, God—what God enables within us and asks of us. *Adikon* then refers to falling short of God's call upon our lives. The context helps determine the specific meaning.)

3. Ted claims that the word "this" in "And *this* is what some of you used to be" (v. 11) refers back to "the unrighteous" [judge, implied], v. 1 (and implied through v. 6). The more obvious referent is the list of those who are wrongdoers, which immediately precedes the comment (vv. 9-10). And, yes, Paul does mean to describe some of "those presently in the church." Although he is very specific, saying "and this is what some of you *used* to be." Various ones in the Corinthian Christian community lived this way in the past. Then they were "washed," "sanctified" and "justified." Thus they no longer live in this way; they live as those who are being sanctified rather than like the unrighteous/wrongdoers.

4. I have two problems here with Ted's interpretation. First, the central subject is the church and what the church is to be; it is not unrighteous judges. Additionally, I wonder if Ted has not here shown some of his cards. Any behavior, to be wrong for Ted, must be shown to cause immediate and obvious harm (*immediate* and *obvious* are important here). Thus for Ted each of these vices has to be redefined so they fit that definition. (I am intending to address this a bit more fully in my response to Ted's next question.)

5. This is Anthony Thiselton's translation. For his justification and discussion of it see: Thiselton, *First Epistle to the Corinthians*, 408-13. (I added the word "sexually" because "sexually immoral person" is what the word *pornois* means.)

6. And, as I argued earlier, hospitality clearly has a place in the Christian community. But, as indicated by this passage, within the Christian community hospitality is to be tied to retaining our identity as a community that is sanctified in Christ.

7. Hays, *First Corinthians*, 92-93.

8. Kenneth Bailey makes the argument that Paul begins a new section with 6:9 that continues to the end of the chapter. See: Bailey, "Paul's Theological Foundation for Human Sexuality." Whether we want to follow Bailey in that claim, the following comments are important: "[Bailey] points out that of the ten 'vices' listed in 6:9-10, five allude to sexual issues, which directly relate to 5:1-13 and 6:12-20; while a further five relate to issues of greed and grasping, eating and being drunk, which are taken up explicitly in 11:17-34. In Bailey's incisive study the specific significance of Paul's 'list' for issues at Corinth becomes undeniable" (Thiselton, *First Epistle to the Corinthians*, 448).

9. Of course sexual immorality, adultery, idolatry, and homosex-

ual practice can all be connected to violent and unjust practices. But they are not by definition. All the terms are broader than that.

10. Hays, *First Corinthians*, 98. It seems to me what you have done is to *reduce* the meaning of the whole to the second of these three points. But as Hays's full discussion (92-101) shows, all three concerns together equal much more than simply a contemporary understanding of social justice.

11. Thiselton, *First Epistle to the Corinthians*, 419.

12. Hays, *First Corinthians*, 97.

13. The relevant phrases from the Greek translation of Leviticus (without accent marks) are: Leviticus 18:22: *meta **arsenos** ou koimethese **koiten** gunaikos*; Leviticus 20:13: *os an koimethe meta **arsenos koiten** gunaikos.* (As you can see in Leviticus 20:13 the two words are, in fact, right next to each other.)

14. Of course I have provided an overly simple summary of a complicated debate. For a superb and nuanced summary of the debate see: Thiselton, "Vice Lists, Catechesis, and the Homosexuality Debate (6:9-10)," in *First Epistle to the Corinthians*, 440-53. For a fuller picture of the debate see: Boswell, Christianity, *Social Tolerance, and Homosexuality*, 106-7, 335-53; D. Wright, "Homosexuals or Prostitutes?" and "Translating *Arsenokoitai*"; Petersen, "Can *Arsenokoitai* Be Translated By 'Homosexuality'"; Dale B. Martin, "*Arsenokoitês* and *Malakos*: Meanings and Consequences," in *Sex and the Single Savior*, 37-50, 201-6; and Gagnon, *Bible and Homosexual Practice*, 303-39 (and essays on his website).

15. Boswell quoted in Wright, "Homosexuals or Prostitutes?"

16. There should be no need to document the patent absurdity of the claim that the Old Testament does not inform morality in the New. Nonetheless, for one study that shows the absurdity and its relevance for the passage we are examining see: Rosner, *Paul, Scripture, & Ethics*.

17. Johnson, "Scripture & Experience," 14-17.

18. Even if your interpretation of *malakos* is correct, you still must make a few more significant (and not yet justified) steps to see this as strong evidence for forbidding all possible same-sex intimate partnerships. For one thing, how does the reference to static "passive" and "active" partners speak to on-going *mutual* relationships? Secondly, how does this reference to *male* practices have relevance for female same-sex partners?

19. Of course these matters can be debated, especially in relation

to the translation of specific verses. However, it appears that most translators agree that it is distorting always to translate the words with *dik* as a root as some form of the word "just."

20. Let me state what is perhaps obvious: the verbal parallel with the Greek translation of the Old Testament still stands even if one isn't convinced that the wrongness of homosexual practice was assumed among average Jews at the time of Jesus and Paul. It's just that the significance of the verbal parallel seems even more apparent if Judaism was more or less of one mind about homosexual practice.

21. The most thorough discussions I have seen of this topic are: Gagnon, *Bible and Homosexual Practice*, 43-183 and DeYoung, *Homosexuality*, 23-136, 265-68. But compare: Scroggs, *New Testament and Homosexuality*, 66-98; Nissinen, *Homoeroticism in the Biblical World*, 37-56, 89-102; Greenberg, *Construction of Homosexuality*, 135-41, 190-202; and Crompton, *Homosexuality & Civilization*, 32-48.

22. Bader-Saye, "Violence, Reconciliation, and the Justice of God," 536, 538.

23. I would recommend *The Interpreter's Dictionary of the Bible* and *The Anchor Bible Dictionary*. But any good one would do. Note: in the New Testament we are dealing with one Greek root word, variously translated, depending on context, by some form of the word just or righteous. In the Old Testament the vocabulary is a bit more complicated, but there is a similar interrelationship between justice or righteousness (depending on the context).

24. We also must note that, biblically, *our* faithfulness is only possible because of what God has done for us. Thus we must keep in mind that salvation and sanctification (or holiness) are topics that are vitally connected to any full discussion of righteousness/justice.

25. I was reminded of this through an explicit discussion of this general concern and then an attempt to use such a category through reading a book on mission recently. In this case I thought it was in fact illuminating because of the nature of the category combined with the rich way in which it was explicated. See: C. Wright, *Mission of God*.

26. However, I do want to qualify this statement. Just because this particular issue might not be the most important issue does not mean it is unimportant. I would agree with J. Andrew Kirk: "to minimize the importance of right sexual relationships on the grounds that there are more substantial issues of injustice and abuse is to make a false choice.

The Gospel is directed toward all forms of dissonance between God's world of righteousness and our world of unrighteousness." Kirk, "The Gospel in Context: The Case of Same Gender Relations," in *Mission under Scrutiny*, 189.

27. I believe everything I have said here. But I have intentionally said it here in abbreviated form. Of course all of these statements must be held together with what I have said throughout the book.

Chapter 7

1. Three of the best discussions I have seen along these lines are: Jenson, "Holiness in the Priestly Writings in the Old Testament," in *Holiness*, 93-121; deSilva, *Honor, Patronage, Kinship & Purity*, 241-315; and Bockmuehl, "Keeping It Holy," in *I Am the Lord Your God*, ed. Braaten and Seitz. Also see Klawans, *Impurity and Sin in Ancient Judaism*.

2. Plantinga, *Not the Way It's Supposed to Be*, 10.

3. "Vandalizing shalom" is the wonderful expression of Plantinga, *Not the Way It's Supposed to Be*, 7.

4. For a rich understanding of sin see the wonderful book by Plantinga already named. Also see Biddle, *Missing the Mark*.

5. See my comments on the Presbyterian Church document in chapter two, above (and see references there).

6. On this see: Roberts, *Creation & Covenant*; Van Leeuwen, *My Brother's Keeper*; and Rhoads, *Taking Sex Differences Seriously*.

7. Gold, "Getting Real," 6.

8. I have alluded to these matters and pointed to some of the most relevant literature in the last main section of my longer essay. Also see the new book by Blankenhorn, *Future of Marriage*. Though I certainly don't agree with all of it, nonetheless, as someone who is quite concerned about the welfare of marriage and children, he has provided a carefully argued and well-documented book.

9. Since I have referred to Christian tradition numerous times, I should name one thing. I think some of my fellow Anabaptists are insufficiently appreciative of the wisdom we can gain from Christian tradition. I learned this from John Yoder. As Yoder said, "The clash is not tradition versus Scripture but faithful tradition versus irresponsible tradition." John Howard Yoder, "The Authority of Tradition," in *Priestly Kingdom*, 69. If we undervalue the tradition across time we are likely to overvalue contemporary wisdom and insight.

10. You have raised the issue of other "exceptions" that have been made. Simply put, divorce by most of us is still considered a sin and a serious sin at that. But it is instructive to discuss "concessions" we have made in this regard and how they might or might not be instructive for this discussion. (See the various writings by David Instone-Brewer on divorce and remarriage.) A number of writings I have already referenced offer insightful reflections on the problem with a total divorcing of the act of sex from the possibility of procreation and the rearing of children. Most would not see this only in relation to homosexual practice.

11. See the references regarding different dimensions of the issue in the last main section of my longest essay.

12. One of my normal small acts of resistance in the present "war on terrorism" is to refuse to use the term "9/11." Instead I refer to September 11, 2001. This small gesture is intended to resist the simplistic and too often nationalistic interpretations of this single day.

13. In addition to what I've said above, let me point, one last time, to the illuminating essay: Linda Woodhead, "Sex in a Wider Context," in Davies and Loughlin, *Sex These Days*, 98-120.

14. My repeated comments about males and females are not intended to underwrite the gender "essentialism" that you worry about. Rather they are intended to take seriously many studies that have been done, some of which I have referenced.

15. For one account of the zeitgeist regarding sexual issues as shaped by the media over the last fifty years see: Streitmatter, *Sex Sells!* Also see: Regnerus, *Forbidden Fruit*.

Chapter 8

1. E. Achtemeier, "Righteousness in the OT," and P. Achtemeier, "Righteousness in the NT"; "Righteousness," *Anchor Bible Dictionary*: Vol. 5, 724-73. Though I wouldn't want to make too much of it, nonetheless it is interesting that the *Interpreter's Dictionary of the Bible* doesn't have an entry under "justice" and the *Anchor Bible Dictionary* only has a few pages under "justice," though, of course, both dictionaries discuss justice under the overarching category of "righteousness."

Bibliography

Abraham, William J. "United Methodists at the End of the Mainline." *First Things* 84 (June/July 1998): 28-33.

Achtemeier, Elizabeth R. "Righteousness in the OT." In *Interpreter's Dictionary of the Bible*, s.v.

Achtemeier, Paul J. "Righteousness in the NT," in *Interpreters' Dictionary*, 91-99.

Anchor Bible Dictionary. David Noel Freedman, ed. New York: Doubleday, 1992.

Bader-Saye, Scott. "The Freedom of Faithfulness." *Pro Ecclesia* (Fall 1999): 437-58.

Bader-Saye, Scott. "Violence, Reconciliation, and the Justice of God." *Crosscurrents* (Winter 2003): 536-42.

Bailey, J. Michael. *The Man Who Would Be Queen: The Science of Gender-Bending and Transsexualism*. Washington: Joseph Henry Press, 2003.

Bailey, Kenneth E. "Paul's Theological Foundation for Human Sexuality: 1 Corinthians 6:9-20 in the Light of Rhetorical Criticism." *Theological Review* 3 (1980): 27-41.

Balch, David L., ed. *Homosexuality, Science, and the 'Plain Sense' of Scripture*. Grand Rapids, MI: Eerdmans, 2000.

Banner, Michael. *Christian Ethics and Contemporary Moral Problems*. Cambridge, UK: Cambridge University Press, 1999.

Barr, James. *The Semantics of Biblical Language*. New York: Oxford University Press, 1961.

Bartchy, Scott. "Table Fellowship," in Joel B. Green, Scot McKnight, and I. Howard Marshall, eds., *Dictionary of Jesus and the Gospels*. Downers Grove, IL: InterVarsity Press, 1992. 796-97.

Bayer, Ronald. *Homosexuality and American Psychiatry: The Politics of Diagnosis*. Princeton: Princeton University Press, 1987.

Behr, John. *Asceticism and Anthropology in Irenaeus and Clement*. New York: Oxford University Press, 2000.

Bell, Daniel M., Jr. "Jesus, the Jews, and the Politics of God's Justice." *Ex Auditu* 22 (2006): 87-112.

Bercier, Barry. "Diverse Diversities," *First Things* (January 2004): 22-27.

Berry, Wendell. *Sex, Economy, Freedom & Community*. New York: Pantheon Press, 1993.

Biddle, Mark E. *Missing the Mark: Sin and Its Consequences in Biblical Theology*. Nashville: Abingdon Press, 2005.

Biesecker-Mast, Gerald. "Mennonite Public Discourse and the Conflicts over Homosexuality" *Mennonite Quarterly Review* 72.2 (April 1998): 275–300.

Blankenhorn, David. *The Future of Marriage*. New York: Encounter Books, 2007.

Bonhoeffer, Dietrich. *Dietrich Bonhoeffer Works, Vol. 4: Discipleship*, trans, Barbara Green and Reinhard Krauss, ed. Geffrey B. Kelly and John D. Godsey. Minneapolis: Fortress Press, 2001.

Borg, Marcus. *Jesus: A New Vision*. San Francisco: HarperSanFrancisco, 1987.

Boswell, John. *Christianity, Social Tolerance, and Homosexuality: Gay People in Western Europe from the Beginning of the Christian Era to the Fourth Century*. Chicago: University of Chicago Press, 1980.

Boswell, John. *The Marriage of Likeness: Same-Sex Unions in Pre-Modern Europe*. London: HarperCollins, 1995.

Braaten, Carl E. and Christopher R. Seitz, eds. *I Am the Lord Your God: Christian Reflections on the Ten Commandments*. Grand Rapids, MI: Eerdmans, 2005.

Bradshaw, Timothy, ed. *The Way Forward? Christian Voices on Homosexuality and the Church*. London: Hodder & Stoughton, 1997. 2nd edition, Grand Rapids, MI: Eerdmans, 2003.

Brawley, Robert L., ed., *Biblical Ethics and Homosexuality: Listening to Scripture*. Louisville: Westminster John Knox Press, 1996.

Brooten, Bernadette J. *Love Between Women: Early Christian Responses to Female Homoeroticism*. Chicago: University of Chicago Press, 1996.

Brown, Peter. *The Body and Society*. New York: Columbia University Press, 1988.

Bruckner, James K. "Justice in Scripture." *Ex Auditu* 22 (2006): 1-9.

Brueggemann, Walter, et al., *To Act Justly, Love Tenderly, Walk Humbly*. New York: Paulist Press, 1986. [reprint: Eugene, OR: Wipf & Stock, 1997]

Brueggemann, Walter. "Biblical Authority: A Personal Reflection." *The Christian Century* (January 3-10, 2001): 14-20.

Brueggemann, Walter. *Genesis*. Atlanta: John Knox Press, 1982.

Brueggemann, Walter. *Interpretation and Obedience: From Faithful Reading to Faithful Living*. Minneapolis: Fortress Press, 1991.

Brueggemann, Walter. *The Book That Breathes New Life*. Minneapolis: Fortress Press, 2005.

Brueggemann, Walter. *The Covenanted Self*. Minneapolis: Fortress Press, 1999.

Brueggemann, Walter. *Theology of the Old Testament*. Minneapolis: Fortress Press, 1997.

Bruner, Frederick Dale. *Matthew, A Commentary: Vol. 2: The Churchbook*, 2nd ed. Grand Rapids, MI: Eerdmans, 2004.

Budziszewski, J. "Just Friends." *First Things* 87 (November 1998): 60-63.

Budziszewski, J. "The Illusion of Moral Neutrality." *First Things* 35 (August/September 1993): 32-37.

Burr, Chandler. *A Separate Creation: How Biology Makes Us Gay*. New York, NY: Bantam Books, 1997.

Butler, Sara. "Sex or Gender?" *First Things* 154 (June/July 2005): 43-47.

Carey, John J. "Body and Soul: Presbyterians on Sexuality." *The Christian Century* 108 (May 8, 1991): 516-20.

Carter, Craig A. *Rethinking Christ and Culture: A Post-Christendom Perspective*. Grand Rapids, MI: Brazos Press, 2006.

Clapp, Rodney. *Border Crossings: Christian Trespasses on Popular Culture and Public Affairs*. Grand Rapids, MI: Brazos Press, 2000.

Clapp, Rodney. *Families at the Crossroads: Beyond Traditional and Modern Options*. Downers Grove, IL: InterVarsity Press, 1993.

Collins, Raymond F. *Sexual Ethics and the New Testament*. New York: Crossroad, 2000.

Comstock, Gary David and Susan E. Henking, eds. *Que(e)rying Religion: A Critical Anthology*. New York: Continuum, 1997.

Comstock, Gary David. *Gay Theology Without Apology*. Cleveland, OH: Pilgrim Press, 1993.

Countryman, L. William. *Dirt, Greed & Sex: Sexual Ethics in the New Testament and Their Implications for Today*. Philadelphia: Fortress Press, 1988.

Crompton, Louis. *Homosexuality & Civilization*. Cambridge, MA: Harvard University Press, 2003.

Davies, Jon and Gerard Loughlin, eds. *Sex These Days: Essays on Theology, Sexuality and Society*. Sheffield, England: Sheffield Academic Press, 1997.

Davis, Ellen F. and Richard B. Hays, eds. *The Art of Reading Scripture*. Grand Rapids, MI: Eerdmans, 2003.

Dawn, Marva. *Sexual Character*. Grand Rapids, MI: Eerdmans, 1993.

deSilva, David A. *Honor, Patronage, Kinship & Purity: Unlocking New Testament Culture*. Downers Grove, IL: InterVarsity Press, 2000.

DeYoung, James B. *Homosexuality: Contemporary Claims*

Examined in Light of the Bible and Other Ancient Literature and Law. Grand Rapids, MI: Kregel Publications, 2000.

Douglas, Mary. *Purity and Danger: An Analysis of the Concepts of Pollution and Taboo.* London: Routledge, 1966.

Dunn, James D. G. Dunn. *Romans 1–8*, Word Biblical Commentary. Dallas: Word Books, 1988.

Dunnam, Maxie D., and H. Newton Malony, eds., *Staying the Course: Supporting the Church's Position on Homosexuality.* Nashville: Abingdon Press, 2003.

Edwards, George. *Gay/Lesbian Liberation: A Biblical Perspective.* New York: The Pilgrim Press, 1984.

Eller, Vernard. *Towering Babble.* Elgin, IL: Brethren Press, 1983.

Elliott, Neil. *Liberating Paul: The Justice of God and the Politics of the Apostle.* Maryknoll, NY: Orbis Books, 1994.

Ellison, Marvin M. and Sylvia Thorson-Smith, eds. *Body and Soul: Rethinking Sexuality as Justice-Love.* Cleveland, Ohio: Pilgrim Press, 2003.

Estlund, David M. and Martha C. Nussbaum, eds, *Sex, Preference, and Family.* New York: Oxford University Press, 1997.

Farrow, Douglas. "Beyond Nature, Shy of Grace." *International Journal of Systematic Theology* 5 (November 2003): 261-86.

———. *Nation of Bastards: Essays on the End of Marriage.* Toronto: BPS Books, 2007.

Fone, Byrne. *Homophobia: A History.* New York: Metropolitan Books, 2000.

Fowl, Stephen E. *Engaging Scripture.* Oxford: Blackwell, 1998.

Fretheim, Terence E. "Genesis," in Leander Keck, ed. *New Interpreter's Bible: Volume I.* Nashville: Abingdon Press, 1994.

Friedman, Ellen G. and Corinne Squire. *Morality USA.* Minneapolis: University of Minnesota Press, 1998.

Furnish, Victor Paul. *The Moral Teaching of Paul: Selected Issues.* Nashville: Abingdon Press, 1979.

Gagnon, Robert A. *The Bible and Homosexual Practice.* Nashville: Abingdon Press, 2001.

Garber, Marjorie. *Vice Versa: Bisexuality and the Eroticism of Everyday Life*. New York: Simon & Schuster, 1995.

George, Robert P. and Jean Bethke Elshtain, eds. *The Meaning of Marriage*. Dallas: Spence Publishing, 2006.

Goddard, Andrew. *God, Gentiles and Gay Christians: Acts 15 and Change in the Church*. Cambridge, UK: Grove Books Ltd., 2001.

Gold, Kari Jenson. "Getting Real." *First Things* (January 1994): 6-7.

Gorman, Frank H. *Leviticus: Divine Presence and Community*. Grand Rapids, MI: Eerdmans, 1997.

Gorman, Michael J. *Cruciformity: Paul's Narrative Spirituality of the Cross*. Grand Rapids, MI: Eerdmans, 2001.

———. *The Apostle of the Crucified Lord*. Grand Rapids, MI: Eerdmans, 2004.

Greenberg, David F. *The Construction of Homosexuality*. Chicago: University of Chicago Press, 1988.

Grieb, A. Katherine. "'So That In Him We Might Become the Righteousness of God' (2 Cor 5:21): Some Theological Reflections on the Church Becoming Justice." *Ex Auditu* 22 (2006): 58-80.

Griffiths, Paul J. "Proselytizing for Tolerance." *First Things* (November 2002): 30-34.

Grimsrud, Ted and Howard Zehr. "Rethinking God, Justice, and the Treatment of Offenders." *Journal of Offender Rehabilitation* 35.3/4 (2002): 259-85.

Grimsrud, Ted and Loren L. Johns, eds. *Peace and Justice Shall Embrace: Power and Theopolitics in the Bible*. Telford, PA: Pandora Press U.S., 2000.

Grimsrud, Ted. "Pacifism and Knowing: 'Truth' in the Theological Ethics of John Howard Yoder." *Mennonite Quarterly Review* 76.3 (July 2003): 403-16.

———. "Violence as a Theological Problem." *Justice Reflections* 10 (2005): 1-25.

————. *God's Healing Strategy: An Introduction to the Bible's Main Themes*. Telford, PA: Pandora Press U.S., 2000.

Grenz, Stanley. *Welcoming but not Affirming: An Evangelical Response to Homosexuality*. Louisville: Westminster John Knox Press, 1998.

Hallie, Philip P. *Lest Innocent Blood Be Shed*. New York: Harper & Row, 1979.

Hamlin, E. John. *Judges: At Risk in the Promised Land*. Grand Rapids, MI: Eerdmans, 1990.

Hanigan, James P. *Homosexuality: The Test Case for Christian Sexual Ethics*. New York: Paulist Press, 1988.

HarperCollins Bible Dictionary, Paul J. Achtemeier ed. San Francisco: HarperSanFrancisco, 1996.

Harrisville, Roy A. and Walter Sundberg. *The Bible in Modern Culture: Baruch Spinoza to Brevard Childs*, 3rd ed. Grand Rapids, MI: Eerdmans, 2002.

Hays, Richard B. "Awaiting the Redemption of Our Bodies." *Sojourners* 20 (July 1991): 17-21.

————. "Relations Natural and Unnatural: A Response to Boswell's Exegesis of Romans 1." *Journal of Religious Ethics* 14 (Spring 1986): 184-215.

————. *First Corinthians*. Louisville: John Knox Press, 1997.

————. *The Moral Vision of the New Testament: A Contemporary Introduction to New Testament Ethics*. San Francisco: HarperSanFrancisco, 1996.

Hefling, Charles, ed. *Our Selves, Our Souls & Bodies*. Cambridge, MA: Cowley, 1996.

Helminiak, Daniel A. *What the Bible Really Says About Homosexuality*. San Francisco: Alamo Square Press, 1994.

Herman, Didi. *The Antigay Agenda: Orthodox Vision and The Christian Right*. Chicago: University of Chicago Press, 1997.

Hiebert, Paul. *Reflections on Missiological Issues*. Grand Rapids, MI: Baker Books, 1994.

Holben, L. R. *What Christians Think About Homosexuality: Six*

Representative Viewpoints. North Richland Hills, TX: Bibal Press, 1999.

Hunter, James Davison. *Before the Shooting Begins: Searching For Democracy in America's Culture Wars*. New York: Basic Books, 1994.

Hunter, James Davison. *Culture Wars: The Struggle to Define America*. New York: Basic Books, 1991.

Husbands, Mark and Daniel J. Treier, eds. *The Community of the Word*. Downers Grove, IL: InterVarsity Press, 2005.

Interpreter's Dictionary of the Bible, George A. Buttrick, ed., Nashville: Abingdon Press, 1962.

Interpreter's Dictionary of the Bible, supplementary volume. Keith Crim, ed. Nashville: Abingdon Press, 1976.

Jenson, Philip. "Holiness in the Priestly Writings in the Old Testament," in Stephen C. Barton, ed. *Holiness: Past & Present*. London: T & T Clark, 2003: 93-121.

Jenson, Robert W. *Systematic Theology, Volume 2: The Works of God*. New York: Oxford University Press, 1999.

Johnson, Luke Timothy. "Scripture & Experience" *Commonweal* (June 15, 2007): 14-17.

——. *Scripture & Discernment: Decision Making in the Church*. Nashville: Abingdon Press, 1996.

Johnson, William Stacy. *A Time to Embrace: Same-Gender Relationships in Religion, Law, and Politics*. Grand Rapids, MI: Eerdmans, 2006.

Jones, Stanton L. and Alex W. Kwee. "Scientific Research, Homosexuality, and the Church's Moral Debate: An Update." *Journal of Psychology and Christianity* 24/4 (Winter 2005): 304-16.

Jones, Stanton L. and Mark A. Yarhouse. *Homosexuality: The Use of Scientific Research in the Church's Moral Debate*. Downers Grove, IL: InterVarsity Press, 2000.

Keeping Body and Soul Together: Sexuality, Spirituality, and Social Justice. Louisville: Office of the General Assembly, Presbyterian Church (USA), 1991.

Kenneson, Philip D. *Beyond Sectarianism*. Harrisburg, PA: Trinity Press International, 1999.

———. *Life On the Vine*. Downers Grove, IL: InterVarsity Press, 1999.

King, Michael A. *Fractured Dance: Gadamer and a Mennonite Conflict Over Homosexuality*. Telford, PA: Pandora Press U.S., 2001.

———. *Trackless Wastes & Stars to Steer By*. Scottdale, PA: Herald Press, 1990.

Kirk, J. Andrew Kirk. *Mission under Scrutiny: Confronting Contemporary Challenges*. Minneapolis: Fortress Press, 2006.

Klawans, Jonathan. *Impurity and Sin in Ancient Judaism*. Oxford, UK: Oxford University Press, 2000.

Kraus, C. Norman, ed. *To Continue the Dialogue: Biblical Interpretation and Homosexuality*. Telford, PA: Pandora Press U.S., 2001.

Kreider, Roberta Showalter, ed. *From Wounded Hearts: Faith Stories of Lesbian, Gay, Bisexual and Transgendered People and Those Who Love Them*. Gaithersburg, MD: Chi Rho Press, 1998; 2nd edition, Kulpsville, PA: Strategic Press, 2003.

———. *The Cost of Truth: Faith Stories of Mennonite and Brethren Leaders and Those Who Might Have Been*. Kulpsville, PA: Strategic Press, 2004.

———. *Together in Love: Faith Stories of Gay, Lesbian, Bisexual, and Transgender Couples*. Kulpsville, PA: Strategic Press, 2002.

Kuefler, Matthew, ed. *The Boswell Thesis*. Chicago: University of Chicago Press, 2005.

Lakoff, George. *Moral Politics: What Conservatives Know That Liberals Don't*. Chicago: University of Chicago Press, 1996.

Levine, Baruch. *Leviticus*, JPS Torah Commentary. New York: Jewish Publication Society, 1989.

Lewontin, Richard. *The Triple Helix: Gene, Organism and Environment*. Cambridge, MA: Harvard University Press, 2000.

"Marriage." In *Anchor Bible Dictionary*, s.v.

Martin, Dale. *Sex and the Single Savior*. Louisville: Westminster John Knox Press, 2006.

McCarthy, David Matzko. *Sex and Love in the Home*. London: SCM Press, 2001.

McCarthy, Matzko. "Homosexuality and the Practices of Marriage," *Modern Theology* 13.3 (July 1997): 371-97.

McMinn, Lisa Graham. *Sexuality and Holy Longing*. San Francisco: Jossey-Bass, 2004.

Meeks, Wayne A. *The Origins of Christian Morality*. New Haven, CT: Yale University Press, 1993.

Meilaender, Gilbert. "Sexuality," in *The New Dictionary of Christian Ethics & Pastoral Theology*. Downers Grove, IL: InterVarsity Press, 1995.

———. "The First of Institutions." *Pro Ecclesia* VI/4 (Fall 1997): 444-55.

———. "What Sex Is—And Is For." *First Things* (August 2000): 44-49.

Mendus, Susan, ed. *The Politics of Toleration*. Edinburgh, UK: Edinburgh University Press, 1999.

Michael, Robert T., et al. *Sex in America: A Definitive Survey*. Boston: Little, Brown and Co., 1994.

Miles, Carrie A. *The Redemption of Love: Rescuing Marriage and Sexuality from the Economics of a Fallen World*. Grand Rapids, MI: Brazos Press, 2006.

Miles, Margaret R. *Fullness of Life: Historical Foundations for a New Asceticism*. Philadelphia: Westminster Press, 1981.

Milgrom, Jacob. "Leviticus." In *Interpreter's Dictionary of the Bible*, (supplementary vol.) s.v.

Miller, Patrick D. *The God You Have: Politics, Religion, and the First Commandment*. Minneapolis: Fortress Press, 2004.

Moberly, Walter. "The Use of Scripture in Contemporary Debate About Homosexuality." *Theology* 103 (July-August 2000): 251-58.

Morse, Jennifer Roback. *Smart Sex: Finding Life-Long Love in a Hook-Up World*. Dallas: Spence Publishing, 2005.

Murray, Stuart. *Explaining Church Discipline*. Kent, UK: Sovereign World, 1995.

Myers, David G. and Letha Dawson Scanzoni. *What God Has Joined Together: The Christian Case for Gay Marriage*. San Francisco: HarperSanFrancisco, 2005.

Nation, Mark Thiessen. "The Fruit of the Spirit or Works of the Flesh? Come Let Us Reason Together." *Interface: A Forum for Theology in the World* [Australia] 9/1-2 (May/October 2006): 76–99.

———. "Salvation in an Age of 'Moralistic, Therapeutic Deism.'" unpublished paper.

Nation, Mark Thiessen and Samuel Wells, eds. *Faithfulness & Fortitude: In Conversation with the Theological Ethics of Stanley Hauerwas*. Edinburgh, UK: T & T Clark, 2000.

Nelson, James B. and Sandra P. Longfellow, eds. *Sexuality and the Sacred: Sources for Theological Reflection*. Louisville: Westminster John Knox Press, 1994.

Newman, Elizabeth. *Untamed Hospitality: Welcoming God and Other Strangers*. Grand Rapids, MI: Brazos Press, 2007.

Nissinen, Marti. *Homoeroticism in the Biblical World: A Historical Perspective*. Minneapolis: Fortress Press, 1998.

O'Toole, Robert F., S.J. *Who Is a Christian? A Study in Pauline Ethics*. Collegeville, MN: Liturgical Press, 1990.

Orr, H. Allen. "What's Not in Your Genes." *The New York Review of Books* 50 (August 14, 2003).

Osborn, Eric. *Ethical Patterns in Early Christian Thought*. Cambridge, UK: Cambridge University Press, 1976.

Paglia, Camille. *Vamps & Tramps*. New York: Vintage Books, 1994.

———. "The Joy of Presbyterian Sex." *The New Republic* (December 2, 1991): 24–25.

———. *Sex, Art, and American Culture*. New York: Vintage Books, 1992.

———. *Sexual Personae*. New York: Vintage Books, 1990.

Petersen, William L. "Can *Arsenokoitai* Be Translated By 'Homosexuality.'" *Vigilae Christianae* 40 (1986): 187-89.

Peterson, David, ed. *Holiness & Sexuality: Homosexuality in a Biblical Context*. Milton Keynes, UK: Paternoster Press, 2004.

Peterson, Eugene H. *Christ Plays in Ten Thousand Places: A Conversation in Spiritual Theology*. Grand Rapids, MI: Eerdmans, 2005.

————. *Eat This Book*. Grand Rapids, MI: Eerdmans, 2006.

Plantinga, Cornelius, Jr. *Not the Way It's Supposed to Be: A Breviary of Sin*. Grand Rapids, MI: Eerdmans, 1995.

Platten, Stephen, Graham James, and Andrew Chandler, eds. *New Soundings: Essays in Developing Tradition*. London: Darton, Longman, & Todd, 1997.

Pohl, Christine D. *Making Room: Recovering Hospitality as a Christian Tradition*. Grand Rapids, MI: Eerdmans, 1999.

Porter, Stanley E. and Anthony R. Cross, eds. *Baptism, the New Testament and the Church*. Sheffield, UK: Sheffield Academic Press, 1999.

Radner, Ephraim. *Leviticus*. Grand Rapids, MI: Brazos Press, 2008.

Radner, Ephraim and Philip Turner. *The Fate of Communion: The Agony of Anglicanism and the Future of the Global Church*. Grand Rapids, MI: Eerdmans, 2006.

Rae, Murray A. and Graham Redding, eds. *More Than a Single Issue*. Hindmarsh, South Australia: Australian Theological Forum, 2000.

Ramsey Colloquium, The. "The Homosexual Movement," *First Things* (March 1994): 15-20.

Regnerus, Mark D. *Forbidden Fruit: Sex & Religion in the Lives of American Teenagers*. New York: Oxford University Press, 2007.

Reno, Russell R. *In the Ruins of the Church*. Grand Rapids, MI: Brazos Press, 2002.

Rhoads, Steven E. *Taking Sex Differences Seriously*. San Francisco: Encounter Books, 2004.

Ridley, Matt, *Nature via Nurture: Genes, Experience, and What Makes Us Human*. New York: Harper Collins, 2003; 2nd ed., *The Agile Gene: Genes, Experience, and What Makes Us Human*. New York: Harper Collins, 2004.

"Righteousness." In *Anchor Bible Dictionary*, s.v.

Roberts, Christopher Chenault. *Creation & Covenant: The Significance of Sexual Difference in the Moral Theology of Marriage*. New York: T & T Clark, 2007.

Rogers, Eugene F., Jr. *Sexuality and the Christian Body*. Oxford, UK: Blackwell Publishers, 1999.

Rogers, Jack. *Jesus, the Bible, and Homosexuality: Explode the Myths, Heal the Church*. Louisville: Westminster John Knox, 2006.

Rolheiser, Ronald. *Seeking Spirituality*. London: Hodder & Stoughton, 1998.

Rosario, Vernon A. *Science and Homosexualities*. New York: Routledge, 1999.

Rosenblum, Nancy L., ed. *Liberalism and the Moral Life*. Cambridge, MA: Harvard University Press, 1989.

Rosner, Brian S. *Paul, Scripture, & Ethics: A Study of 1 Corinthians 5-7*. Grand Rapids, MI: Baker Books, 1999.

Rousselle, Aline. *Porneia: On Desire and the Body in Antiquity*, tran. Felicia Pheasant. Oxford, UK: Basil Blackwell, 1988.

Rudy, Kathy. *Sex and the Church: Gender, Homosexuality, and the Transformation of Christian Ethics*. Boston: Beacon Press, 1997.

Ruether, Rosemary Radford. *Christianity and the Making of the Modern Family*. Boston: Beacon Press, 2000.

Satinover, Jeffrey. *Homosexuality and the Politics of Truth*. Grand Rapids, MI: Baker Books, 1996.

Scanzoni, Letha Dawson and Virginia Ramey Mollenkott. *Is the Homosexual My Neighbor?* New York: Harper & Row, 1978; 2nd ed. San Francisco: HarperSanFrancisco, 1994.

Schmidt, Thomas E. *Straight & Narrow? Compassion & Clarity in the Homosexuality Debate*. Downers Grove, IL: InterVarsity Press, 1995.

Schmookler, Andrew Bard. *Debating the Good Society: A Quest to Bridge America's Moral Divide.* Cambridge, MA: MIT Press, 1999.

Scott, Kieran and Michael Warren, eds. *Perspectives on Marriage,* 2nd ed. New York: Oxford University Press, 2001.

Scroggs, Robin. *The New Testament and Homosexuality.* Philadelphia: Fortress Press, 1983.

Seitz, Christopher and Kathryn Greene-McCreight, eds. *Theological Exegesis: Essays in Honor of Brevard S. Childs.* Grand Rapids, MI: Eerdmans, 1998.

Seligman, Adam B. "Tolerance, Liberalism and the Problem of Boundaries," *Society* (January/February 2004): 12-16.

"Sexuality and Justice-Love," *The Christian Century* 108 (May 8, 1991): 519.

Shaw, Brent D. "A Groom of One's Own? The Medieval Church and the Question of Gay Marriage," *The New Republic* 211 (July 18 & 25, 1994): 33-41.

Siker, Jeffrey S., ed. *Homosexuality in the Church: Both Sides of the Debate.* Louisville: Westminster John Knox Press, 1994.

Smith, Christian. *Christian America? What Evangelicals Really Want.* Berkeley: University of California Press, 2000.

Smith, Mark D. "Ancient Bisexuality and the Interpretation of Romans 1:26-27." *Journal of the American Academy of Religion* 54.2 (Summer 1996): 223-56.

Snyder, C. Arnold. *Following in the Footsteps of Christ: The Anabaptist Tradition.* Maryknoll, NY: Orbis Books, 2004.

Stein, Edward. *The Mismeasure of Desire: The Science, Theory, and Ethics of Sexual Orientation.* Oxford, UK: Oxford University Press, 1999.

Stout, Jeffrey. "How Charity Transcends the Culture Wars: Eugene Rogers and Others on Same-Sex Marriage." *Journal of Religious Ethics* 31 (Summer 2003): 169-80.

Streitmatter, Rodger. *Sex Sells! The Media's Journey from Repression to Obsession.* Boulder, CO: Westview Press, 2004.

Stuart, Elizabeth and Adrian Thatcher, eds. *Christian Perspectives on Sexuality and Gender*. Grand Rapids, MI: Eerdmans, 1996.

Stuart, Elizabeth. *Just Good Friends: Towards a Lesbian and Gay Theology of Relationships*. London: Mowbry, 1995.

Swartley, Willard M. *Homosexuality: Biblical Interpretation and Moral Discernment*. Scottdale, PA: Herald Press, 2003.

————, ed. *Essays on Peace Theology and Witness*. Elkhart, IN: Institute of Mennonite Studies, 1988.

Taylor, Daniel. "Deconstructing the Gospel of Tolerance." *Christianity Today* (February 11, 1999): 43-52.

Terry, Jennifer. *An American Obsession: Science, Medicine, and Homosexuality in Modern Society*. Chicago: University of Chicago Press, 1999.

Thiselton, Anthony. *The First Epistle to the Corinthians*. Grand Rapids, MI: Eerdmans, 2000.

Van Leeuwen, Mary Stuart. *My Brother's Keeper: What the Social Sciences Do (and Don't) Tell Us About Masculinity*. Downers Grove, IL: InterVarsity Press, 2002.

Vasey, Michael. *Strangers and Friends: A New Exploration of Homosexuality and the Bible*. London: Hodder & Stoughton, 1995.

Veyne, Paul, ed. *A History of Private Life, Vol.1: From Pagan Rome to Byzantium*. Cambridge MA: Harvard University Press, 1987.

Via, Dan O. and Robert A. J. Gagnon. *Homosexuality and the Bible: Two Views*. Minneapolis: Fortress Press, 2003.

Volf, Miroslav. *Exclusion and Embrace*. Nashville, TN: Abingdon Press, 1996.

Wallace, Catherine M. *For Fidelity: How Intimacy and Commitment Enrich Our Lives*. New York: Vintage Books, 1998.

Wannenwetsch, Bernd. "Old Docetism—New Moralism? Questioning a New Direction in the Homosexuality Debate." *Modern Theology* 16 (July 2000): 353-64.

Watson, Francis. *Agape, Eros, Gender: Towards a Pauline Sexual Ethic*. Cambridge, UK: Cambridge University Press, 2000.

Watts, Gary L. "An Empty Sexual Ethic." *The Christian Century* 108 (May 8, 1991): 520-21.

Webster, John. *Confessing God.* New York: T & T Clark, 2005.

White, Mel. *Stranger at the Gate: To Be Gay and Christian in America.* New York: Simon & Schuster, 1994.

Wiesner-Hanks, Mary E. *Christianity and Sexuality in the Early Modern World.* New York: Routledge, 2000.

Williams, Bruce A., O. P., "Homosexuality and Christianity: A Review Discussion," *The Thomist* 46 (1982): 609-25.

Wink, Walter, ed. *Homosexuality and Christian Faith: Questions of Conscience for the Churches.* Minneapolis: Fortress Press, 1999.

Wold, Donald. *Out of Order: Homosexuality in the Bible and the Ancient Near East.* Grand Rapids, MI: Baker Books, 1998.

Wolf, Christopher, ed., *Homosexuality and American Public Life.* Dallas: Spence Publishing, 1999.

Wolf, Christopher, ed., *Same Sex Matters.* Dallas: Spence Publishing, 2000.

Wood, Peter. *Diversity: The Invention of a Concept.* San Francisco: Encounter Books, 2003.

Wright, Christopher J. H. *The Mission of God: Unlocking the Bible's Grand Narrative.* Downers Grove, IL: InterVarsity Press, 2006.

Wright, David F. "Homosexuals or Prostitutes? The Meaning of *Arsenokoitai* (1 Corinthians 6:9, 1 Timothy 1:10)." *Vigilae Christianae* 38 (1984): 125-53.

———. "Translating *Arsenokoitai* (1 Corinthians 6:9; 1 Timothy 1:10)." *Vigilae Christianae* (1987): 396-98.

Wright, N. T. "The Letter to the Romans." *The New Interpreter's Bible, Vol. 10,* ed. Leander Keck. Nashville: Abingdon Press, 2002. 393-770.

———. *The Last Word: Beyond the Bible Wars to a New Understanding of the Authority of Scripture.* San Francisco: HarperSanFrancisco, 2005.

Wright, Tom. *Paul for Everyone: The Pastoral Letters*. Louisville: Westminster John Knox Press, 2004.

Yancey, Philip. "Exploring a Parallel Universe: Why Does the Word Evangelical Threaten So Many People in Our Culture?" *Christianity Today* (November 2005): 128.

———. "Why I Don't Go to a Megachurch." *Christianity Today* (May 29, 1996): 80.

Yoder, John Howard. *The Christian Witness to the State*. Scottdale, PA: Herald Press, 2002 [original 1964].

———. *The Politics of Jesus*, 2nd edition. Grand Rapids, MI: Eerdmans, 1994.

———. *The Priestly Kingdom*. Notre Dame: University of Notre Dame Press, 1984.

The Authors

Ted Grimsrud is Professor of Theology and Peace Studies at Eastern Mennonite University. He is an author and editor of numerous books including *Embodying the Way of Jesus: Anabaptist Convictions for the 21st Century* (Wipf and Stock, 2007); co-editor, *Transforming the Powers: Peace, Justice, and the Domination System* (Fortress, 2006).

Mark Thiessen Nation is Professor of Theology at Eastern Mennonite Seminary. Well-known as a scholar and editor of John Howard Yoder books, his titles have included *John Howard Yoder: Mennonite Patience, Evangelical Witness, Catholic Convictions* (Eerdmans, 2006) and *Karl Barth and the Problem of War and Other Essays* by John Howard Yoder (Cascade, 2003).